Fly-Fish
BETTER

D1010030

0 11557 03216 1

Fly-Fish
BETTER

Practical Advice on Tackle, Methods, and Flies

ART SCHECK

STACKPOLE
BOOKS

Published by
STACKPOLE BOOKS
5067 Ritter Road
Mechanicsburg, PA 17055
www.stackpolebooks.com

Printed in the U.S.A.

First edition

10 9 8 7 6 5 4 3 2 1

Photos and drawings by Eleanor Scheck and Art Scheck
Cover photo by Eleanor Scheck
Cover design by Caroline Stover

Library of Congress Cataloging-in-Publication Data
Scheck, Art.
  Fly fish better : practical advice on tackle, methods, and flies / Art Scheck.
    p. cm.
  Includes index.
  ISBN 0-8117-3216-9 (alk. paper)
  1. Fly fishing. I. Title.

SH456.S36 2005
799.12′4—dc22

2004021312

ISBN 978-0-8117-3216-1

Contents

Acknowledgments

Our daughter Ellie gave up Saturdays and Sundays in the spring-time to stand in rivers and take pictures of her crazy dad waving a long stick and trying not to fall in. It was good to spend time out-doors with her again.

Dr. Bill Chiles helped on both sides of the camera, as model and photographer, and introduced me to some wonderful southern waters.

In his letters, Lefty Kreh shared wisdom on knots and the testing thereof.

Umpqua Feather Merchants, Orvis, Scientific Anglers, and Frog Hair collectively provided more than a mile of tippet material, most of which I broke testing and comparing knots.

As always, my greatest thanks go to my wife, Mary Jo, for her patience and encouragement. She makes projects like this one possible.

Shorter versions or parts of the following chapters were articles for *American Angler* magazine:

"A Comfortable Load," in the May–June 2003 issue.

"Basic Leadership Skills," in the November–December 2002 issue.

"Saltwater-Style Rigging for Freshwater Fish," in the May–June 2001 issue.

"The Fine Points of Angling," in the July–August 2003 issue.

"Positive Buoyancy," in the July–August 2002 issue.

"Lessons from the Salt," in the November–December 2001 issue.

"Appropriate Force," in the September–October 2003 issue.

Preface

Novice fly fishers can learn the rudiments of the sport from any number of good books. Experts and specialists can pick from hundreds of volumes devoted to advanced fly fishing and narrow topics. This book aims to land between the extremes, to offer some ideas and advice beyond the scope of beginners' primers while still exploring a sufficient range of topics to serve all-around anglers who fly-fish in freshwater streams and rivers. My hypothetical readers have been enjoying this sport for at least a few years, fish for trout and probably some warmwater species, have learned most of the rudiments, and would like to improve their skills and knowledge.

I don't have much to say about specific hatches or particular fly patterns. Those are important, of course, but real and artificial flies tend to be local or regional topics, and they're ably covered by many other writers. The chapters of this book deal with topics other than bugs: some of the mechanics of fly tackle, leaders and rigging, techniques and methods for using various types of flies, the whereabouts of fish and the general kinds of food that they eat between hatches, and tricks that can make fly fishing a little less frustrating and a little more fun. I won't insult your intelligence by claiming that this book will carry every reader to some hyper-advanced level of expertise. But I hope that most freshwater fly fishers will find some useful ideas between these covers; I've tried to make this a practical book for practical fly fishers.

Three of the best tips that I can share do not require whole chapters, so I'll pass them along here.

First, work on your casting, even if you've been fishing for decades. Very few fly fishers, including me, cast well enough, and no one can cast too well. Fresh- and saltwater guides universally agree that if they could magically impart one skill to their clients, they would give them the ability to throw the line. Take lessons, study good casting books such as those by Ed Jaworowski, and practice what you learn. Better fishing depends mostly on better casting.

Second, use your feet. We've all heard that 10 percent of the anglers catch 90 percent of the fish. I don't know if that's true, but I've noticed that 90 percent of the anglers seem to occupy the 10 percent of water nearest the parking areas. Let other guys jostle for space under the bridge. You'll find a better experience if you follow the path upstream or downstream until it becomes faint and narrow, and then press on for another quarter of a mile. It's astonishing how many anglers simply refuse to walk more than a few hundred yards. The summer before I started this book, a friend introduced me to a lovely stream high in the southern Appalachians, a fast, rough, pristine little river full of wild brown and rainbow trout. From the nearest paved parking area, we have to hike two-thirds of a mile to a footbridge that crosses the stream. Granted, it's a steep two-thirds of a mile. But my friend tells me that in 1997, the last year in which the owners of the land kept written records, anglers made seventy-seven visits to this marvelous place. For about 80 percent of the year, no one tried to catch those wild trout.

Hoof it. At worst, you'll get some exercise.

Third, enjoy the great variety that American waters offer. Perhaps, like many anglers, you love trout more than other fish. Fine. But why scorn the bass and panfish that flourish in so many of our streams? I once baffled a good-natured Briton by remarking that he came from an impoverished angling culture. When he asked what I meant, I pointed out that his homeland lacks crappies, blue-gills, rock bass, smallmouths, largemouths, Kentucky spotted bass, and pickerel; when he went fly-fishing at home, he had to settle for trout or salmon. My British friend thought that I was joking. I wasn't. We're lucky to have our warmwater fish. Sometimes they'll test us; compared with some river bass I've met, brown trout are pushovers. And when warmwater fish aren't fussy, they're more fun than an angler has any right to expect to have.

Cast better, walk a little farther, appreciate whatever fish your local waters provide. Those are three of the secrets of happy anglers. The fourth, I think, is curiosity, an eagerness to learn new tricks and understand how things work. This book's purpose is to share such tricks and understanding as I've acquired. I hope you find it useful.

1

Cast 90 Feet—Whether or Not You Want To

The colorful fly-rod ad in the glossy magazine was a fair specimen of its type. It showed an angler firing an astonishing length of line over the water, his casting arm extended until his shoulder tendons creaked and his six-inch-tall loop zooming toward the distant horizon of the beautiful setting. The headline said something about never settling for second-best performance. Beneath the photo, a dozen lines of copy made reference to the rod's ultra-high-modulus fibers, revolutionary resin system, and groundbreaking taper design. No fish is out of reach for an angler using one of these rods, the ad implied.

We shouldn't be too hard on companies that commission ad agencies to create such messages. This is America, and Americans want the latest, coolest, fastest, highest-performance stuff, even if we don't always need it or know how to use it. Take a look around. Folks who drive barely well enough to negotiate parking lots buy 300-horsepower cars that look great creeping along at 12 miles an hour in urban traffic jams. Citizens purchase computers more powerful than anything NASA had for the Apollo program so that they can send ungrammatical e-mail and dirty jokes to friends who don't have time to read the stuff anyway. Consumers bring home

A high-modulus, high-performance, extra-fast-action fly rod is a marvelous casting tool. But is it the right tool for this kind of fishing? Softer, slower-action rods make more sense for many anglers.

stereos that can reproduce frequencies inaudible to the human ear and generate enough volume to make concrete buildings crumble, and then listen to talk radio or collections of music with such titles as *Greatest Dentist-Office Hits of the Seventies.*

There's no harm in any of those things, of course—a certain amount of overcapacity, perhaps, but no real harm. Fly fishers, however, can do themselves some harm when they blithely accept the notions that the possession of an allegedly high-performance fly rod somehow translates into high-performance angling and that the latest, hottest long-distance rod is always the best one to use. In fly fishing, overcapacity can hurt you.

Not that I have anything against the newest, lightest, highest-modulus fly rods. In many circumstances, they are wonderful casting implements, light and crisp and a joy to use. Most of them are also tougher and less likely to break than their forerunners were.

But too many anglers don't understand that when it's applied to a fly rod, the term "high-performance" doesn't refer to what the rod *does*. A fly rod doesn't do anything. If it's truly a high-performance model, a rod *lets* or perhaps helps a very good fly caster do certain things in certain situations. The rod's qualities might or might not matter to you or me; sometimes they might even hinder us from fishing well.

Before considering why a high-performance, high-modulus rod might not be the best one to have, perhaps we should spend a minute looking at what happens when we cast and thinking about the differences between this year's most-hyped line launcher and a fly rod made, say, twenty-five years ago. This line of inquiry is more complicated and involved than many anglers suspect.

BEND AND STRETCH AND TRY NOT TO COLLAPSE

Obviously, a fly rod bends when you make a cast with it. How easily and deeply it bends and how vigorously it straightens ("recovers" is the usual term) determine its casting properties. So far, it's all pretty simple. But the event of bending is not so simple as it seems. A typical graphite fly rod is a tapered tube. This tube consists not of a solid substance (as, say, a copper pipe does), but of several materials. The carbonized fibers that make the rod springy run lengthwise. A plastic resin holds the carbonized fibers together. You can think of a graphite rod blank as a hollow, tapered bundle of long, extremely thin wires held together by epoxy glue. That's a crude picture, but it suits our purpose.

When a rod bends, the fibers on the outside of the curve are stretched. They don't like stretching, and they want to return to their original length. That's why the rod straightens when the load is removed. The "modulus" that anglers and rod companies make such a big deal of is a truncation of "modulus of elasticity," a measurement or mathematical description of how a material behaves when stretched. A high-modulus fiber resists stretching more and returns to its original length more forcefully than a low-modulus fiber does. Graphite is a higher-modulus material than fiberglass, and that's the main reason that a graphite rod is stiffer than a glass one.

Every time you cast, then, you stretch part of your fly rod. As the rod bends, another thing happens: The tube's cross section wants to go out of round. That's true of any tube, as you can demonstrate by bending a plastic drinking straw. Bend the straw more than a little bit, and it suddenly kinks and collapses at one point. Anyone who has tried to bend electrical conduit without a proper tool has experienced this same problem.

If a fly rod's cross section goes out of round under stress, the tube kinks and collapses, and the rod breaks. A tubular fishing rod must maintain its round cross section under considerable strain. Rod builders use the term "hoop strength" to refer to this requirement. With fiberglass, hoop strength wasn't an issue. Most glass rods were (and many still are) made with woven cloth in which equal numbers of fibers lie at right angles to one another; half the fibers run lengthwise, and the other half run across the blank. The crosswise fibers form hoops and, not surprisingly, provide hoop strength. That's why most fiberglass rods are so tough; they have loads of built-in resistance to deforming and kinking because half of the fibers contribute to structural integrity.

For the most part, the carbonized fibers that give a graphite fly rod its power and spring run along only the lengthwise axis. Since these lengthwise fibers do not form hoops, they contribute nothing to hoop strength. If made with materials available in the 1970s, when graphite fishing rods first came on the market, a fly rod consisting only of carbon fibers and plastic resin would collapse and break instantly when bent.

Blank makers had to find ways to build hoop strength into carbon-fiber tubular rods. The easiest way is to use a layer of woven fiberglass called "scrim." Fiberglass scrim works perfectly well, and many rod manufacturers still use it in some or all of their blanks. Its main drawback is that it adds a little weight.

That's where rod technology stood circa 1980—lengthwise graphite fibers to provide stiffness and spring, a layer of woven fiberglass scrim to provide hoop strength, and a plastic resin to hold the whole works together. This arrangement had two advantages over all-fiberglass rods, as least on paper. First, graphite rods bent less deeply and straightened more forcefully than glass rods did. Generally, that translates into longer and more accurate casts. Second, graphite rods weighed less than their glass counterparts, because graphite lets a blank designer use less material to produce a desired degree of stiffness. Graphite isn't inherently lighter than fiberglass—a pound of one weighs as much as a pound of the other—but a graphite fishing rod simply contains less stuff than a glass rod built for the same job.

The benefit of lower weight lies not in reduced exertion for anglers, but in better casting. If two rods were made with materials of identical modulus, the lighter one would recover more quickly. Less mass also means less jiggling or bouncing that throws shock waves into a fly line and robs distance and accuracy from the cast.

So far, all the news is good for everyone. When graphite sticks hit the market, fly fishers instantly had lighter, crisper rods with which they could make longer, more accurate presentations that required fewer false casts. Anglers had never had it so good; fish had never had things so tough.

But progress marches relentlessly onward. Sometimes, theory outpaces practice.

MORE EQUALS BETTER—OR DOES IT?

You might recall the scene in *Casablanca* in which the beautiful young refugee woman faced with a tough decision asks Rick his opinion of M Renard, the police captain played by the immortal Claude Rains.

"He's like other men, only more so," Rick replies.

That's a good analogy for what has happened with graphite fly rods over the past twenty years: They've become more so. Fly rods have changed because of the natural and laudable inclination of engineers and designers to take any product to a higher level, the pressures of a crowded marketplace, and the buying public's love of buzzwords and five-second explanations of complicated topics.

If graphite is better than fiberglass, then higher-modulus graphite must be better than lower-modulus stuff. If x-modulus fibers do all manner of wondrous things for fishermen, then $2x$-modulus fibers must do twice as many good things or do them twice as well—or both, in the arithmetic of marketing.

And so the race begins. Finding higher-modulus material wasn't hard. Indeed, the fibers used in the stiffest, highest-performance fly rods are, by the standards of larger industries, only medium-modulus material. The trick was finding ways to use higher-modulus graphite to make tubular rods that didn't break. As I understand it, the challenge was not so much overcoming any inherent brittleness of materials as finding ways to maintain and improve hoop strength in rods made with them while also keeping weight to the bare minimum.

The technical details of rod-design progress don't matter to this discussion. Besides, they're beyond the ken of most laymen (or at least this layman). It's sufficient to note that rod makers have adopted new resins that in themselves provide greater hoop strength, and that they've found ways to make scrim with carbon fibers rather than fiberglass. Thanks to those and some other innovations, manufacturers can now employ higher-modulus graphite than they could a decade ago. On paper, and often in practice, that means lighter fly rods that throw lines faster, farther, and straighter.

The newer materials also lend themselves to increasingly powerful and aggressive blank designs, and that's why some of us run into problems with some contemporary fly rods. It's not that the materials are innately bad or wrong; they're not. But they allow and even encourage blank designers to make rods that are simply too damn stiff for the kinds of fishing that many of us enjoy. Many high-performance fly rods are designed with the help of champion casters, and they just don't work very well in the hands of an average guy fishing at modest distances.

"No problem," you say. "I use a 6- or 7-weight line with my new 5-weight UltraBlaster rod, and it works fine."

Well, okay, but that seems a bass-ackwards approach to things. No matter what the label on the rod says, you're fishing with a 6- or 7-weight outfit. Didn't you want a 5-weight rig in the first place?

Fly fishing begins with the line. We throw our fat, heavy lines because our lures are too light to throw by themselves. You cannot cast a Hare's Ear nymph with a spinning rod; you have to sling a

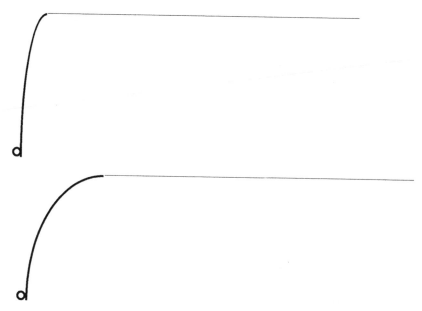

In the hands of an average angler trying to make a short- or medium-range cast, an overly stiff, powerful fly rod bends only a little *(top)*. The caster ends up doing more work and finds the rod tiring to use. A softer rod that bends more deeply *(bottom)* will make this angler's casting easier and more pleasant. The right rod isn't necessarily the one that can throw the most line.

length of thick, plastic-coated string and let that heavy line drag the fly to its destination. By definition, fly fishing consists of casting the weight of the line rather than the weight of a bait, lure, float, or sinker. The fly fisher's lure is a passenger, not a projectile.

I choose a 4-weight line for some jobs because it has enough mass and no more. Naturally, any fly I can cast with a 4-weight outfit is even easier to cast with a 6-weight rig. But the thicker, heavier line makes for less graceful deliveries that might spook more fish. And the lighter line lets me use a lighter, more limber rod that gives me greater pleasure when playing a fish, particularly such specimens as I catch.

Having picked a line, I now want a rod that will let me cast as much of the string as I need to and have fun doing it. This is where many stiff, high-performance rods designed for heroes don't work for me and many other anglers. Such rods are designed to carry and propel a great deal of fly line, often much more than we need to throw. With a short line, they don't load well, and casting with them is actually more work than it is with my older, softer, technically inferior sticks. It's a lot less pleasurable, too. This is why some of us have returned to glass rods for much of our fishing: They work beautifully in our worlds, and they feel nice.

I can cast pretty well, particularly when I follow my own advice and practice between outings. Call me a braggart, but I'd say that I'm slightly above average. My backcast is strong and fast and tight, and I can double-haul. I build my own rods and understand how they work.

In fresh water, though, I do nearly all of my fishing at ranges of 50 feet or less. The rivers and streams that I like best do not require (and often don't permit) 60-foot casts. When I fish a bigger river, I try to break it into manageable 50-foot chunks and fish each section carefully with a length of line that I can easily control and mend. On a lake or pond, it's usually better to move the boat than to make a longer cast; 40 feet of line allows me more control over a popper or a bass than 80 feet does. Even saltwater angling does not always require heroic casts. Most of the guides with whom I've discussed the subject agree that speed and accuracy often matter very much in the salt, but that sheer distance matters less often. And when a guy does need to make 100-foot casts all day, chances are that he'll use a shooting-taper line, which means that he'll carry only 30 to 40 feet of line in the air.

Some anglers do need to cast far with a conventional, full-length fly line. But experience and observation suggest that most of the time, most of us don't. Let's examine a couple of medium-distance casts and see what happens when we make them.

Suppose the target is 45 feet away, and you need to reach it with a 9-foot, 5-weight trout outfit. (It's very instructive to go outside and actually measure 45 feet.) Your leader is 9 feet long. The rod forms part of the length of the cast; let's be conservative and say that the rod contributes 7 feet, since it's not perfectly horizontal as the line rolls out toward the target. So, when the fly alights on the target, you will have 29 feet of fly line outside the rod. Almost certainly, though, you shot some of that line on the presentation cast. Again, we'll be conservative and say that you shot 5 feet of fly line. At the start of the delivery cast, then, you had 24 feet of fly line outside the rod.

Of course, that line is not all the same diameter. The line's thin tip and part of its front taper weigh very little and therefore contribute very little to loading the rod. Let's be safe and set aside the first 4 feet of the fly line as too light to put much load on the rod.

That means that you expect to load the rod with only 20 feet of relatively heavy fly line to make your 45-foot presentation.

But what if the rod was designed to load most effectively with 35 feet of line outside the tip, and then only in the hand of an expert caster who can move a fly rod much faster than the rest of us can? These days, that's not unlikely. With your paltry 20 feet of line, the rod functions merely as a lever and not as a powerful, efficient spring. You have to push the rod hard to make it bend, and even then the line barely wafts toward the target. With an unusually wind-resistant fly, you might not be able to make the cast at all. After half an hour of forcing the rod to bend, you're exhausted.

We can run the exercise from the other direction. Let's say that a softer, lower-modulus 5-weight rod loads well and recovers smoothly with the belly and just a little of the rear taper of a weight-forward line outside the tip. If you have 7 feet of front taper and tip, 25 feet of belly, and 2 feet of rear taper in the air, you have 34 feet of line outside the rod. Add 9 feet for the leader and 7 feet for the rod's contribution. With the fat part of the line outside the rod, you should be able to shoot a fair amount of the thinner running line; let's say 10 feet.

Do the math: $34 + 9 + 7 + 10 = 60$ feet. So a rod that loads easily and well with just the fattest part of a weight-forward line in the air—a rod, in other words, that behaves like an old-fashioned fly rod—will let you easily hit targets 60 feet away.

Go out in the yard and measure 60 feet. Be honest, now: How often do you fish beyond that distance in fresh water? And how well can you manage and mend that much line?

These strike me as realistic numbers, but a lot of high-performance fly rods don't work well with them, because the rods are designed to carry and throw considerably more line. With 25 feet of string outside their tips, these rods simply don't bend very much. That's not a criticism of the rods or the folks who make them. Today's most powerful fly rods are astonishing casting tools. They're just not the *right* casting tools for the fishing that a lot of us do.

Don't fault manufacturers for making and promoting their supersticks. For one thing, the high-performance rods have plenty of uses. More important, many anglers don't think about the subtleties of casting and fishing. A "Cast Farther!" headline in an ad is a convenient handle for customers to grab and a simple, powerful message for the advertiser to use. Before we blame rod companies for selling us stuff that we don't need, we should ask ourselves if we've bothered to learn anything about the products and their functions. We buy Formula 1 race cars for driving in a subdivision with a 25-mile-per-hour speed limit. Whose fault is that?

Perhaps the greatest irony is that our collective obsession with sheer distance and sexy buzzwords eclipses the truly good news about fly rods. The new resins and manufacturing methods that permit the use of higher-modulus fibers also can make *all* fly rods a little lighter and a lot more durable. Rods that fire a mile of line are useful to only a handful of anglers. But big improvements in rod-making technology benefit all of us. Somehow, that message gets lost in the hype.

APPROPRIATE PERFORMANCE

So how does a garden-variety, reasonably proficient fly fisher go about picking a rod? First, don't even ask what a rod weighs or what kind of graphite it contains or how it compares to this or that high-end rod. None of those things matter in the real world; all of them are symptomatic of what a friend in the trade calls "yuppie equipment anxiety." And it seems to me that when fishing tackle serves as a status symbol, the real point of going fishing has been lost.

You want a rod that works pleasantly, easily, and comfortably in your world. Start by paying attention to how you fish. On average, how far do you cast? Bring an indelible marker when you go fishing, and mark the line where you grab it at the end of a cast; the mark will let you perform realistic tests with a rod that you're contemplating buying. Do you make many roll casts? You might want to test a rod with a slower action. Do you usually pick up only half (or less) of the line that you originally cast? In this case, you certainly don't want the stiffest fly rod in the shop. How well do you cast after, say, three hours of hard fishing? If you tire as quickly as I do (a problem caused by too much time at a desk), you want a forgiving rod, not a lightning-fast superstick that demands perfect form and timing every cast.

Selecting a new fly rod is a personal business. But I'd bet that if you approach the job thoughtfully, you'll decide that you're happiest with something other than the sexiest, trendiest, highest-performance rod in the store. You will probably settle on something that feels softer and slower than the line cannons touted in glossy ads, a rod that actually bends with 20 to 25 feet of line outside the tip-top, one that just plain feels smooth and good as you cast. Nearly every rod company makes such rods. Sometimes they cost a little less than the supersticks; sometimes they sell for much less. They are perfectly good, indeed sometimes superior, fly rods. There is no correlation—none whatsoever—between dollars spent and happiness achieved.

And you'll find that you fish very well and have lots of fun with your new rod. You will have achieved the only kind of "high-performance" angling that means anything.

What if you sometimes need to reach out farther, to hit a target 65 or 70 feet away? Chances are that you can, at least if your casting is any good. And, as explained in the next chapter, there are things you can do with lines to alter the casting characteristics of a fly rod. For instance, if you expect to pick up and carry much more line than usual, try a 4-weight double-taper string on a nominally 5-weight rod.

Besides, distance comes mostly from technique and form, both of which come from instruction and practice. Worry about equipment *after* you have become such a good caster that you can throw an entire fly line with the cheapest entry-level 6-weight rod in the shop.

Some years ago, I spent a few days in the Keys with an extraordinary fly fisher. I had a new 9-weight rod that I'd made with an inexpensive, fairly heavy, relatively slow, first-generation-graphite blank. It was what I could afford. My host asked to try my new rod. He noted right away that although it might have been good for bass fishing, my homemade rod wasn't right for casting to bonefish. Too soft, too slow, not crisp enough, he pointed out as he false-cast. Flats fishing demands a rod that builds line speed *right now*, my host said, one that can deliver a fly with only one or two false casts.

He was right, of course. My new rod was a lousy tool for flats fishing. But even as my friend pointed out my rod's shortcomings, I noticed that he was casting most of the line. I don't mean that he was shooting it—he was carrying about 80 feet of Bonefish Taper in the air, and making it look easy. When he uncorked a final cast, all the rest of the fly line and some backing shot through the guides, and the fly plopped down well over 100 feet away.

But he didn't like the rod. Too soft and slow.

A fine caster, and that chap certainly is, can make a short-range rod do long-range work, and he can generally do it without breaking a sweat. A typical caster, however, cannot do the opposite; he can't make a long-range rod work well and smoothly at 30 feet. The mechanics of the thing are against him. He'd have more fun with a softer stick.

If you buy a 200-watt stereo and never turn the volume knob above 1, your easy-listening elevator music will still sound okay. If you never find out how fast your 300-horsepower car can go, you can still enjoy driving it around town at a sedate pace. And if your zillion-megahertz, umpteen-gigabyte computer never does anything harder than send birthday greetings to Aunt Lulabelle, neither it nor you will suffer.

In fly casting, though, you use a special type of spring that works best within a certain range of loads. Here, overcapacity isn't merely wasteful; it can be counterproductive. And catching a trout or bass 50 feet away is sufficiently high performance for me, thank you.

2

A Comfortable Load

Every beginning fly fisher learns the difference between casting a fly and casting a lure. A spin fisher throws a dense object that tows thin monofilament line, while a fly fisher casts a heavy line that carries a practically weightless fly. Next, the beginner learns that this difference accounts for the moral, intellectual, and spiritual superiority of fly fishers over all other humans.

The first part of the lesson is true, but casting with fly tackle and casting with other gear also have similarities. Whether he uses spinning, plug-casting, or fly tackle, an angler throws an object that has mass and weight. Some anglers toss plugs and jigs; others sling pieces of plastic-coated string. They all use a law of inertia—an object at rest wants to stay that way, much like a guy watching a ball game on TV—to store energy in a springy rod.

But many fly fishers don't think in terms of throwing weights, of bending a rod by accelerating against the inertia of a mass. If we did think that way at least occasionally, we would better understand how our tackle works, make our rods more versatile, and avoid some casting problems.

SPECIFICATION OR RECOMMENDATION?

The term "5-weight line" refers to a specification, an actual weight. Industry standards say that the first 30 feet of a 5-weight fly line (exclusive of the skinny, level tip) weigh 140 grains. For a 6-weight string, the specification is 160 grains. One ounce equals 437.5 grains.

The term "5-weight *rod*" means one that in the estimate of its maker, and under the conditions for which it was designed, works best with a 5-weight line. That's not quite the same as a specification.

Rod designers differ in their tastes. One might feel that a 5-weight rod should load and unload—bend and straighten, that is—smoothly and easily with 25 feet of fly line in the air. Another might believe that a 5-weight stick should have the guts to carry 50 feet of line. These two chaps will design different sticks.

Designers also need to address different segments of the market. An expert caster who has trained his hand to produce extremely high tip speed at exactly the right instant can handle a relatively stiff 5-weight rod with an extra-fast action. He can make a high-performance blank work, and he probably does a lot of long-range fishing. A beginning or casual angler with a slower hand and less-than-perfect timing probably feels more comfortable using a more flexible 5-weight rod that bends more deeply and straightens a little more slowly.

Both of our hypothetical rods are legitimate, useful 5-weights. One is for a habitual 70-foot caster; the other is for a 25-foot caster. Which is better depends entirely on one's point of view and style of fishing.

If we were all perfectly rational, we would buy exactly the right fly rods for our various purposes and fishing styles. But we're not and we don't. Besides, none of us casts a fixed length of line. And so we need to make certain adjustments.

ADAPT TO THE LOAD

Among the phalanx of rod tubes in my office closet is one that contains a plug-casting stick rated for ¼- to ¾-ounce lures. Think about that for a minute. According to the maker, the heaviest lure that this rod can handle weighs *three times* as much as the lightest lure. Translated into fly-casting terminology, that's like a fly rod that can cast a 140-grain or a 420-grain line—a rod that's suitable for both trout lines and billfish lines. (Well, almost; the analogy is not exact.)

My plug rod can indeed handle a wide range of lure weights. But it behaves differently with different weights, and so must I. With a ¼-ounce surface plug, I have to pop the rod pretty hard, using a lot of wrist, keeping my thumb on the spool a little longer, and throwing the lure with a low, flat trajectory. When I throw a sinking crankbait or jig that weighs more than half an ounce, I make a longer, slower stroke and release the spool a bit earlier, and the lure travels in a higher arc. At either extreme, casting with this rod calls for more attention and effort than casting a ⅜-ounce lure does. With a ⅜-ounce Jitterbug or crankbait, casting with this plug rod becomes nearly effortless, and I become deadly accurate. But I can still cast lures considerably lighter or heavier than those of the ideal weight.

If he's halfway adept, any spin fisherman changes his casting style when he changes lures. With a light spinner, he casts with a short, quick snap of the wrist, and the lure flies with a flat trajectory. When he replaces the little spinner with a jighead three times as heavy, our friend casts with a longer, slower motion, almost lobbing the lure, which follows a higher, curved trajectory.

A good fly caster makes similar adjustments because he, too, changes the amount of weight he casts. For a while, he might indeed have 140 grains of fly line outside the tip-top of his 5-weight rod. Then he enters some rough pocket water hemmed in by trees, shortens his line, and casts 110 grains. A hundred yards upstream, where the stream opens up, the angler spots three trout rising in a long stretch of dead-calm water, and he starts throwing 160 grains.

That's a difference of nearly ⅛ ounce between the lightest load and the heaviest. A reasonably good caster feels how his rod behaves differently when he makes longer or shorter casts, and he adjusts his stroke accordingly. With the shorter line, he probably makes a shorter, very quick stroke. When he lengthens the line beyond his normal range, a good caster also lengthens his stroke, makes certain to accelerate the rod smoothly over the entire length of the stroke, and probably moves the rod through a wider arc so that he can let the powerful butt section do more of the work. He can handle a range of loads.

So can a fly rod, of course. These days, many rods work well with 25 or 50 feet of line in the air. Still, a given rod works best within a certain range of weights, and sometimes a rod's ideal load range does not coincide with an angler's current needs. Maybe the angler struggles to make accurate short casts, or perhaps he can't get a long cast to turn over. It's time to adjust the load.

OVERLINING A ROD

A fly rod is a type of spring, a device for storing and releasing energy. The amount of energy temporarily stored in a fly rod during a casting stroke results from two factors: mass and acceleration. A great caster accelerates the rod tip to a higher speed than the rest of us do. Since he also makes more long casts than most of us do, he wants a rod that can handle a greater mass of line. A great caster can store more energy in a fly rod than an average caster can.

The average guy can have a problem when he buys a stiff, high-performance rod designed for or by the great caster. Mr. Typical simply doesn't put enough energy in the rod; he casts a shorter line (less mass) than the expert throws, and his hand doesn't attain the same speed that the expert's does. He doesn't load the rod, and his feeble casts waft slowly in the general direction of the target.

This angler would do well to overline his rod. That is, he should use a 6-weight line with his nominally 5-weight stick. The extra mass will help load the rod, and the line will travel with more zip.

Casting instructors take note: I'm not recommending heavier lines as solutions to casting problems. Good technique has no replacement. But there's no denying that some high-modulus rods are made for better-than-average casters. When a novice buys one, he has a tool that doesn't work for him. Using a line one weight

Every rod works best within a certain range of loads. A very short line can be tricky to cast because it puts virtually no load on a fly rod. For short-range angling like this, many fly rods work better with lines one or even two weights heavier than those their manufacturers recommend.

heavier than the rod's nominal rating will make the tool work better.

Casters take note: Don't rely on equipment to cure casting woes. The best money that you will ever spend will go toward casting instruction. But overlining a rod, particularly a stiff one, can help while you're learning. You will probably find that the need to overline diminishes with experience. As your form improves and your hand learns to move the rod faster, you can go back to the recommended line. Your 5-weight rod might need to throw a 6-weight string for a year, but then, as your skills and distance improve, it will begin to work well with the lighter line.

Even a good caster might want to overline a rod when he fishes at shorter-than-normal distances. When an angler takes his favorite 4-weight rod to a small stream on which an average cast uses 15 feet of line, he might want to switch to a 5- or even 6-weight line. A rod that's a 5-weight on a big river might be a 6-weight at a bluegill pond.

For a fly rod to work, it needs to bend. In some circumstances, overlining is the best way to put an adequate bend in the stick.

UNDERLINING

These days, few rods need lines lighter than those recommended by their makers. In some situations, though, underlining a rod can help. A very soft 4-weight rod designed for close-quarters fishing might work fine for 20-foot casts on a mountain brook. But on slightly bigger water that requires 30- or 35-foot casts, the soft little rod lacks the muscle to get the job done with a 4-weight line. It bends all the way down past the stripping guide, whimpers, and then recovers too slowly to throw a good loop. But with a 3-weight line—that is, with less mass attached to the tip—the rod can recover with enough zip to propel a tidy cast 30 feet.

If you own a soft rod, you might want to have two lines for it— the recommended line and another that's one weight lighter. The lighter string will let you carry more line in the air and cast a little farther while still enjoying the fun of playing trout or panfish on a lively rod.

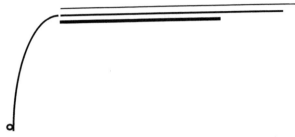

The recommended fly line *(middle)* might indeed work best for most fishing. In extreme situations, however, a heavier or lighter line can keep the rod operating within its preferred load range. On a small stream where all the casts are very short, a line one weight heavier *(bottom)* will load the rod more effectively than the recommended line. If the angler expects to pick up and carry an extra-long line all day, he might do better by dropping down one line weight *(top)* to avoid overloading the rod.

Underlining isn't just for short, rubbery, fiberglass brush rods. Some fast-action, 9- or 9½-foot rods have very soft tips. They work fine with 30 feet of the recommended line but collapse when asked to carry much more than that. Dropping down one line weight can help a rod with a squishy tip reach targets 45 or 50 feet away.

Some types of fishing entail making long casts with a fairly constant amount of line. A guy fishing a streamer in a broad river might make a 60-foot cast, mend his line once or twice while the ersatz minnow swings across the current, retrieve the fly only a couple of yards, and then pick up 50 feet of line to repeat the process. When he fishes a dry fly on the same river, the angler might make a 60-foot up-and-across cast, manage the drift by dint of skillful mending, retrieve just enough line to take up the slack, and then pick up more than 40 feet of fly line. In neither case does the fisherman shoot or retrieve a lot of line. Rather, he picks up and carries a fair amount of string. He might find that lifting 50 feet of the recommended line overloads the rod. This is another good time to use a lighter line. And since he's not shooting for distance, this angler might also want to change the type of line, replacing his usual weight-forward 6-weight with a double-taper 5-weight. He'll find that the lighter, double-taper line makes long pickups easier and simplifies mending.

HOW MUCH DO LINES DIFFER?

Fly lines differ in weight less than many anglers realize. Consider the standards for a range of common trout-fishing lines:

3-weight: 100 grains
4-weight: 120 grains
5-weight: 140 grains
6-weight: 160 grains
7-weight: 185 grains.

That's not much of a spread. A 6-weight line is only 1.14 times as heavy as a 5-weight; a 5-weight is only 1.17 times more than a 4-weight; and a 7-weight line weighs less than twice as much as a 3-weight.

Yet a 6-weight rig certainly *feels* a lot different than a 4-weight outfit. This seems to indicate that a fly-fishing outfit is a finely tuned, specialized instrument. Even a mediocre plug rod can handle a range of lures from, say, 5/16 to 5/8 ounce. But no one would expect a fly rod to handle both 3-weight and 7-weight lines.

If fly rods are that specialized, then maybe we need to pay attention to the loads we ask them to carry. Perhaps overlining and underlining are valuable strategies, good ways to keep a rod operating within its best load range. And maybe, considering the small differences among lines (a 5-weight and a 6-weight differ by less than 0.05 ounce), we should experiment more. Maybe it's worth thinking of a 5-weight rod as a 4/5/6.

SINKING LINES AND SHOOTING TAPERS

A sinking line weighs no more than a floater. It's just denser. Still, some anglers go up one line weight when they use sinking lines. A caster can pick up 40 feet of floating line, putting a good bend in the rod. With a sinking line, an angler generally brings the fly close, makes a roll cast to lift the line to the surface, and then picks up. He makes the first backcast with only a little line, perhaps not enough to load the rod. A line one weight heavier will load the rod right away. And since a sinking line shoots so well, the angler can make fewer and shorter false casts, carrying less line in the air. His rod carries the same load that it would with a floater, but the load is packed into fewer feet of line.

Many experts recommend using a shooting taper at least one weight heavier than a full-length line—a 7-weight head on a nominally 6-weight rod, and so on. The reason is that a shooting taper is a fixed amount of weight, whereas a full-length line is a variable weight. With a shooting taper, the load is always the same; once the head and a little running line are outside the rod, the caster lets go. He never carries more or less line. So he can use a head that puts the maximum effective load on the rod.

THE RIGHT LINE

I once had an expensive 7-weight rod with which I cast a 6-weight line. When I used the recommended line—and I tried several brands and tapers—I cast poorly. With a 6-weight line, I looked like a champ. Perhaps the problem was mine; maybe some innate defect made it necessary for me to use a line one weight too light. No doubt a casting guru would have put a 7-weight line on my rod and thrown a mile of it. But the rod didn't belong to a casting guru. It belonged to me. And in my hand, it was a 6-weight stick.

By and large, the labels on fly rods are trustworthy. But remember that a rod's line-weight rating is a recommendation, not a measurement. If all your rods cast beautifully at all ranges with the recommended lines, count yourself lucky. If not, then borrow a few "wrong" lines for a few days and see how your rods like them. You might solve a problem. At the very least, you will probably find out that most of your rods are more versatile than you thought.

3

Basic Leadership Skills

Sooner or later, it happens to every fly fisher. You're standing there minding your own business, enjoying some peace and quiet and hoping to catch a fish, when a stranger with a spincast outfit appears. He watches you cast a few times before piping up.

"Isn't that line awful fat?" the stranger asks. "Looks like about two-hundred-pound test. You're not gonna catch any whales or tiger sharks here, pal."

One's reply is a function of personality. A good person might tell the stranger about the mechanics of fly fishing. I'm more likely to say that only a fool fishes with wimpy line when the white marlin are running upstream to spawn. That explanation usually gets rid of a stranger.

But the stranger has inadvertently hit on one of fly fishing's unique problems. By necessity, fly line is pretty fat. Even if you could affix a fly directly to the line, no fish is going to bite an Adams attached to a hunk of thick, opaque, plastic-coated string.

And so you have to use a thin, nearly invisible (you hope) link between the fly line and fly. While it solves some problems, a leader creates others, at least sometimes. You have to cast the thing, and you have to get it to turn over and straighten at the end of the cast. It doesn't always cooperate.

If you doubt that a leader affects casting, try this experiment. Replace the entire leader on your 5-weight outfit with 18 inches of 20-pound-test monofilament. Attach a fly and note how easily, how powerfully, and how far you can cast. The fly will hit the water like a brick, but you can throw it a mile. Then replace the 18-inch leader with 15 feet of plain 4-pound monofilament or an equal length of 30-pound nylon. With either, you won't be able to cast worth a damn.

Leaders affect casting and presentation, and sooner or later, every fly fisher has trouble getting a leader to behave. Countless articles and book chapters have been devoted to fly-fishing leaders. And still we have trouble with them.

Maybe we make them more complicated than necessary. I'm not suggesting that leaders are simple. They're not. But they shouldn't cause endless trouble and confusion, either. Getting a reasonably good leader to do its basic jobs—straightening at the end of each casting cycle and dropping the fly with a modicum of delicacy—is not a complicated business.

Leaders come in two main varieties: hand-tied and knotless. When I was a kid, I learned that serious fly fishers always tied their own leaders. The knotless, extruded jobs were for beginners, dilettantes, and oafs. Maybe part of this view derived from snobbery, but the advocates of hand-tied leaders had a point. Thirty years ago, most knotless leaders were wretched things with tapers that simply didn't work. Getting one to straighten at the end of the cast was quite a feat. Even in the 1980s, I bought some extruded leaders that would have defied the best efforts of a champion caster (which I wasn't, and still ain't).

Nowadays, though, all of the major fly-fishing companies sell knotless, extruded leaders that work well. Nearly everyone starts out with this sort of leader, and many good fly fishers stick with them. But even though a one-piece tapered leader seems like a pretty simple piece of equipment, many anglers still don't understand it.

ACCUSE THE RIGHT CULPRIT

Let's begin with the most common headache: The leader collapses in a tangled heap at the end of the cast. We've all dealt with this. What's the problem?

It's probably not the leader. If you're using a 9-foot leader from any of the major companies, and you're throwing a garden-variety trout fly, don't automatically blame a pileup on the leader. Look first to your casting.

It's possible to have a bad leader or one that's wrong for the job that you want it to do. These days, though, most knotless leaders are at least pretty good; some are excellent. If you can't straighten a name-brand, 9-foot leader with a size 14 dry fly at the end, most (if not all) of the solution lies in casting instruction and practice. That's good news, because you *can* learn to cast well enough to make a reasonably good leader turn over and straighten. Efficient casting also lets you make a leader do tricky things, such as land with slack in it.

LEADER TERMINOLOGY

Whether it's extruded or tied by hand, a tapered leader has three parts. The butt is the fat end that attaches to the fly line. It should make up at least a third of the leader's total length, because its mass largely determines how well the rig turns over and straightens. The butt of a well-designed, hand-tied leader usually takes up 50 to 60 percent of the leader's length. Years ago, extruded leaders typically had short butt sections, but most modern knotless leaders have adequately long butts. In the United States, we measure leader butts in thousandths of an inch: 0.021, 0.022, or whatever.

In the middle or taper section, the leader's diameter decreases rapidly. Depending on whose formula you're reading, the taper section should constitute 20 to 30 percent of the leader's total length. In that short distance (2 to 3 feet, typically), the diameter of the line drops from, say, 0.021 inch at the butt to 0.008 inch or even smaller. This part of the leader is the transition from the heavy, powerful butt section to the thin, supple tippet.

The tippet is the skinny end to which you attach the fly. American and British anglers describe tippets with the X system, which has nothing to do with breaking strength. But the X system does tell us the thickness of a tippet. It's called the Rule of 11. Subtract the X number from 11, and the result is the material's diameter in thousandths of an inch. A 4X tippet, then, has a diameter of 0.007 inch: $11 - 4 = 7$. A 6X tippet has a diameter of 0.005 inch: $11 - 6 = 5$.

LEADER LENGTH

The three most common lengths for knotless trout-fishing leaders are 7½, 9, and 12 feet. All other things being equal, a shorter leader is easier to turn over than a longer one. Does that mean that you should use a 7½-footer? Not necessarily. For one thing, the greater the distance between the fat, opaque fly line and the fly, the more likely you are to fool a fish into eating the lure. And again, all other things being equal, a longer leader presents the fly more delicately and allows it a better drift.

So, should you use a 12-foot leader? Well, it depends. Can you get it to turn over and straighten *today,* at your present level of casting skill? Even the best leader won't do you any good if the cast ends in a tangled mess.

You need to consider several things when picking a leader. Your casting ability is one. Do not doubt that you can learn to make perfect dry-fly presentations with a 12-foot or longer leader. But if you don't cast well enough to do that today—be honest, now—use a 9-foot leader. You can move up to the 12-footer as your casting improves.

Consider the fly, too. A big Marabou Muddler is easier to throw with a 7½-foot leader than with a 12-footer. Dry flies don't weigh anything, but a big, bushy one—a size 10 Royal Wulff, say—can have considerable wind resistance. You'll find that fly easier to cast with a 9-foot leader than with something a lot longer.

If you're fishing below the surface, think about depth. With a floating line, a streamer or wet fly will swim deeper on a 9-foot leader than on a 7½-footer. For streamer fishing, a more powerful outfit—a 6-weight instead of a 4-weight—can let you use a longer leader, which in turn lets you fish a little deeper.

Is it windy? If it is, you'll find a shorter leader easier to cast.

How big is the stream? What's the water like? On a fast mountain brook hemmed in by shrubbery, you're not going to make long casts. With a shorter leader, you'll have more fly line in the air to load the rod. Here, I'd use a 7½-foot leader. But on a calm pool in a midsize river with plenty of room, you want the longest leader you can cast; try the 12-footer here.

By and large, a 9-foot leader is the most versatile and manageable length for trout fishing. It's long enough for most dry-fly and nymph fishing on most streams, and short enough to let you sling most streamers and big nymphs. By adding a longer tippet, you can make a 10-foot leader for more delicate work.

Carry a 7½-footer in case the wind picks up or you need to heave a beast of a fly. And work on your casting until you can turn over a 12-foot leader.

You can tie the leader to the fly line with a nail knot, but many anglers (I'm one) use loop-to-loop connections between their lines and leaders. Such an arrangement lets you replace a leader without

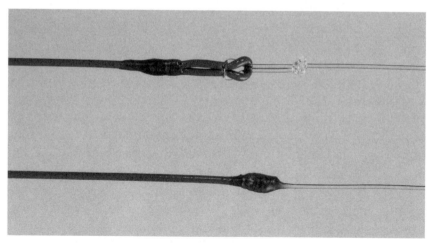

A nail knot coated with Pliobond or something similar is one of the traditional ways to connect a leader to a fly line *(bottom)*. With some modern fly lines, however, the nail knot is not a particularly strong connection. With any line, replacing the entire leader entails cutting off the old nail knot and tying a new one. I much prefer a loop-to-loop junction *(top)*. It's a stronger connection that works with any fly line, and it permits fast, easy leader changes in the field.

having to tie knots in the field. Most fly shops sell braided loops for the ends of fly lines. Or you can double the tip of the fly line to make a ⅜-inch-long loop and secure it with two back-to-back nail knots tied with 8-pound monofilament (or 1X or 2X tippet material). Coat the knots with Pliobond, Loon UV Knot Sense, or something similarly flexible. The coating protects the nail knots from abrasion and nicks; it has nothing to do with their strength. Then tie a small perfection loop in the butt end of your leader, and join the line and leader by interlocking the loops. To change leaders, simply undo the connection. This method beats tying a new nail knot every time you want to change leaders.

ADDING TIPPET MATERIAL

As you change flies, the tippet becomes shorter until eventually you have to add more material to the leader. Fly fishers love to argue over the best knot for this. Some prefer the blood or barrel knot; others swear by the surgeon's knot. The surgeon's knot is easier to tie, but it usually consumes more line than a blood knot because a surgeon's knot has long tag ends (the leftover line that doesn't become part of the knot). Tradition favors the blood knot.

I'd long preferred the blood knot on the assumption that it was stronger, but I had no evidence to support my belief. So, as I did with line-to-hook knots, I spent many hours tying and breaking test rigs. Each rig consisted of three pieces of monofilament; two were joined with knot A, and the third piece was attached with knot B. I'd pull on each rig until something broke, and then record which knot had failed. In some rigs, all three pieces of line had the same diameter; for instance, all three were 5X material. In other rigs, the center section was heavier, such as a piece of 4X with lengths of 6X tied to both ends. Altogether, I made and broke hundreds of rigs constructed of various tippet materials.

It turns that both the blood-knot and the surgeon's-knot advocates are all wet. In light materials, neither is the best knot (indeed, neither is particularly good). By far the strongest knot for connecting two light lines—0.011 inch or thinner, say—is a strange-looking junction that some knot experts call a ligature knot. In *Practical Fish-*

ing Knots, the book from which I learned it, Lefty Kreh and Mark Sosin call it the simple blood knot. But since the connection bears scant resemblance to the regular blood knot that we all know, ligature knot strikes me as the better label.

In one knot-against-knot test after another, the ligature knot trounced all comers. There's simply no comparison—it always beats any other tippet knot I've found.

The ligature knot's performance prompted me to do a few tests with a digital scale. Five 6X test rigs made with blood knots, which previous tests had shown to be consistently stronger than a surgeon's knot in this material, broke at an average of 2.15 pounds. Each rig failed at the blood knot.

Then I tested three 6X test rigs made with ligature knots. In all three, the line itself broke at least an inch from the knot; none of the ligature knots failed. All three knots achieved 100 percent efficiency, breaking the line at an average of 3.33 pounds.

That's a difference, according to my scale, of 1.18 pounds—in 6X material! Even if the scale was a little bit off, we can still use the relative numbers. The ligature-knot rigs broke at 153.5 percent of the strength of the blood knots. That is, they were more than half again as strong. That's a huge difference.

That sort of disparity almost certainly wouldn't persist over the course of hundreds of tests conducted with a variety of lines. But in dozens of tests that pitted one connection against another, the ligature knot beat every other knot. It works in nylon and light fluorocarbon, and it will accommodate lines that differ by 0.002 inch in diameter.

Nothing's perfect, and the ligature knot has a few drawbacks. It's simple to form but a bit tricky to tighten properly. Practice it at home before using it in the field. It uses a bit more line than, say, the surgeon's knot. And it becomes progressively harder to tighten as the line's diameter increases. I can manage it in nylon up to 0.011 inch and fluorocarbon up to about 0.009 inch. In 3X and lighter materials, the ligature knot is fairly easy to tie and tighten, and it provides supreme strength and security. It adds significantly to the strength of a trout or smallmouth-bass leader.

Learn this knot. It's so much better than any of the more popular tippet knots in that it actually allows you to use a better, stronger knot at the fly. You'll find illustrated instructions at the end of the chapter.

The popular and often-recommended surgeon's knot was a consistent loser in my tests. In a batch of thirty-five nylon test rigs that pitted surgeon's or triple surgeon's knots against blood knots, the blood knots won thirty-three contests. Blood knots won 95 percent of the time in another batch of test rigs. In one group of tests made with fluorocarbon material, the Orvis tippet knot beat the surgeon's and triple surgeon's knots 92 percent of the time. The surgeon's knot (standard or triple) loses to the ligature knot 100 percent of the time.

That's bad news for anglers who love the surgeon's knot for its speed and simplicity. There is, however, an alternative that's just as fast, easy, and economical to tie but consistently stronger. This knot goes by several names, including the Orvis tippet knot and the Christopher knot. It's a simple figure eight with an extra wrap. Figure-eight knots have been used for centuries to join ropes, and I suspect that the Orvis tippet knot (that seems the better-known name) has been around forever, or at least since the days of silkworm-gut leaders.

In tests with nylon, the Orvis tippet knot came out about even with the blood knot. When the lines were identical in diameter, the blood knot won a slight majority of the contests. When the lines differed by 0.001 or 0.002 inch, the Orvis tippet knot won slightly more than half the time. In tests with fluorocarbon, the Orvis tippet knot consistently beat the blood knot. You can find illustrated instructions for this knot at the end of the chapter.

The ligature knot is the undisputed strength champion in the tippet materials that we use for most freshwater fishing. If it strikes you as too troublesome to tie (but _please_ try to learn it—it's that good), then use an Orvis tippet knot with a fluorocarbon tippet, and a blood knot or Orvis tippet knot with nylon. If you've been using the surgeon's knot, reconsider your choice. Other junctions beat it consistently.

Knotless leaders taper almost imperceptibly, which can make it tough to know when you need to add tippet. Try this method. Take a brand-new 9-foot, 4X leader, measure back 24 to 30 inches from the tip, and cut it there. Tie on a 30-inch piece of 4X material with a ligature knot. The knot becomes a marker; it lets you see that the tippet is getting short. When you need a new tippet, cut back the 4X material attached to the main leader to a length of about 8 inches, and tie the fresh tippet to that. If you want a slightly longer, finer leader, cut the 4X stuff back to a length of 12 to 16 inches, and add about 24 inches of 5X to it. You can treat each of your new leaders similarly, replacing its tippet at home so that you will have a reference mark in the field.

After adding tippet material a few times, and particularly if you've caught a few fish, replace the entire tippet section. That is, cut the leader right behind the original ligature knot, and then tie on a fresh 30-inch piece of material. This eliminates the chance of losing a fish to a knot that has become weaker through enduring repeated strains.

TIPPET DIMENSIONS

The longer and finer the tippet, the more bites you'll get. That's true with pretty much any kind of fly. The problem, sometimes, is getting a long, skinny tippet to straighten.

The relationship between the size of a fly and the specifications of a tippet is not absolute, because flies come in so many varieties. A heavily hackled, size 12 Fanwing Royal Coachman and a size 12 nymph have very different aerodynamics; the former is nearly weightless and very wind-resistant, whereas the latter is fairly dense and streamlined.

A dry fly won't travel far under its own momentum. Your leader and tippet have to drag the fly to its destination. With most dry flies, you can divide the hook size by three to get a rough idea of the right tippet diameter. Try these matchups: with a size 12 dry fly, use a 3X or 4X tippet; with a size 14 fly, 4X or 5X; size 16, 5X or 6X; size 18 and 20, 6X or 7X. Try to use at least 2 feet of tippet with a floating fly.

Wet flies, larvae, pupae, and most nymphs actually let you use lighter tippets than you would with dry flies the same size. You don't have to "turn over" a size 12 Gold-Ribbed Hare's Ear nymph. If you get the fly moving at a good clip, it will sail to its destination without much help; the tippet simply has to stay out of the way. I've long used 5X and even 6X tippets for nearly all nymphs and wet flies size 8 and smaller. A thinner tippet lets a fly sink more quickly and gives it more freedom of movement as it drifts. Here, too, try to use at least 24 inches of tippet.

Once you get them moving, many streamers also sail pretty well. Unless I'm throwing an immense size 2 Muddler or Woolly Bugger, I hardly ever go heavier than 3X with a streamer. With small and midsize trout streamers, I generally use 4X and even 5X tippets. These are lighter than the conventional wisdom recommends. But the lighter the tippet, the better a streamer's or bucktail's action, and the more rapidly it can sink. Besides, a skinnier line is less visible to the fish. You do, however, need to produce a fair amount of line speed, which comes not from a mighty heave, but from longer casting strokes that accelerate smoothly and stop smartly. Saltwater anglers routinely use 10-pound-test tippets with 5-inch streamers tied on size 1/0 hooks. That's like using 6X with a size 4 Muddler. With good casting technique, it's not hard.

BUT PROBLEMS

Many leader problems derive from casting flaws. Sometimes, though, a leader's butt section can cause troubles.

If a leader's butt is much stiffer than the fly line to which it's connected, you're going to have casting problems. This is rarely an issue if you use a name-brand, freshwater knotless leader with a 5-, 6-, or 7-weight line. Some leaders have butt sections that are a tad heavy and stiff for some 4-weight lines. With a 3-weight or lighter line, you really have to pay attention to the stiffness of the leader butt.

Here's how to check it. Grab the fly line about 8 inches away from its connection to the leader, and hold the leader at the same distance from the junction. Bend the line and leader butt into a U. If the line seems to bend much more readily than the leader, try switching to a leader with a thinner or more supple butt section. Ask your local fly shop for help.

An overly short leader butt can also impair casting. Draw the leader butt between your thumb and forefinger. If you detect a marked decrease in diameter within the first few feet, try another brand that has a longer butt section. You'll find that your casts start turning over more reliably.

A BASIC KIT

You need the ability to make some adjustments on the water. But do you really need to be ready for every imaginable situation? How often do you fish size 22 dry flies and size 2 streamers on the same day with the same outfit? On any given outing, you can get by with a small kit.

For trout fishing, start with a couple of 9-foot leaders, one tapering to 4X or 5X, and the other ending with 3X. The finer leader will handle most of your dry-fly, wet-fly, and nymph fishing; it will probably be your workhorse. Use the heavier one for streamers and perhaps for big nymphs.

Pick up a 7½-foot, 2X or 3X leader for casting big or heavy flies, particularly on breezy days. Get a 12-footer with a 5X or 6X tip for fishing slow, calm water.

Those four will cover most of your trout fishing. Rig all of them with small perfection loops in their butts. Put a braided or nail-knot loop on the end of your fly line. Now you can swap leaders quickly and easily. Unless you regularly cast immense streamers to huge trout, spare 3X through 6X tippet material will cover all your needs.

Your 7½- and 9-foot trout leaders with 3X or 4X tippets will work fine for panfish angling. On most days, I prefer the 9-footer, because even panfish will spook from a fly line that splashes down too close to them. On a breezy day, though, the shorter leader is easier to cast.

A heavy trout leader, say a 9-footer tapering to a 2X or 3X tippet, will handle most smallmouth flies. When you fish for largemouths, things become a tad more complicated. Years ago, many bass fishermen used heavy, 6-foot leaders, because delivering a big, wind-resistant bug is easier with such a rig. Over time, we learned that we can catch more bass with longer leaders—indeed, a largemouth bass in clear water is every bit as wary as an old brown trout—and these days, most bass anglers use 9-foot or even longer leaders.

Most manufacturers make specialty bass leaders with heavy (0.026-inch or thereabouts) butts. If you fish for largemouths with an 8- or 9-weight outfit and big bugs or streamers, these heavy-butt leaders work fine. But if you use a 6- or 7-weight rig and slightly smaller flies for bass (as many anglers do), you will probably find a leader with an 0.026-inch butt too heavy and stiff for the line to carry and turn over. With a light bass outfit, a 9-foot, 1X or 2X trout leader usually works better. Just because the label on a package says "Bass Leader" doesn't mean that the contents are right for *all* largemouth fishing. If you're going to cast well, your rod, fly line, leader, and fly have to work as an integrated, balanced system.

In time, you will acquire a lot more leaders. We all do. Maybe you'll start tying your own, experimenting with lengths, materials, and taper designs. Eventually, you might carry a wallet full of specialized leaders ranging from 7 to 16 feet, with tippets from 1X to 8X—and that's just for trout fishing. Perhaps you'll overhaul your leader for each new pool or run, as some experts do. Or you might adopt the unusual but very simple leader system described in the next chapter, a loop-to-loop setup that provides the greatest possible strength and saves you from ever having to tie leader knots in the field.

The endless tinkering is part of the fun of fly fishing. And you do need more than one leader. For most trout fishing, though, a small, simple assortment of leaders and tippet material will do the job. The main thing is to use any leader well. Perfect your casting first, and then worry about making tiny adjustments in the taper section of a 15-foot leader.

TYING THE LIGATURE OR SIMPLE BLOOD KNOT

Lefty Kreh and Mark Sosin named this connection the simple blood knot in their 1991 book, *Practical Fishing Knots.* In *The Complete Book of Fishing Knots*, British author Geoffrey Budworth says that "it is in fact a multiple form of another knot altogether—the ligature knot." I defer to Kreh and Sosin in all things piscatorial, but I like the serious sound of "ligature," and that's what I call this knot. Besides, Mr. Budworth seems to have a point: This line-to-line junction is fundamentally different from a standard blood knot.

You can call it the Mystical Magic Double Seven Knot for all I care, or name it after your cat. The main thing is to learn and practice it. Tied properly, the ligature knot creates an extraordinarily strong connection. In some materials, I have seen it achieve 100 percent efficiency. The blood and surgeon's knots aren't even in the same league, particularly in very light lines. Combined with a high-strength knot at the fly, the ligature knot will let you land more and bigger fish.

Tightening this knot is a bit of a chore. You have to pull first on the tag ends to close the wraps partway, then on the main lines, then on the tags again, and then on the main lines to tighten the knot all the way. With some lines, you can get away with pulling once on the tags and once on the standing lines—but don't count on it. The knot's tremendous strength makes it worth the effort. Be sure to lubricate the knot before beginning to tighten it.

I find the ligature knot difficult to tighten in lines above 0.011 inch. With modern nylon tippet material, though, that translates to at least 12-pound-test line. In 3X (0.008 inch) and lighter materials, you should have no trouble tightening this knot. Learn it with 4X nylon.

Colored wire takes the place of monofilament in three of the four following photos. The fourth shot, of the tightened knot, shows dyed-black nylon line.

The black wire coming from the left represents the end of the leader. The gray wire is the new tippet. Put the left-hand (black) line on top of the right-hand line, making sure that you have at least 4 inches of line above the point at which they cross.

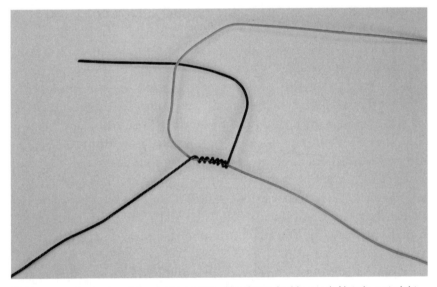

Make seven wraps around the right-hand line (the tippet, in this case). Not six, not eight—seven. Bring the tag end of the leader (the line with which you made the wraps) behind the tag end of the tippet. This detail is important.

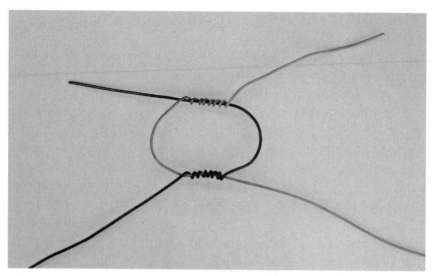

Once again, make seven wraps from left to right, this time wrapping the tag end of the tippet around the end of the leader. Note that in both wraps, the line that does the wrapping begins on top of the other line. You will produce a boxy arrangement that looks like this.

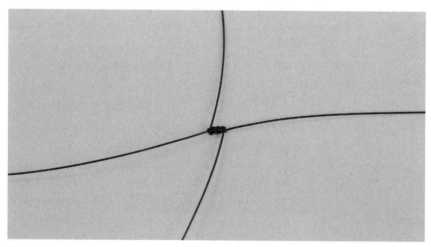

Dip the knot in water, and begin closing it by pulling on the tag ends. Then let go of the tags and pull on the main lines. Pull the tags again. Finish tightening the knot by pulling on the main lines with steady force. This takes a little practice; don't give up if your first few attempts go badly. The knot should finish with the tags at opposite ends and perpendicular to the main line, like these. Clip the tag ends close to the knot.

TYING THE ORVIS TIPPET–CHRISTOPHER KNOT OR IMPROVED FIGURE EIGHT

This knot's simplicity suggests that it has probably been discovered by many anglers over the years. The Orvis website says that the knot was developed by Perk Perkins, the company's CEO, who named it the Orvis tippet knot. In 2001, *American Angler* magazine ran an article about a line-to-line connection called the Christopher knot; structurally, it is identical to the Orvis tippet knot. No matter what one calls it, this knot is simply a figure eight with an extra wrap made with the end of the leader and the tippet—an improved figure eight, as it were. Figure-eight knots of various sorts have been used since the days of wooden sailing ships, and it seems likely to me that someone must have employed this knot back when gut leaders were hot stuff.

Although it's simple and fast, this connection consistently proves stronger than the more popular surgeon's and triple surgeon's knots. In fluorocarbon, it regularly beats the blood knot; in nylon, the two are about equal. Unlike the blood knot, the improved figure eight easily accommodates light lines that differ by 0.002 or even 0.003 inch; in other words, you can use it to attach 5X material to 3X.

The natural temptation is to add one more wrap with the end of the leader and the tippet. Resist the urge. Tests indicate that adding another wrap does nothing to improve the knot and sometimes detracts from its strength.

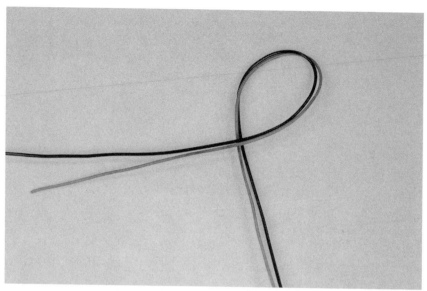

The black wire represents the end of the leader; the gray wire is the new tippet. Overlap at least 4 inches of the lines. Bend the lines into a loop, bringing the end of the leader and the new tippet behind the standing part of the leader.

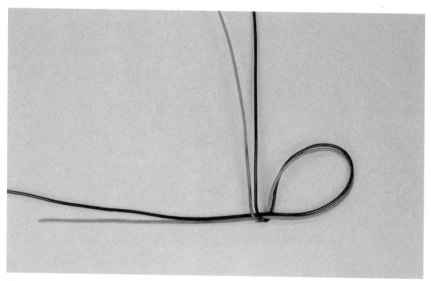

Bring the end of the leader and the new tippet up in front of the overlapped lines. Pinching all four strands at the crossover point makes the rest of the knot very easy to tie.

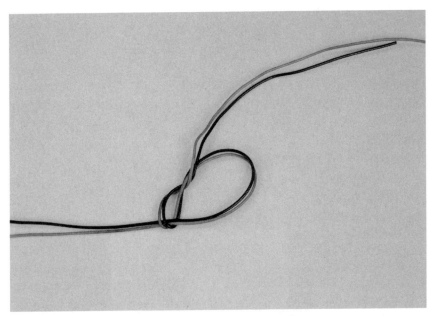

Pass the end of the leader and the entire tippet through the loop from the back side.

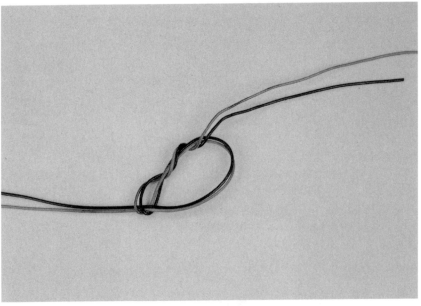

Make one more complete wrap with the end of the leader and the entire tippet.

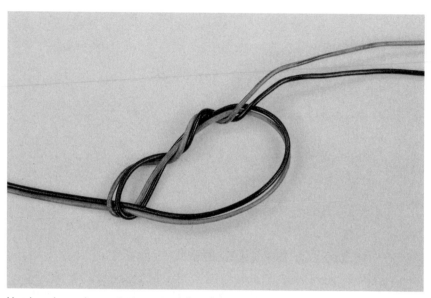

Here's a closer view so that you can follow the path of the lines. This is a very simple knot.

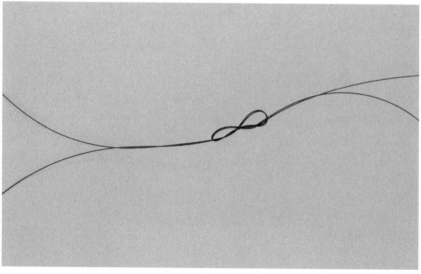

This photo and the next show dyed-black monofilament. Tighten the knot as you would a surgeon's knot, by pulling evenly on all four strands. As you begin tightening the knot, it will assume an obvious figure-eight shape, but with one extra wrap on the right side.

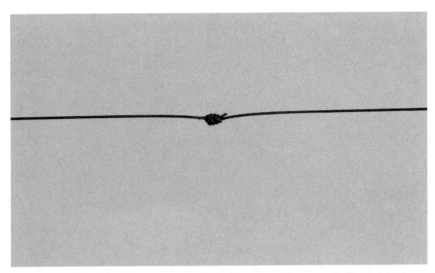

Lubricate the knot and tighten it all the way. Pull hard on all four strands. The finished improved figure eight is fatter than a blood knot, but shorter. It contains less line and therefore weighs less.

4

Saltwater-Style Rigging for Freshwater Fish

Even if he has never had much interest in striped bass, bonefish, or red drum, a trout fisherman can do himself a world of good by attending a saltwater fly-fishing school. For one thing, the saltwater guys really know how to cast. It's not a question of muscle, but of form and technique, and the principles that let an angler throw a mile of 9-weight line also make him a more efficient short-range caster with a 4-weight outfit.

Saltwater fly fishers also understand the subtleties of baitfish flies. They have to. A saltwater angler succeeds or fails according to his knowledge of bait. Although I've never been more than a lukewarm saltwater fly fisher, the designs of marine flies have shaped the ways in which I tie and fish freshwater streamers. My streamer boxes contain none of the traditional New England and northeastern patterns, but they hold lots of phony minnows based on successful saltwater flies.

Third, fly fishing in the salt requires superior rigging knowledge and skills. Again, it's a matter of necessity. A trout fisherman usually plays his quarry, but a tarpon or permit angler *fights* his, and he needs strong tackle. My salty friends didn't merely teach me a few new knots; they taught me to think about leaders and connections in a new way. And once again, what I learned carried over into freshwater fishing. For the past fifteen years, a saltwater system has been my standard rigging method for freshwater angling.

Yes, I know it's delusional to believe that I always *need* the strongest possible system when I fish for trout, bass, or panfish. Where I most enjoy fishing for trout, old twine would work fine as backing, because a guy could go a lifetime without seeing it. Most guys do. But hope springs eternal, and I know in my bones that someday I will hook a shockingly big trout or smallmouth in a place where he has room to run. I'd like to be ready.

Besides, saltwater-style rigging provides not only strength, but also consistency. My tackle has three loop-to-loop junctions: backing to fly line, line to leader, and main leader to tippet. I make the loops at home, sitting in a chair under a good light and with all my gadgets handy. Except for tying flies to tippets, I've eliminated tying knots in the field; I go years at a stretch without knotting tippet material to a leader. In doing so, I've eliminated many chances to make bad connections. I can *always* count on my rigging.

Those loops also simplify making changes. Whether I want to swap lines on a reel, replace an entire leader, or switch to a lighter or heavier tippet, I can do it quickly and without fussing with knots. I do not miss the frustration of trying to tie a leader knot in poor light or with stiff, cold fingers.

Since the loops let me change lines, leaders, or tippets quickly and easily, they also make my outfits more versatile. In a minute or two, I can swap a 10-foot, 6X leader for an 8-foot, 3X rig, changing a 5-weight line from a trout outfit for casting small dry flies to a bream outfit for throwing balsa poppers. When the trout seem uninterested in insects, I can quickly replace an entire dry-fly leader with a quick-sinking streamer rig equipped with tiny lead weights.

This style of rigging has worked beautifully for virtually all of the fly fishing I've done since the late 1980s, and I think that it will work just as well for you. Let's go through the entire system and you'll see what I mean.

BACKING TO FLY LINE

In his book *Fly-Fishing for Bonefish*, Chico Fernández reports the results of some tests that he, Bob Stearns, and Frank Steele conducted. Although these three saltwater experts knew from decades on the water which backing-to-line connection to use, they wanted to test various junctions to see how knots stack up against one another and whether test data would support conclusions drawn from experience.

Chico's book has the full account of the backing-to-line tests. A condensed version might go like this: Use only a loop-to-loop system to connect backing to fly line; no other connection is nearly as strong. Popular and often-recommended connections such as the nail knot and Albright special performed poorly in the tests that the three anglers conducted.

On every fly reel you own, connect the backing to the line with a loop-to-loop junction. The loop in the backing needs to be long enough to pass over a spool of fly line or a reel. In most freshwater outfits, a loop about 14 inches in length is plenty long enough.

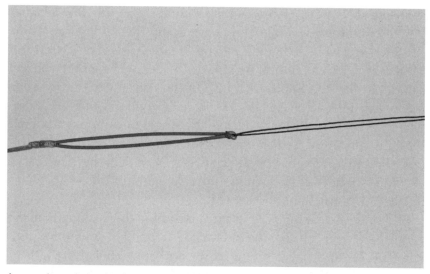

A properly made loop-to-loop junction is the strongest connection between the backing and fly line. If you rig all of your fly lines with loops, you can remove a line from a reel and replace it with another in a few minutes without having to tie any knots.

You can use either of two methods to put a loop in the backing. Most (though not all) Dacron backings permit you to make a spliced loop. Splicing a loop in braided Dacron takes a bit of dexterity and a tool, but a spliced loop is very strong and perfectly smooth.

Your other choice is to tie a Bimini twist in the backing. This is how I usually do it, simply because I like tying Biminis and do not enjoy monkeying around with homemade splicing needles. The Bimini twist produces a long loop while retaining practically 100 percent of the line's strength. It's a long, narrow knot that easily passes through the guides on a fly rod.

Although it's more complex than, say, a clinch knot, the Bimini twist is not difficult to master. Many fly fishers seem to regard tying a Bimini as an act of black magic possible only for those who have served a long apprenticeship in the dark arts. Baloney. Anyone with average coordination can master this knot in one lesson from a good teacher. The Bimini twist can be difficult to learn from printed instructions (it was for me), and perhaps this is why so many freshwater anglers fear it. The best way to learn is to have someone show you. After watching a good rigger tie a few Biminis, you'll wonder why you haven't been using this knot all your life.

It's worth noting that in *Practical Fishing Knots*, Lefty Kreh and Mark Sosin put the Bimini twist near the beginning of the chapter called "Knots You Should Know." In the comments that precede the instructions, Kreh and Sosin say, "Although developed for big-game trolling, the Bimini ranks as the single most important knot for light tackle and fly fishing." Amen. Learn the Bimini twist. It is not something exotic or specialized—it is among the basic, absolutely essential fly-fishing knots. The end of this chapter has illustrated instructions and some tips.

Enough preaching. After tying a Bimini in the backing to make a long loop, you can coat the knot with Pliobond or something similar. The coating has nothing to do with the knot's strength; it merely makes the Bimini a little smoother so that it might pass through the rod guides more easily. But since the Bimini is such a tidy knot anyway, many anglers don't bother coating it.

Make the loop in the tail end of the fly line with a pair of nail knots. Bend back the end of the line to make a loop 1 to 2 inches in length. With 10-pound-test nylon monofilament (or 1X tippet material), tie a six- or seven-wrap nail knot around both legs of the fly-line loop. Trim the tag ends of the first knot, and then tie another nail knot next to the first one. After trimming the tags of the second nail knot, clip the tag end of the fly line. Give the nail knots and about ½ inch of the fly line a couple coats of Pliobond or a coat of Loon UV Knot Sense to make the assembly smooth.

A nail-knot loop tied with 10-pound mono is stronger than the fly line itself. I'm not speculating here. I've made such rigs and pulled on them until something broke, and the fly line has always failed before the loop.

When you join the backing to the fly line, snug up the connection very carefully so that the interlocking loops form a square knot. The loop in the backing will probably want to flip back on itself and form a girth hitch or, to use the more elegant British term, a lark's-head layout. Don't let that happen. If it forms a girth hitch, the backing loop becomes much weaker. Guide and manhandle the loops so that they form a square knot, and then pull hard on the rig so that the backing dents the fly-line coating a little.

Loop-to-loop rigging works with any fly line—floating or sinking, opaque or clear. That's not true of the nail knot or even the Albright special, both of which can make poor connections to fly lines with single-strand or braided-monofilament cores.

Always make sure that a loop-to-loop connection forms a square knot, as shown by this wire model. If either of the loops flips back on itself to form a girth hitch, the line will fail under little strain. A connection that looks like this one is absolutely secure.

In fresh water, I may never need all the strength that loops provide, but that hardly justifies knowingly using second-rate rigging methods. Besides, the loop-to-loop setup has another benefit: It lets me quickly change entire lines. I own more fly lines than reels, which means that some of my reels have to do several jobs. One week, a reel might hold a standard 5-weight line for dry-fly fishing; the next week, when I go fishing for big bluegills, the same reel might hold a 5-weight line with a shorter front taper and head. Another reel might carry a floating 8-weight line for most of the year, but then hold a clear, slow-sinking line when I make a trip to the coast.

Because all my fly lines have loops, I can swap lines in a few minutes without having to tie any knots. When I'm away from home for more than a day, I often carry a couple of spare lines in my gear bag. If I damage a line while fishing, I can easily replace it, again without tying any knots. The fewer knots I tie in the field, the happier I am. I'd rather do my rigging under a good light in my office.

Rigging all your lines and reels with loops takes a little more time up front, but it saves time in the long run. It also makes your tackle stronger and more reliable. There's really no point in doing it any other way.

LINE TO LEADER

A loop-to-loop junction at the front end of the fly line permits instant leader changes. I don't often replace an entire leader while fishing, but I like to have the option of doing so without having to tie knots, and I'm very happy to have a quick-change connection after a fish damages a leader by dragging it across rocks, submerged timber, or dock pilings.

Many anglers have long employed loops to connect leaders to fly lines. Years ago, I used to nail-knot a foot of 0.021-inch mono to the tip of a fly line, tie a small perfection loop in the end of the mono, and connect my leader to that. Some anglers still do it that way. But it's a poor method, because that foot of heavy mono comes off the reel with a pronounced curl. The line "remembers" the diameter of the spool, and no amount of pulling will remove the curl from a short piece of stiff, 0.021-inch nylon. Besides, a nail knot is not an especially secure connection to some fly lines.

These days, many anglers equip fly lines with braided, slip-on loops. Braided loops generally work okay, but a nail-knot loop works better and costs nothing. It also floats better than a slip-on loop; indeed, a nail-knot loop largely eliminates the problem of having the tip of the line sink after you've been fishing for a while.

Double the tip of the line to make a small loop. Secure the loop with a pair of six-turn nail knots tied next to each other. On a 6-weight or lighter fly line, use 8-pound-test mono for the nail knots; to make a loop in a 7-, 8-, or 9-weight line, use 10-pound monofilament. The finished loop should be between ⅜ and ½ inch long. Coat the nail knots with something to make them smooth and protect them from nicks.

To attach the leader, tie a small perfection loop in the butt. Poke the end of the fly line through the loop in the leader. Then pull the

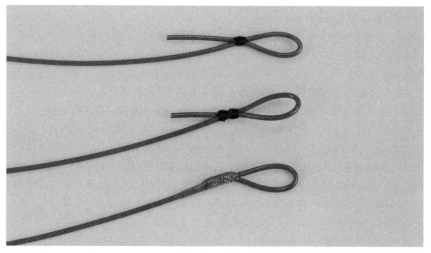

Making a nail-knot loop on the end of a fly line. *Top:* Double the line back on itself to make a loop, and secure the loop with a nail knot tied with 8- or 10-pound monofilament. This mono was dyed black to make it easier to see. *Middle:* Tie another nail knot next to the first. *Bottom:* Clip the tag end of the fly line, and cover the nail knots with Pliobond, Loon UV Knot Sense, or another flexible coating.

leader through the loop in the end of the fly line. Snug up the connection, and you're ready to fish. Should you want to replace the entire leader or remove it to clean the line, you can do so without having to mess around with knots. You will also have a very strong, secure connection between line and leader.

Some folks who prefer theory to practice (and this sport has lots of them) will argue that such an arrangement cannot cast well, that a loop-to-loop junction will inevitably "hinge" or somehow fail to "transmit energy" as the cast rolls out toward the target. Granted, interlocking loops make a heavier and bulkier connection than, say, a needle knot, and if I had to turn over a 15-foot leader with a 2-weight outfit all day, I'd probably not rig with loops. But I've used nail-knot loops with 4- through 9-weight outfits since the 1980s, with leaders up to 12 feet or more in length and every imaginable sort of fly, and my experience has been that loop-to-loop junctions cast just fine—every bit as well as leaders nail-knotted to fly lines. I'd hate to fish without my loopy leaders.

TIPPETS, WITH A TWIST

Trout anglers who have reached A Certain Age know the anguish of trying to poke a 7X tippet through the eye of a size 22 fly in poor light. For me, tying a piece of skinny tippet material to the end of a leader is even worse. Knotting 7X monofilament makes me crazy and nervous. Should I clip off all of the old tippet or just add to it? If I do cut off the entire tippet, will I have trouble tying a piece of 0.004-inch nylon to the end of a leader that now measures 0.006 inch or more? Should I tie a Stu Apte improved blood knot (which makes me even crazier) just to be sure? How do I *know* that whatever knot I've tied is completely trustworthy?

The minute I heard about it many years ago, a leader with a loop-to-loop tippet struck me as the best invention since largemouth bass. No more fumbling with or fouling up blood knots while standing in fast water.

My early loop-to-loop tippets had a few reliability and performance problems. As I became interested in saltwater fly fishing and made the acquaintance of anglers smarter than I am, I learned a much better way to make tippets with loop connections, and I discovered that a saltwater rigging method intended for heavy leaders and big flies works beautifully with trout leaders, fine tippets, and small flies. After using this saltwater-style leader for fifteen years, I have so much confidence in it that I'm reluctant to use anything else.

The leader has two components joined by means of loops: the butt and taper section, and the tippet. The butt and taper (or middle) section is much like that of a standard leader, except that it ends with a piece of medium-weight mono (0.011 to 0.013 inch, depending on the leader) that has a small loop in the end. Connected to that loop is a special Bimini tippet. That's right: I tie Bimini twists in trout-weight tippet material. It's actually easier than tying them in 12-pound-test mono or 20-pound-test backing.

This saltwater-style leader has several advantages. First, the loop-to-loop junction between the main leader and the Bimini tippet is very strong. With this setup, the weakest link in your system is the tippet-to-fly knot. If you attach the fly with a superior knot (we'll look at this topic in the next chapter), the entire rig is amazingly strong; you can use a 5X tippet and have a stronger system than some anglers have with 3X.

Second, Bimini tippets are absolutely reliable, because you make them at home, where you can work in good light and take your time. In the field, you no longer tie knots to attach tippets. By eliminating tippet knots tied in a hurry or in poor light and with cold fingers, the Bimini tippet also eliminates the likelihood of mistakes that create weak spots—sometimes very weak spots—in leaders. When you loop on a premade, saltwater-style tippet, you *know* that you have a full-strength connection. It's a good feeling.

Third, you will save time on the water by not having to tie knots. When you need a new tippet, unloop the old one and loop on a new one. Since the main leader can typically accommodate at least four sizes of tippets—3X through 6X, for instance—you will also save time by not having to overhaul a leader's taper section

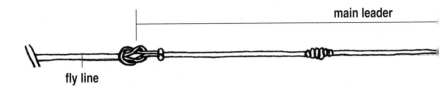

when you switch from a light tippet to a heavier one. You can replace a 6X tippet and size 18 caddis with a 3X tippet and size 4 weighted sculpin in about a minute.

Fourth, you can tie Bimini tippets so that you can change the performance of the entire leader simply by switching from one tippet to another. A single butt-and-taper section can serve as the foundation of a powerful, 9-foot leader for fishing a big streamer, or as the foundation of an 11-foot (or longer) leader that turns over a 6X tippet with all the delicacy you could want. We'll see how this works a little later.

Finally, you no longer have to fish with a stack of tippet wheels stuffed into a pocket or dangling from a contraption attached to your vest. A small leader wallet will hold enough Bimini tippets for a couple days of fishing, plus a few spare main leaders. When I go on a trip, I throw a few tippet spools into my tackle bag so that I can tie Bimini tippets in the evening to replace those I used during the day. When I fish locally, I restock my leader wallet after I get home. I haven't carried spools of tippet material in my vest since the late 1980s. Leaving the tippet wheels behind frees up room in my vest for important stuff like candy bars or cigars.

Bimini tippets have many advantages over conventional leaders and no significant drawbacks that I've discovered in fifteen years of using them. Let's build one of these saltwater-style leaders so that you can see how it works.

The Main Leader

A typical leader has a butt section made of one or two pieces of heavy monofilament. Then comes the taper section, in which the diameter decreases rapidly. Generally, the end of the taper section

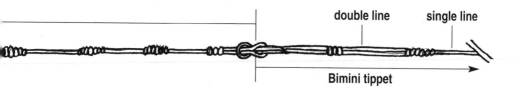

A saltwater-style, loop-to-loop leader eliminates having to tie tippet knots in the field and provides the greatest strength and reliability at the junction of the main leader and tippet. It's a versatile rig, too, since one main leader can accommodate a range of tippet sizes and lengths.

has to be within two or three thousandths of an inch of the tippet's diameter. So a traditional leader with a 5X tippet might start out with 0.021-inch mono, progress through diameters of 0.019, 0.017, 0.015, 0.013, 0.011, and 0.008, and terminate in a length of 0.006 (5X) material. Naturally, the length of each piece of every conceivable leader is a topic of endless debate among fly fishers.

A loop-to-loop leader is simpler: It uses one or two fewer pieces, and you don't have to worry as much about the diameter of the final piece. Part of the tippet section—the double line created by the Bimini twist—serves to continue the leader's taper. The main leader, therefore, can end with somewhat heavier line than in a traditional setup. Most of my trout leaders consist of five or six pieces of mono, not counting the Bimini tippet.

Construct the main leader as you normally would, using blood knots to join pieces of progressively thinner line. Here's one formula for an all-around leader for a 5- or 6-weight outfit. It will work with any soft to moderately stiff nylon monofilament.

36 inches of 0.021 mono, with a perfection loop in the butt end;
24 inches of 0.019;
  6 inches of 0.017;
  6 inches of 0.015;
  6 inches of 0.013;
  6 inches of 0.011, with a small perfection, surgeon's, or nonslip mono loop in the end.

That makes a 7-foot main leader with a two-piece, 60-inch butt section. Add a short, 3X Bimini tippet, and you'll have a total length of about 9 feet. Switch to a 5X Bimini tippet made with 12 inches of double line and 36 inches of single line, and you'll have an 11-foot dry-fly leader.

Every leader formula is a compromise or a custom job suited to a particular application, so feel free to alter the specifications. That basic 7-foot main leader works well for a wide range of fishing with 5- and 6-weight outfits, and it will work with some 4- and 7-weight rigs. For a 4-weight or lighter line, though, you might want to construct a leader that begins with 0.019 material and tapers to 0.010 or even 0.009 if you plan to fish entirely with light tippets. With a 7- through 9-weight outfit, you might want to start with 0.023 material and taper to 0.015 or 0.013, again depending on the tippets that you anticipate using.

You have some flexibility when tying leaders. Whether the butt section consists of a single piece or two pieces (as in the formula above), it should make up 50 to 60 percent of the leader's total length. As long as you follow that general rule, your leaders should perform well.

The Bimini Tippet

Now for the business end of the rig. Since we've already built a general-purpose main leader for a trout outfit, let's give it a 4X Bimini tippet. Peel a couple yards of line off the spool, but don't clip the line yet. Double the material to create an open loop about 20 inches long. Twist the loop and tie a Bimini twist. If you don't know this knot, study the step-by-step instructions at the end of the chapter and practice it with 10-pound-test or lighter line. Better yet, ask an experienced rigger to show you.

After tying the Bimini, you have a 4X line with a roughly 15-inch loop on the end. (Don't worry about the exact length.) Or, to look at it the way a saltwater angler does, you have a single line that turns into about 15 inches of double line. That double line is the whole point of the Bimini twist: It turns one strand into two while maintaining the full strength of the line.

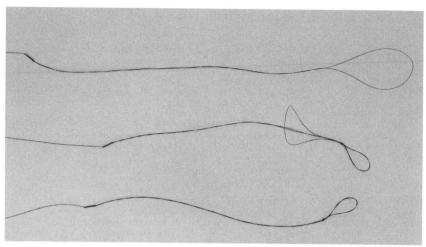

Finishing a Bimini tippet. *Top:* The Bimini twist *(far right)* turns a single line into a double line; that is, it creates a long loop. *Middle:* Fold the double line back on itself, and tie a small surgeon's loop with all four strands. *Bottom:* Clip the leftover line after tying the surgeon's loop. The tippet is now ready to be attached to the main leader by means of a loop-to-loop junction. (Ignore the kink next to each Bimini twist; the hot dye bath that made the line suitable for photography also put some strange bends in it.)

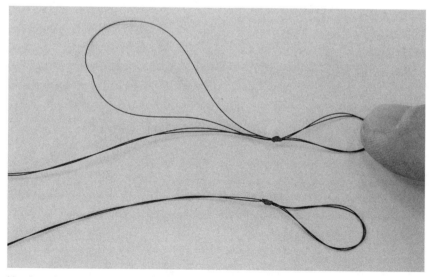

Here's a closer view of the connection end of a Bimini tippet. *Top:* The double line folded back on itself, and a surgeon's loop tied with all four strands. *Bottom:* The finished tippet.

About 10 inches from the Bimini twist, fold the loop back on itself. That is, double the double line. Now tie a surgeon's loop with all four strands. Try to keep the surgeon's loop as small as you can. If you're confused, study the photos. It's really very simple, though difficult to explain. After tying the surgeon's loop with all four strands of mono, clip the leftover line.

Here's what you now have: a single 4X line (still connected to the tippet spool) that turns into about 10 inches of double line that ends with a pair of perfectly even, concentric loops. Three feet away from the Bimini twist, clip the single line. Your Bimini tippet is complete. After a little practice, you can knock out one of these rigs in less than a minute. Honest. I do it all the time.

The end of the main leader is relatively heavy mono—0.011 inch. At the end of the Bimini tippet, you have that double loop— two thicknesses of 4X line, in other words. So, the junction will con-

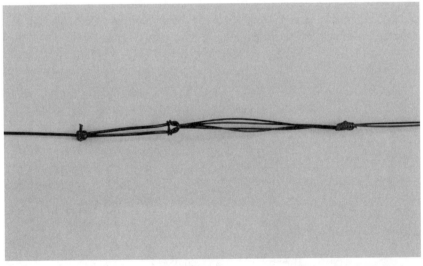

Dyed-black line showing the junction of the main leader and the Bimini tippet. The main leader *(left)* terminates in a small perfection loop. The Bimini tippet *(right)* has a double-thickness surgeon's loop on the end. A loop-to-loop connection joins the two components. This arrangement casts nicely and eliminates most worries about the relative diameters of lines; a single main leader can accommodate four sizes of tippets.

sist of a double-thickness loop on the tippet snugged up against a loop of fairly stout mono at the end of the main leader. That's a very strong, reliable connection. If you tied a halfway decent Bimini, you have retained 99-point-something percent of the strength of the virgin line. You can now use an extra-strong knot to attach the fly without risk of busting off an entire tippet. If you tested the entire rig on a scale, you'd find that even your lightest leader is a full pound or more stronger than the conventional leaders that your friends use.

That double-thickness loop at the end of the tippet also eliminates most worries about the relative diameters of the tippet material and the end of the main leader. You wouldn't want to knot a 4X (0.007-inch) tippet to a main leader that ends with 0.011-inch monofilament; the disparity in diameters is too great unless you use an improved blood knot. But you can attach any Bimini tippet from 7X to 3X to that main leader. The connection will be perfectly strong, and the transfer of casting energy will be smooth.

You'll probably notice that the double line coming from the Bimini has a slight twist. That is, the two strands curl around each other several times in the 10-inch length of the double line. That usually happens with a Bimini, and in this case it's a good thing. The gentle twist keeps the two strands together when you cast, largely eliminating the possibly of the fly fouling or tangling in the double line should you throw an egregious specimen of tailing loop.

CUSTOMIZING THE LEADER'S PERFORMANCE
You control how long the double line will be on each Bimini tippet. If you want 2 feet of double line, tie a long Bimini twist, and then tie the surgeon's loop out near the end of the rig. If you want 2 inches of double line, tie a Bimini with a shorter loop, and then make the surgeon's loop only 2 inches from the Bimini twist. This means that you can customize not only the overall length of a tippet section, but also its casting behavior, because the double line acts as a continuation of the leader's taper section.

Our general-purpose, 7-foot main leader ends with a piece of 0.011-inch mono equipped with a small loop. Let's say that you want to rig for casting weighted Woolly Buggers or smallmouth poppers. Tie some 3X Bimini tippets that have just a few inches of double line and only 18 or 20 inches of single line. After connecting one of those tippets to the main leader, you'll have a powerful rig that turns over a streamer or smallmouth bug with authority. The entire length is a tad under 9 feet.

The next day, you anticipate casting small dry flies to picky trout. Remove the stout tippet, and replace it with a 6X Bimini tippet that has 18 inches of double line and 36 inches of single line. The entire leader is now 11½ feet long. That foot and a half of double 6X material serves as a long continuation of the leader's taper section. It functions as a brake when the leader turns over, and your tippet and fly will waft gently to the water. Without having tied any knots, you've transformed a muscular big-fly leader into a delicate dry-fly leader.

Generally, my 3X and 4X tippets have 8 to 10 inches of double line. The 5X and lighter tippets that I use for dry flies and small wets or nymphs have 12 inches or more of double line. Heavy tippets for casting poppers or warmwater streamers have 6 inches or less of double line.

You will almost certainly want several other main leaders for different types of fishing and various outfits. Try the formulas in the following table. The top row lists the length of each main leader (exclusive of the Bimini tippet) and the floating lines with which it's most useful. Below each heading are the lengths of the leader's sections; the final section, of course, ends with a small loop. The left-hand column specifies the diameters of the sections. With these four formulas and the one above, you can make leaders for nearly everything from panfish to pike. Depending on the lengths of the tippet sections, your five finished leaders will range from about 8 feet to roughly 12 feet, and, collectively, they'll accommodate tippets as light as 8X and as heavy as 12-pound-test with a wire bite tippet for pike. That covers most freshwater fishing.

Material	8 ½ feet, 5- to 7-weight	6 feet, 4- to 7-weight	7 ½ to 8 feet, 4-weight and lighter	7 feet, 8- and 9-weight
0.023				36 inches
0.021	42 inches	36 inches		24 inches
0.019	24 inches	18 inches	36 to 42 inches	8 inches
0.017	10 inches	6 inches	24 inches	8 inches
0.015	10 inches	6 inches	10 inches	8 inches
0.013	8 inches	6 inches	8 inches	
0.011	8 inches		6 inches	
0.010			6 inches	

Make up Bimini tippets in the range of sizes you expect to need. As you tie tippets, store them in a leader wallet with labeled compartments. It's wise to carry a couple of spare main leaders. Even if you prepare eight tippets in each size and three spare leaders, the whole kit still fits in a pocket.

Then go fishing. When you need to replace a tippet, undo the loop-to-loop connection, attach the fresh tippet, and get back to work, confident that you're fishing with the strongest leader you've ever used. When other anglers cuss as they try to tie on fresh tippets in the gloaming, you'll loop on a ready-made piece of terminal tackle and enjoy the evening rise. Later, at home, check your tippet inventory and tie replacements for those you used.

A UNIVERSAL SOLUTION? WELL, ALMOST . . .

Some anglers who've never used this kind of leader will look at it and, with all the certainty of a medieval pope, pronounce it wrong and bad. Don't listen to them; try it for yourself. You'll find that though it looks unconventional, a loop-to-loop leader with a Bimini tippet performs beautifully, turning over smartly and presenting the fly as neatly as a regular leader. I use them to cast small dry flies to trout, balsa poppers to bass, and yarn crabs to redfish.

But nothing is always perfect, and there are a few outfits with which I'd prefer a leader knotted directly to the fly line. Neatly made loops aren't very big, but they're bigger than a nail or needle knot. If I know that I'll need to fish a leader longer than 12 feet, I also know that the line-to-leader connection will have to come through the tip-top and several running guides every time I land a fish. In this case, I'd rather have a leader nail-knotted directly to the fly line. But I'll still use a Bimini tippet

I enjoy trout fishing with short rods. With a 9- or 10-foot leader and a 7-foot rod, I'm going to pull the leader butt through the tip-top and five or six small running guides every time I bring a trout to hand. So a couple of my small reels have lines with nail-knotted leaders. Even here, though, the leaders have Bimini tippets.

WHAT ABOUT KNOTLESS LEADERS?

You can use Bimini tippets with a knotless leader, but you need one that has a sufficiently thick tip. The loop-to-loop connection requires a main leader that terminates with a diameter between 0.009 (for very light trout tippets) and 0.013 inch (for heavy trout or smallmouth tippets). You can't tie a loop in the end of a 5X knotless leader, attach a 3X Bimini tippet, and expect the rig to cast very well.

Here are some possibilities. Start with a short, heavy knotless leader—a 7½-foot 1X or 0X model with a butt diameter of 0.022 inch. Cut a couple inches off each end, and then tie small perfection loops on both ends. You now have a main leader about 7 feet long with a 0.010- or 0.011-inch tip, and it should work well enough with 3X to 7X Bimini tippets.

Or you can begin with a longer leader and do some tinkering. For instance, you could start with a 12-foot, 3X knotless leader with an 0.024-inch butt. Cut a foot off the fat end, then snip about 3 feet off the skinny end, which should bring you back to a diameter of at least 0.010 inch. Tie a small perfection loop in each end of the now 8-foot main leader, loop on a 4X Bimini tippet, and go outside for some test casting. If the rig performs poorly, trim the main leader from the thin end, cutting off a few inches at a time.

You can perform such experiments with old leaders and, once you've figured out what works for you, modify a few new ones. If you have a micrometer, the work goes faster.

But if you're going to go through all that trouble (not to mention tying Bimini tippets), you might as well learn to tie your own leaders. In the long run, you'll save money by tying your own; and right off the bat, you'll have customized leaders that perform better.

THE QUICK-SINK LEADER

Many anglers who use loop-to-loop connections carry a short piece of sinking fly line (or even lead-core line) that has a loop on each end. My friend Dr. Bill Chiles always has a 3-foot piece of high-density line coiled up in a vest pocket. When he wants to drag a streamer or a big stonefly nymph across the bottom of a pool, he loops the sinking line to the end of his fly line, adds a short leader, and then ties on the fly. Throwing such a rig isn't like casting a floating line, but Bill makes it looks easy, even with a 3-weight. And he catches a lot of good trout in the high-gradient southern Appalachian streams that he loves.

A weighted leader accomplishes much the same thing as a piece of fast-sinking fly line. Construct a main leader like our 7-foot, general-purpose model. That leader has five blood knots: four in the taper section and one in the butt section. You're interested in the three smallest knots in the taper section and the knot that forms the loop in the end of the leader. Cut four ¾-inch pieces of fine or medium weighting wire that fly tiers use. Lead wire is easier to work with, but some jurisdictions permit only lead-free wire and sinkers. On the back side of each blood knot—that is, the side facing the butt end of the leader—wrap a piece of wire tightly around the monofilament. Wrap the final piece of wire behind the loop on the leader's tip. Put a drop of superglue, Pliobond, Flexament, or even nail polish on each coil of wire to keep it in place.

You'll find that this sort of leader casts pretty well, helps a streamer or nymph get down in a hurry, and keeps the fly deep. At the end of each presentation, make a strong roll cast to bring the weighted leader to the surface, and then begin the backcast. Use longer, smooth casting strokes and throw a loop that's wider than usual.

To make a weighted leader for streamer, wet-fly, or nymph fishing, wrap short pieces of fine fly-weighting wire above the last two or three blood knots and the perfection loop to which the Bimini tippet is attached. Coat the wire wraps with superglue, vinyl cement, Pliobond, nail polish, or whatever to protect them and keep them in place. This unusual rig is surprisingly pleasant to cast.

You can make quick-sink leaders in an infinite range of weights by varying the thickness of the weighting wire, the length of each piece, and the number of pieces. Remember, though, that you need to cast the thing, so don't get carried away with the lead. A leader with five 2-inch-long pieces of heavy lead wire might seem just the ticket for swinging a Woolly Bugger through fast, deep water, but you'll need a tarpon outfit to throw the rig. A lightly weighted leader casts easily, but it still makes a difference with a streamer or nymph.

TYING THE BIMINI TWIST
Saltwater-style rigging with loops and Bimini twists provides superior strength and reliability, more convenience in the field, and greater versatility. Tying a Bimini isn't hard. Explaining how to do it is. Don't let the following sequence scare you; it contains a certain

amount of redundancy. Most of the photos show my hands tying a Bimini with black, 30-pound-test braided line. In a few places, the "live-action" photos are supplemented by pictures of wire models that I hope will make the steps easier to understand.

Learning how to tie the Bimini twist is one of the most important skills a fly fisher can acquire. Practice the knot with 3X (0.008-inch) or 2X (0.009-inch) material; a small spool of 4- or 6-pound-test spinning line costs only a few dollars and has enough material to let you practice this and other knots scores of times. Once you become halfway proficient, you will tie a Bimini twist in no more than half a minute and knock out an entire Bimini tippet in less than a minute. Honest. It's not even within shouting distance of being difficult.

Twenty is the standard number of twists for the loop of a Bimini. With 4X and lighter tippet materials, I generally make twenty-four to twenty-six twists.

The Bimini can be finished in several different ways. The method shown here seems the easiest to me, and it has proved absolutely reliable.

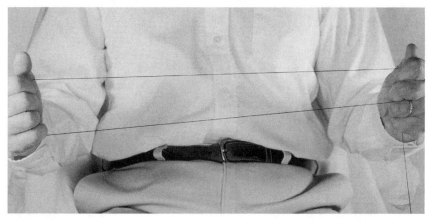

Double the end of the line to make a loop 18 to 24 inches long. The standing line makes the bottom leg of the loop; the tag end is the top leg. Your left hand holds the line, with the tag end pinched between your thumb and the top of your fist.

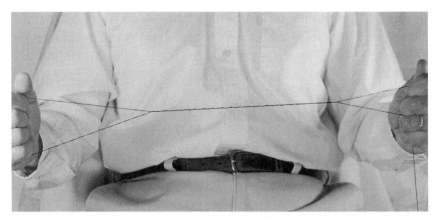

With your right hand, put at least twenty twists in the loop. Rotate your hand as if you're scooping water or dirt toward you. A "twist" is one complete revolution of your hand.

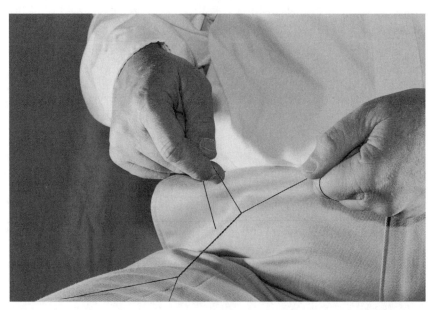

Put the loop over your right knee. Hold the standing line with your left hand and the tag end with your right. Pull the loop firmly against your leg. Separate your hands to compact the twists—that is, to squeeze them into a shorter area. Maintain tension on the lines as you separate your hands.

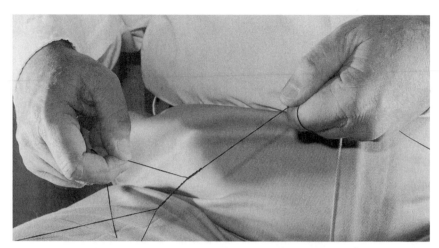

Move your left hand so that it's aligned with the top of the loop. Move your right hand until the tag end is slightly beyond perpendicular to the standing line. Now, let your right hand slowly move inward, relaxing some of the tension on the tag end. As you do this, the tag end will jump up onto the twists and begin forming a series of barrel wraps.

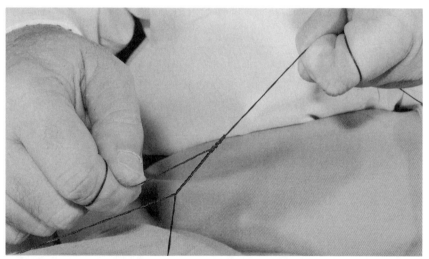

Here's a closer view of this step. My left hand is maintaining tension on the standing line (note that the line is wrapped around a finger for a better grip). My right hand has moved the tag end slightly past perpendicular. As I relaxed some of the tension on the tag end, it hopped up onto the twists and began forming barrel wraps over them; you can see the barrel wraps just below the bottom of my shirt.

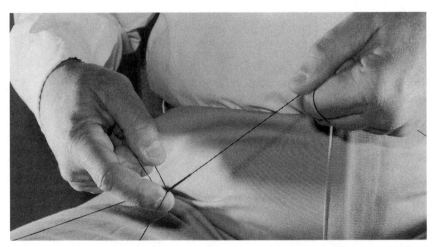

Let the tag end continue to make barrel wraps all the way down to the top of the V. With heavy line such as fly-line backing, you can help the process along by hooking your right index finger in the top of the V. Note that the tag end in this photo has finished making the barrel wraps—it's all the way down to the top of the V and has run into my index finger.

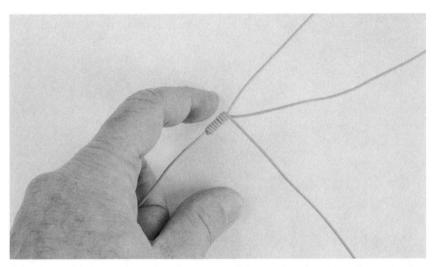

This wire model shows what you want to accomplish: a series of neat barrel wraps ending at the top of the V. It's all one smooth process: Put the twisted loop over your knee, spread your hands to squeeze the wraps into a short space, align the standing line with the top of the V, move the tag end a little past perpendicular, and relax some of the tension on the tag end so that the twists become barrel wraps.

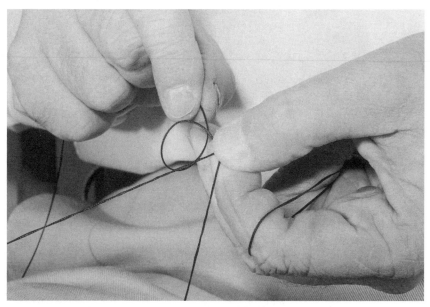

Walk your left hand down the line, and pinch the barrel wraps hard with your thumb and forefinger. With the tag end, make a half hitch around the right leg of the V.

Here's the wire model again. This is the view you will have as you tie the knot, but it's the same step shown in the previous photo: Pinch the barrel wraps to keep them together, and then throw a half hitch around the right leg of the V with the tag end of the line.

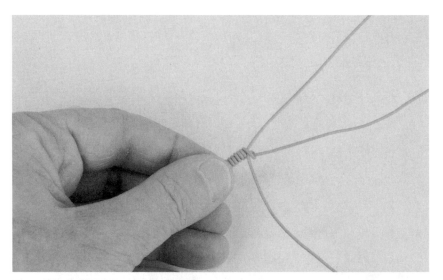

Tighten the half hitch firmly. If you need to, you can now relax for a moment. The hard stuff is done, and the knot will stay together while you take a deep breath. But keep the loop over your knee until the next step.

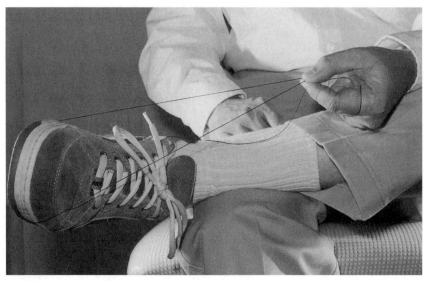

You need to put the loop on something smaller than your thigh to make the final lock on the knot. Your left foot works fine for this job. And yes, I have some shoes that I prefer for tying Biminis. These crepe-soled sneakers are perfect, as is a pair of old moccasins.

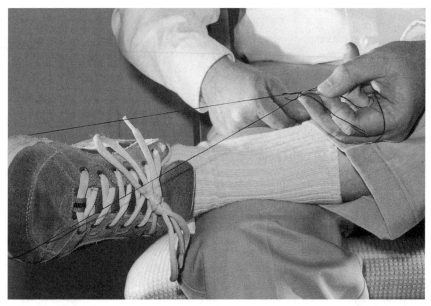

With the tag end, make a big, long half hitch around both legs of the loop. Do not tighten this half hitch.

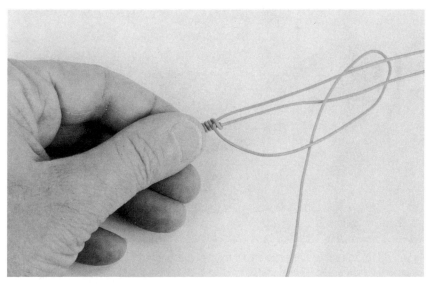

Back to the wire model and your view of the knot. This is another view of the previous step, in which you make a long half hitch around both legs of the loop.

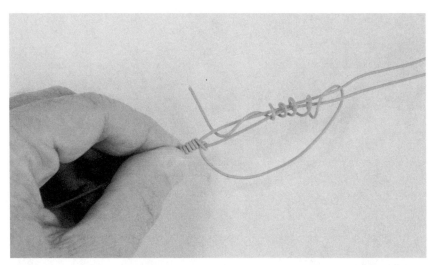

Make several more wraps with the tag end around both legs of the loop. Note that these wraps are inside the half hitch. With backing, make a total of five wraps; with monofilament tippet material, make a total of at least six wraps. After making the wraps, tuck the tag end between the two legs of the loop.

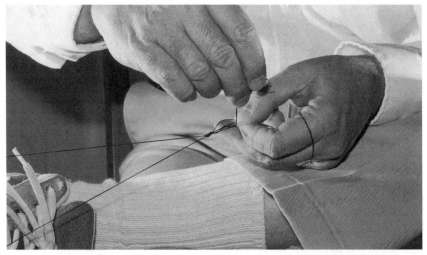

As you make the wraps, it helps to hold the top of the loop—the top of the V, that is—between your left thumb and forefinger to keep the legs of the loop separated a little. This will simplify tucking the tag end between the legs of the loop after you've made the wraps.

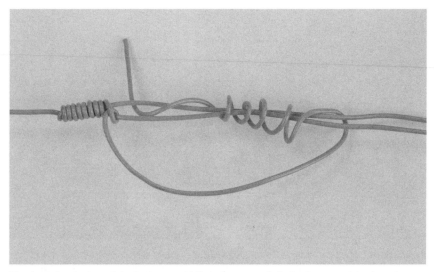

Here's a closer view of the lock wrap. Follow the tag end: At the bottom of the barrel wraps, it makes a half hitch around the right leg of the loop; then it makes a long half hitch around both legs; it makes another five wraps around both legs inside the half hitch; finally, it goes between the legs of the loop.

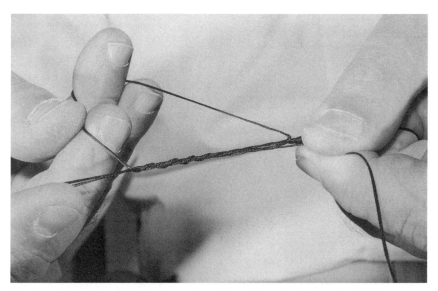

Here's a close-up view of the lock wrap in my heavy black line. Tightening this final stage can be a little tricky.

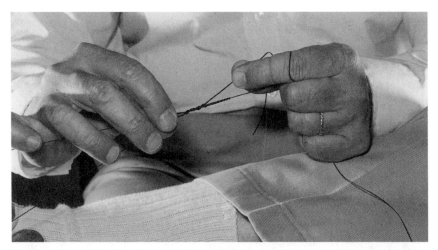

Note that the standing line is wrapped around a finger and then gripped inside the left hand (the one with the wedding ring). This frees the left thumb and forefinger to pull on the tag end. As you gently pull on the tag end, the lock wraps might want to tangle. To prevent that problem, pull the tag end a little, then tease the lock wraps in the direction of your foot to untangle them. Pull on the tag end some more, tease the lock wraps again, and so on until the wraps are almost all the way tight.

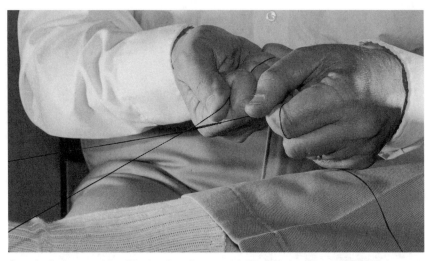

Seat the lock wraps by pulling hard on the tag end. The loop is still over the end of your left foot, and your left hand maintains tension on the standing line while your right hand pulls on the tag.

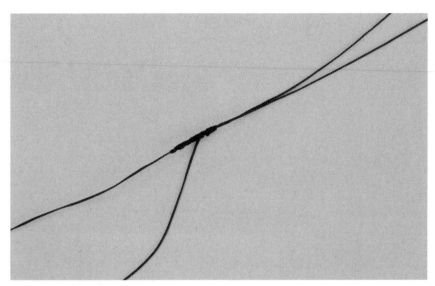

The finished Bimini twist is a long, slender, tidy knot that turns a single line into a double line while retaining virtually (and often literally) 100 percent of the unknotted line's strength. All that remains is to clip the tag end where it exits the side of the knot.

5

The Last Link

A long time ago, an acquaintance who'd heard that I build fly rods came to me with a request. This chap—let's call him Biff—spent a lot of time on a big river where, he claimed, he rarely cast less than 60 feet and hardly ever hooked a trout less than a foot and a half long. Twenty-inchers were common, he alleged. Often, Biff said, he had to cast farther than 70 feet because the big, smart trout wouldn't let him approach any closer. The fish sneered at any fly attached to a tippet heavier than 6X.

I've long believed that one can calculate actual casting distance by multiplying claimed distance by .75 and then subtracting 5. Even so, Biff was trout-fishing at respectable ranges. No doubt he was stretching the length of the trout, too, but the river's reputation supported his claim of casting to better-than-average fish. I figured that Biff was making 40- to 50-foot deliveries to trout that measured 15 or 16 inches. In all but a few places, that's enviable angling.

Biff's problem was that he was breaking off a lot of fish. He was using a very fast, powerful 5-weight rod, the only one he had that would let him cast as far as he needed to. He'd tried half a dozen brands of tippet material and even built special leaders with shock-absorbing butt sections, but nothing helped. Biff's 6X tippets simply couldn't hold the trout—but the fish hooted at flies attached to anything heavier. He hoped that I could make a rod that would solve the problem.

What he needed, Biff explained, was a rod that would fire 70 feet of 5-weight line into the wind, but then protect the frail tippet when a trout rose. He wanted something that cast with the oomph of a saltwater 7-weight and struck a fish with the delicacy of a fiberglass 2-weight. Did I know of such a rod blank?

I didn't, because none existed (or is ever likely to exist). Diplomatically, I told Biff that he was asking for a magic wand, not a fishing rod. On a whim, I asked him which knot he used for attaching the fly.

"Oh, I don't know," Biff said. "That deal where you wrap it around a few times and poke it through."

I fetched a spool of tippet material and a fly, and asked Biff to show me. He tied a clinch knot with three and a half or four turns and pulled it tight—dry. I clipped the fly from the monofilament and retied it with a six-turn clinch lubricated with a little spit. "Try this," I said. "Count the wraps out loud and put some water or saliva on the knot before you tighten it."

"Will it really make a difference?"

"Trust me," I said. "Six wraps. Spit or water."

Biff tried it on his next trip to the famous river. His 6X tippets became stronger, and his need for a magic fly rod vanished.

It's astonishing how little attention freshwater anglers pay to their rigging. Some guys who spend twenty days a year flying to and from fishing lodges have never spent twenty minutes practicing knots. Other anglers who don't flinch at spending $1,200 for a new rod and reel have never spent $12 for a book about knots and rigging. When they break off fish—and they do, in abundance— these blokes look for magazine articles comparing tippet materials, hoping to find a brand that's 3 percent stronger than its competitors. They buy the miracle string and continue to break off fish.

Your rigging is one of the very few parts of fishing over which you have control. It's also one of the most important aspects of fishing. Rigging merits as much thought and practice as casting, and more than selecting flies or understanding aquatic bugs. A guy who attaches flies with "that deal where you wrap it around a few times and poke it through" is wasting his time on the water.

It's too late to wonder about knots after the best fish of the year has made off with your fly. But once you start wondering, you'll find that easy answers are hard to come by.

A TANGLED SUBJECT

Generalities about knots are generally wrong or, at best, true only part of the time. But we can rely on one general statement: *There is no single best knot for attaching every hook to every type of line.*

Be wary of claims about the efficiency of knots. When you read that the Reversed Triple Fubar has 97 percent breaking strength— that it retains 97 percent of the strength of the unknotted line— slam on the brakes. Does the author offer any evidence? Or is he merely repeating a figure that he read in an article by an author who heard the claim from a friend? Angling literature is full of numbers that writers have cribbed (sometimes incorrectly) from one another. Besides, fishing knots have more variables than constants, and it makes no sense to say that the Reversed Triple Fubar or anything else is an *x* percent knot.

Few people have conducted genuinely scientific tests of knots. Think about what's involved. First, the tester must establish the actual breaking strength of the unknotted line. Then he must tie many samples of a particular knot, all attached to identical hooks. Using very accurate equipment, he must strain each knot until it breaks, recording the results and then computing the average breaking strength. Having done all of this, the tester will have data for that one knot—when tied with one size and brand of line, and to one size and model of hook, and by the method that he used to tie it. The knot's efficiency might change with heavier, lighter, softer, or harder line, or when the knot is attached to a hook made of thicker or finer wire.

Do not blindly accept statements about 95 and 98 percent knots. Even if a claim is the product of rigorous testing, it indicates what a knot *can* achieve rather than what it *will always* achieve.

In the field, we sometimes have to think about attributes besides strength. Simplicity matters because it often translates into consistency. This, I think, explains the enduring popularity of the clinch knot. Most of us have used this knot for so many years that we can tie it in poor light and with stiff, half-frozen fingers. On a drizzly late-autumn day, that counts for a lot. Simplicity also matters because we do not all have equally good close-up vision or equally nimble fingers.

The knot can affect a fly's action. Most of the popular knots tighten against the hook eye, creating a rigid connection. A few knots, however, create loops that provide a free-swinging junction between tippet and fly. Loop knots have several benefits. First, the fly has more freedom of movement. A Clouser Deep Minnow attached with a loop has a more pronounced up-and-down action than one attached with a clinch knot. With a loop knot, a popper or slider has more side-to-side movement. Some emerger and midge patterns should hang at an angle or vertically in the surface film, and a free-swinging connection facilitates this.

A loop also lets a fly sink a little faster, at least in still water. With a flexible connection at its nose, a weighted fly, particularly a beadhead pattern or one with metal eyes, can adopt a nose-down attitude that helps it dive during a pause in the retrieve.

A loop knot doesn't care about the relative diameters of the line and the hook wire. A nonslip mono loop tied in 5X material is just as strong with a size 1/0 iron as it is with a size 16 dry-fly hook. With many other knots, that's not true; a clinch knot's strength is affected by the diameter of the wire against which it's tied. A good loop knot can let you fish a big fly on a light tippet. That can help in very clear water.

A knot's economy matters not because fly fishers are cheap, but because we start out with a short piece of terminal tackle. With a plug-casting outfit that holds 180 yards of monofilament, I don't mind using a Palomar knot that consumes 5 inches of line. A 24-inch tippet is a different matter; I'd like to be able to change flies a few times before replacing it. This is why I clung to the clinch knot even as I learned better knots: I wanted to get the most mileage out of a tippet. But I've since learned to use the best knot rather than the one that uses the least line. I go through more tippet material but compensate by drinking cheaper whiskey. One must have priorities.

Other things being equal, it stands to reason that a smaller knot is better than a larger one because the smaller knot is lighter and less visible. If you have a choice, why add a bigger, heavier lump of plastic to the nose of a fly?

Strength is usually the chief consideration with knots, but it's not the only one. An obsessive neurotic can stay busy for years worrying about this stuff.

If knots have so many variables, does an angler have to learn dozens of connections to have any hope of landing fish? Fortunately, no. An angler who masters a few tippet-to-fly knots is ready for anything, at least in fresh water. But he does need more than one, and he does need to master them.

TAKE IT SERIOUSLY

Attaching a fly to your tippet deserves as much care as selecting a fly pattern or deciding how to approach a piece of water. Don't rush the job or treat it as a distraction from fishing.

Operator error is the largest variable in fishing knots. Many anglers doubly handicap themselves by fishing with badly tied second-rate knots. Build every knot carefully. Pretend that you're rigging a big-game leader for one shot at a world-record tarpon, even if you're fishing for small bream at a local pond. Mental habits have a lot to do with fishing success.

Some knots seem to require a third hand. The nonslip mono loop, for instance, requires you to pull in three directions: You need to maintain some tension on the standing line (which means that something has to hold the hook) while pulling on the tag end to draw up the wraps before seating the knot. No matter how dexterous they are, ten fingers often have trouble with the job. The solution is to find something that can hold the hook while one hand keeps tension on the standing line and the other pulls the tag end. Try hooking the fly on a D-ring or zipper pull on your fishing vest

A "third hand" is a useful addition to a fishing vest. This one consists of a jumbo snap swivel attached to a length of old fly-line backing. One end of the backing is tied to a D-ring on my vest. My nippers hang from the other end, and the snap swivel is in the middle.

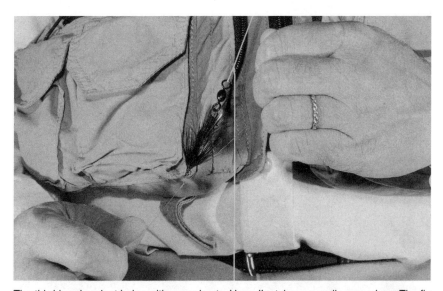

The third-hand gadget helps with some knots. Here, I'm tying a nonslip mono loop. The fly is hooked on the snap-swivel third hand. This allows my right hand to maintain tension on the standing line while my left hand (the one with the wedding band) pulls on the tag end to tighten the knot's wraps.

or tackle bag. Better yet, add "third hands" to your vest, belt pack, and tackle bag. Tie one end of a length of fly-line backing to something secure on your vest or bag (a large D-ring, for instance), and tie a split ring or a large snap swivel to the other end. When it's time to tighten a nonslip mono loop, hook the fly on the split ring or snap. Now you can keep the standing line taut while pulling on the tag end, and the knot becomes simple to tie. I've even clamped hemostats onto my shirt so that I could use one of the finger loops as a third hand.

Lubricate a knot before drawing it tight. Water works fine, and a fisherman always has some handy. Spit also works, but I'm not keen on putting a tippet in my mouth after it has been in a stream or pond. It's possible to ingest the *Giardia* intestinal parasite this way. I've never had giardiasis, but a few friends have, and it sounds particularly grim. Terminal tackle does not go into my yap.

Hook the fly on something solid to tighten a knot all the way. I'm convinced that many anglers lose fish to incompletely tightened knots. It's hard to get a good grip on a size 16 Adams, partic-

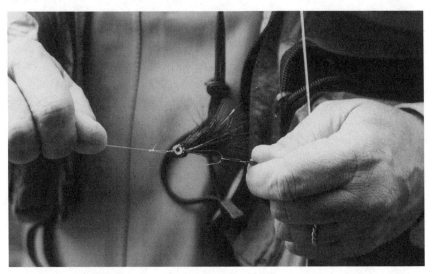

Seat a knot by pulling the hook against something solid. Here, I'm using the big snap swivel attached to my vest with a piece of backing. This method is safer than holding the hook with your fingertips, and it ensures that the knot tightens all the way.

ularly since you don't want to crush the hackles or mangle the wings. And, of course, holding a fly by the bend of the hook while tightening a knot is an excellent way to puncture a finger. Hook the fly onto one of your forceps' finger loops to seat the knot. This simple trick alone will prevent many break-offs.

It pays to sacrifice some tippet material at home tying knots and pulling until they break. Try to develop a feel for the strengths of the materials that you use. Then, in the field, you can seat knots firmly—and one that you formed incorrectly will break in your hands rather than in a fish's mouth.

TESTING KNOTS

Determining that the Reversed Triple Fubar knot is 96.74 percent efficient requires better equipment than I have. But learning whether the Reversed Triple Fubar is stronger than the Improved Murtchison when tied with Brand X material requires no equipment. Cut a piece of tippet material. Attach a hook to one end with a Reversed Triple Fubar. At the other end, attach an identical hook with an Improved Murtchison knot. Pull on the hooks until something busts. Repeat the test nine times, recording the results as you go, and you'll learn which knot is stronger in that material.

It's a crude method, but it does let you pit knot against knot. You can even set up a play-off: The Reversed Triple Fubar beats the Improved Murtchison, the Humdinger Special beats the Flapdoodle Bend, and then Fubar plays Humdinger in the finals. You'll discover which knots work best with the materials you use, and you'll get a *lot* of practice tying knots.

I did just that with several knots, using various tools and gadgets to pull on the hooks. If you test knots this way, wear eye protection and gloves. No matter how careful you are, every now and then a hook or a piece of line will go flying in an unexpected direction. I've had 10-pound-test lines snap and hit my hands hard enough to draw blood.

I broke thousands of test rigs before finishing this chapter. Between my hook-knot tests and my tippet-knot tests, I used about three-quarters of a mile of fishing line. It was all great fun, and it was made affordable by the nice folks at Umpqua Feather Merchants, Scientific Anglers, Orvis, and Frog Hair, who provided many spools of tippet material.

I pulled on each rig until it started to stretch, pulled a little harder, and then broke the rig with a sudden tug. This seems a more useful test than slowly, steadily increasing the pressure until a knot fails. What breaks line in the field is not the fish that swims at a constant speed against the resistance of a smooth and perfectly adjusted drag, but the fish that lunges or thrashes or jumps in the wrong direction. It's the sudden tug that worries me.

Since I broke knots with muscle power rather than a machine, the rate at which the strain increased must have varied from rig to rig. This, too, seems a good reflection of conditions in the field, where every situation is a little different from the last one.

It might be interesting to know which knots perform best under carefully regulated conditions. But I don't fish in laboratories. What I want to know is quite simple: Which knots are least likely to fail when little old human me pulls on the line? I don't pretend that my findings are absolute truth. But neither are they anecdotal evidence based on a couple of lost fish.

No doubt I didn't test some knots that I should have. Perhaps I left out your favorite connection. So run your own tests. Make up ten knot-versus-knot test rigs with identical hooks, pull on each rig until something gives, and tally up the score. You'll be out 6 or 8 yards of tippet material and a little time. But you'll *know*.

FIRST THINGS FIRST

Don't worry about the knot at the hook until you worry about the connection between the leader and the tippet. There's no point in having 3 pounds of breaking strength at the fly and only 2 pounds where the tippet joins the leader. That's surprisingly easy to do. If you tie on a fresh 6X nylon tippet with a surgeon's knot and attach a fly with a nonslip mono loop or Orvis knot, you may well have a rig with 3 pounds of strength at one end and 2 at the other. When you snag a rock or hook a huge fish, you will break off the entire tippet. The Orvis knot's great strength will have been irrelevant.

Much worse, you will have left some durable plastic stuck on the rock or attached to the fish. If you were fishing with a fluorocarbon tippet, you will have left a practically indestructible piece of litter in the stream.

If you persist in attaching tippets with blood knots, surgeon's knots, or even the Orvis tippet knot, then attach your flies with clinch knots. This way, you will most often break the line at the hook rather than at the top of the tippet. Yes, you will have a much weaker rig than you could have with better connections. But that's your problem. Broken-off tippets that you leave behind are a problem for other anglers, the fish, and wildlife. Anglers should not add plastic trash to the environment.

If you use the Bimini tippets described in the previous chapter or the ligature knot covered in chapter 3, then you can use better line-to-hook knots—with nylon. With fluorocarbon, which makes poor line-to-line knots, only a Bimini tippet will let you use one of the stronger tippet-to-fly knots.

Please do not combine a superior hook knot with an inferior tippet knot. Such a rig gives you unwarranted confidence and creates more litter where we least want it.

KNOTS IN NYLON
We can distill the essence of modern fly fishing to a single word: plastic. Before World War II, fly fishers used split-cane or metal rods, braided lines, and gut leaders. The best prewar gear worked very well, but it required a lot of maintenance and cost what was then a lot of money. Cheap rods, lines, and leaders persuaded many budding anglers to take up golf or some other foolishness. In the late 1940s and early 1950s, plastics technology brought us inexpensive, durable, and practically maintenance-free rods, lines, and leaders, and it brought fly fishing within the reach of millions of people. There's some strange irony in here somewhere, but let's not dwell on it.

Nylon monofilament comes in many varieties, and it remains the most popular type of fishing line. Some nylons are supple and elastic; others are much harder and stiffer. For fly fishing, we generally use mono that ranges from moderately soft to very limp and extra-stretchy, though saltwater anglers and some bass fishermen use harder nylon for leaders and tippets. By and large, good knots are easier to tie in soft, stretchy line than in hard, stiff mono.

The following comments are not a comprehensive treatment of line-to-hook knots. But my suggestions are based on experience, advice from experts, and well over a thousand knot-versus-knot tests. If a typical fly fisher combines the information in this chapter with the suggestions in the previous two, he will almost certainly have terminal tackle that is *much* stronger than whatever he's been fishing with.

The Clinch Knot

Bad news first: Of all the knots that I deliberately broke in freshwater tippets, the clinch consistently proved the weakest, with the occasional exception of the Duncan loop. In one small bunch of tests, clinch knots in 6X nylon failed at a paltry 81 percent of the material's baseline strength. That doesn't mean that the clinch is always an 80 percent knot—but it does show how poor it can be in light line.

On the other hand, the clinch knot is simple, consistent, and economical. And it's the responsible choice for an angler who uses a second-rate connection between the leader and tippet.

If you choose to stick with the clinch, tie it well. My tests indicate that a six-turn clinch always beats a five-turn clinch in light nylon. A seven-turn knot is better still, beating the six-turn clinch in 80 percent of my tests.

The line performs some interesting gymnastics as the knot tightens, so always lubricate a clinch before drawing it tight. Pull it up smoothly, not with a jerk, and pull only on the standing line, not on the tag end. Pull *hard* to seat the knot; it pays to deliberately break a few dozen clinch knots to get a feel for how hard you can pull. Don't clip the tag end flush; leave a little room for slippage.

The improved clinch knot seems to offer no improvement. In most of my knot-against-knot tests, the standard and improved versions came out about even. When there was a difference, the standard clinch beat the improved one 60 percent of the time. In this case, indoor tests confirmed my experiences in the field over many years.

Pay attention to the relative diameters of the tippet and the hook wire. If you clinch-knot 6X material to larger and larger hooks (made of thicker and thicker wire), you will reach a point at which the knot won't pull up—it simply slips until it comes undone. If you don't believe me, try clinch-knotting a very fine tippet to the biggest saltwater fly you can find.

The problem is that somewhere between a size 16 dry fly and a size 6/0 marlin streamer, there is a hook with which 6X material makes a clinch knot that *seems* okay but is actually much weaker than you expect. A good trout takes the fly and immediately breaks the knot.

The trick is knowing how large a heavy-wire hook you can use with a clinch-knotted tippet. I've settled on a rough guideline called the Double the X Rule. Double the X size of the tippet, and you'll have a good idea how large a wet-fly or nymph hook you can use. That is, with a 5X tippet and a seven-turn clinch knot, you're probably safe with a size 10 nymph: double 5 and you get 10. With a 6X tippet and the same knot, do not use a nymph or wet fly larger than size 12 (6 times 2). If you want to cast a size 6 streamer and insist on using a clinch knot, use at least a 3X tippet.

Although it performs poorly in light materials, the clinch knot remains useful with heavier tippets. For one thing, you can get it to tighten in virtually any tippet material. The clinch usually works well enough with 0.010-inch and heavier tippets because even a relatively inefficient knot provides enough strength—85 percent of 12-pound-test is still more strain than you can apply with any fly rod short of a tarpon stick. In light tippets, though, it's a poor choice.

The Nonslip Mono Loop

Loop knots have several benefits: more freedom of movement, a slightly faster sink rate, and no worries about the relative diameters of the line and the hook wire. Loops are good; some anglers use them almost exclusively.

The two most popular loop knots for attaching flies are the Duncan loop and the nonslip mono loop described by Lefty Kreh and Mark Sosin in *Practical Fishing Knots*. I had long used the Duncan loop, because it seemed easier to tie. But my tests revealed that there's no contest between the two. When it's tied correctly, the nonslip loop always beats the Duncan loop. Always. In 100 percent of tests. Period. Done.

The nonslip mono loop also beat the clinch knot in 100 percent of my tests, and almost always beat the Palomar and Trilene knots, which are often touted as among the strongest connections. With any nylon that I tried, the nonslip mono loop tied according to Kreh and Sosin's instructions proved as consistently strong as any other knot; that is, no other knot beat it more than half the time. In test rigs made with two nonslip loops, the knot occasionally achieved 100 percent efficiency with the line breaking somewhere between the two knots. In light nylon, the nonslip mono loop appears to be the strength champion. It doesn't do particularly well in the economy department, though that's the least important consideration. It creates no deformation of the line.

With practice, you will make the loop smaller and use less line tying it. When I first tried this knot ten years ago, I used 6 inches of line tying the thing and ended up with a loop 2 inches in length. Now I can make nonslip mono loops less than ½ inch long. This knot often calls for a "third hand," as described earlier in this chapter, since tightening the wraps before seating the knot involves pulling in three directions.

Do not clip the tag end flush. Leave a little stub; ¹⁄₁₆ inch will do. The nonslip loop is a fairly long knot, and it stretches a little under extreme tension.

Do yourself a favor and learn this knot. If you've been using the Duncan loop (also known as the uni-knot) with freshwater tippets, stop. The nonslip mono loop is much stronger and more reliable. Instructions are at the end of the chapter.

The 16-20 Knot

I learned this knot by editing an article written by E. Richard Nightingale for *American Angler* magazine (the piece appeared in the March–April 2002 issue). Mr. Nightingale, the author of a book called *Atlantic Salmon Chronicles*, discovered the knot on his own, but I suspect that knots, like fly-tying tricks, are "invented" by many people, and this one probably has a dozen originators. In a letter written in early 2004, Lefty Kreh told me that this knot has been around since the 1950s, when he knew it as the fisherman's knot. Some folks maintain that the 16-20 is the same as the Pitzen knot, which came from Europe. The more anglers you know, the more you believe in synchronicity.

Mr. Nightingale's name for the knot, the 16-20, derives from "the 16-20 club," which consists of fly fishers who have caught 20-pound Atlantic salmon on size 16 or smaller hooks. He has performed this unusual feat.

Actually, Mr. Nightingale calls it the 16-20 loop knot, because it begins as a sliding loop and finishes by tightening around the standing line. That's a nice distinction, but it creates the wrong impression. The 16-20 knot does not form an open, free-swinging joint. Although it tightens around the standing line, it does so *against* the hook eye. So, I have shortened the name to 16-20, deleting the suggestion of a loop.

The 16-20 has one drawback that doesn't matter in most trout fishing: It doesn't work with heavy line. With 3X and lighter nylon, it's easy to seat properly. Getting a 16-20 knot to seat in 2X and heavier tippets is harder and often impossible. This is a knot for 3X and lighter nylon; you simply can't tie it in heavy stuff.

So why learn it? Because it's a superb knot. In the 3X through 6X nylon materials with which I compared knots, only the nonslip mono loop and Orvis knot proved consistently stronger; the 16-20 trounced every other knot. The 16-20 bested the Trilene knot about 90 percent of the time. It beat the clinch knot every single time, and almost always beat the Palomar knot. Like the nonslip loop, it sometimes achieves 100 percent efficiency.

The 16-20 forms a remarkably small knot. With dry flies, emergers, and small nymphs, that's a good thing. The 16-20 also creates little or no deformation in the line.

Although the 16-20 is a simple knot, it's awkward to learn. The motions and hand positions are not like those involved in making most other knots. I find the 16-20 easiest to form if I start by pulling about 6 inches of line through the hook eye so that I can tie the knot well above the hook, letting the fly dangle below my left hand. The knot slides down to the hook before it tightens.

Tightening the 16-20 is a three-stage process. After forming the knot, pull gently on the tag end to compact the wraps. Don't pull too hard, because the next stage is to slide the knot down to the hook eye. Give the tag end another *gentle* tug to make sure that the wraps are compact (but still not too tight), and then pull hard on the standing line. And I mean hard, because something interesting happens when you pull with enough force. You will feel, and perhaps hear, a click as the knot seats. There's no mistaking the click—you will feel a jolt in the line. When you feel and hear that pop, the knot is seated and finished. You will also notice that the tag end comes out of the front of the knot nearly parallel with the standing line. That's your other indicator that the knot has seated properly. Since you need to pull hard to seat the knot, hook the fly on something solid such as a finger loop on your forceps.

You must feel the click and see the tag end exit the front of the knot almost parallel with the standing line. If either of those does not happen, cut the knot and tie another. More often than not, however, an incorrectly formed 16-20 snaps as you try to seat it. In effect, it has a built-in indicator of strength. Once learned, the 16-20 is childishly simple.

The diameter of the hook wire seems to have little effect on the 16-20's strength. For dry-fly and emerger fishing, where you want a small, tidy connection, the 16-20 knot is remarkably strong and reliable. You'll find instructions after those for the nonslip loop at the end of the chapter. Just remember to use it with 3X and lighter tippets, and remember the click.

The Orvis Knot

Some years ago, the Orvis Company held a contest in which anglers submitted new line-to-hook knots. A gentleman named Larry Becker won, and the knot he submitted is among the strongest, simplest, and most reliable that a fly fisher can use. The Orvis knot is also very small and light.

In 3X and lighter nylon, the Orvis knot always beats the clinch and virtually always beats the Trilene and Palomar knots. I thought that the 16-20 knot was the strongest tight-to-the eye connection in light nylon until I tested it against the Orvis knot. In fifty tests made with 3X through 6X materials, the 16-20 broke twenty-six times and the Orvis knot broke eleven times. In the remaining thirteen cases, neither knot broke; the line parted somewhere between them.

Unlike the 16-20, the Orvis knot works well in heavier lines. It's easy to tie in the fairly stiff, 0.011-inch spinning line that I sometimes use for saltwater and heavy bass-fishing tippets. It's also absurdly simple and almost impossible to screw up.

The Orvis knot does have one drawback: It wants to cock at an angle as it's tightened. If you begin the knot with the hook upright, the line cocks at an upward angle; if you start with the hook upside down, the line ends up cocked downward. You can easily push or pull the finished knot into correct alignment, but it might cock again while you false-cast. How much this matters depends on the fly and the situation. With a bushy dry fly, a cocked knot might result in a twisted tippet. The problem probably will not occur with a size 6 stonefly nymph.

The Orvis knot's great strength and simplicity make it worth using for some, if not most, of your fishing. It seems to work well in virtually any tippet material. Instructions are after those for the 16-20 knot.

The Trilene Knot

Since I'd long used this popular knot and always regarded it as strong and secure, I included it my comparisons. For the most part, it justified my faith. The nonslip mono loop, Orvis knot, and 16-20 consistently beat the Trilene knot in 3X and lighter materials, but the Trilene beat the other knots I tried. In light nylon, it is always stronger than the clinch (winning 100 percent of contests) and usually stronger than the Palomar.

The Trilene knot requires you to pass the tippet through the hook eye twice. That's a problem with a small fly, but also irrelevant, since other knots work better with fine tippets. With a bigger hook, you'll have no trouble poking the tippet through the eye twice. And by a happy coincidence, the Trilene knot seems particularly efficient in heavier materials that you'd use with large flies. In the 0.010- through 0.012-inch nylon lines that I've tried, the Trilene knot beats the Orvis knot more than half the time, always beats the clinch knot, and comes out about even with the nonslip mono loop. I can't explain this; I merely report what I've observed. For attaching a big bass or saltwater fly to a stout tippet, the Trilene knot is an excellent choice.

Tie it with five turns, wet it before drawing it tight (this reduces the knot's tendency to deform an inch or so of line), seat it firmly, and leave at least a ¹⁄₁₆-inch tag end. You can find instructions in any number of books and on many websites.

A Small Group of Nylon Knots

If you use a good connection between the leader and tippet, you can safely use several high-strength knots for attaching flies. To make a free-swinging junction, use the nonslip mono loop. If you want a tight-to-the-eye knot with a 3X or lighter nylon tippet, attach the fly with a 16-20 knot or an Orvis knot. Any of these three knots might even let you drop down a size in tippet diameter, and that translates into more strikes. With a heavy tippet, use the Trilene knot to make a tight-to-the-eye connection.

If you decide to stick with a second-rate tippet knot, then attach your flies with a plain old clinch or a Duncan loop. You will avoid breaking off entire tippets and littering the waterways. But be aware that with some materials, you might have a rig that retains as little as 70 percent of the line's actual breaking strength. I'm not making this stuff up. In one batch of tests made with a digital scale, I watched five consecutive blood knots in 6X nylon fail at an average of 65 percent of the line's baseline strength. Stick with your old knots if you want, but know that you will lose more fish by doing so.

FLUOROCARBON

The outdoor press has lavished oceans of ink on fluorocarbon line without doing a good job of explaining the stuff. Compared with nylon, fluorocarbon has good, bad, and neutral qualities. In the benefits column, fluorocarbon is less visible underwater than nylon, though it is *not* invisible, and it still casts a shadow. It's more abrasion-resistant, too. Fluorocarbon doesn't absorb water; nylon does, and loses strength thereby. These are all good traits.

Fluorocarbon stretches less than nylon. That's desirable in plastic-worm fishing, but fluorocarbon's lack of stretch seems a drawback in trout fishing. Pulling on hundreds of test rigs let me see how much a small, light-wire hook flexes before a 5X or 6X tippet breaks. Believe me, little hooks flex a lot. I'd rather use a more elastic line that provides some cushion for a small hook and the tiny bit of fish flesh in which it's stuck.

Because it's denser than nylon, fluorocarbon sinks faster. Its density can help with a nymph or streamer, but fluorocarbon can sink a dry fly during the drift or when you pick up the line. With a popper or slider that's fished slowly, a fluorocarbon tippet can sag and create a belly of slack that interferes with the fly's action and your ability to strike. So fluorocarbon's density is good or bad according to the situation.

Fluorocarbon is considerably stiffer than nylon of equal diameter. That strikes me as a disadvantage. By and large, I want the most supple tippet possible, at least for freshwater angling.

As I write this, fluorocarbon costs at least twice as much as nylon, and often three or four times as much. That's a drawback; dollars are not so easy to come by that I can ignore the prices of fishing products.

The Knotty Problem

For most anglers, fluorocarbon's biggest drawback is its relatively poor knot performance. Some fluorocarbon materials make better knots than their predecessors did, but they still don't match nylon's efficiency. The softer and more elastic the material, the better it will knot. Because many fluorocarbons resist knotting, they increase the likelihood that an average angler will tie a bad knot, which means that his results are likely to be less consistent than with nylon. When a fish strikes, the material's lack of stretch means that the knots at the ends of the tippet have to absorb the entire shock. If a knot was incompletely seated, it will break under very little strain— perhaps only half of the material's nominal strength. Honest.

The question isn't strength under ideal conditions, but strength in the field, with knots tied by imperfect hands. A perfectly rigged fluorocarbon tippet probably can be almost as strong as a nylon tippet, especially after the latter has absorbed water and lost some of its strength. But fluorocarbon is harder than nylon to rig perfectly and more likely to produce a nasty surprise. To match nylon's predictability, fluorocarbon requires a user with loads of patience and expert rigging skills.

Call me a dinosaur, but I regard fluorocarbon as a specialty product. I might use it for nymphing in an extremely clear, gentle stream populated by nervous trout that see a lot of flies every day. I have little use for fluorocarbon on small, fast mountain streams, and I don't like it for surface fishing. With a streamer or wet fly, I want the cushion that nylon's stretch provides when a fish wallops a fly swinging on a tight line. With a big, heavy nymph, I have more confidence in 5X nylon than in 4X fluorocarbon. That leaves small nymphs in clear, slow streams that get hammered by anglers day after day.

I'm not alone in being a fluoro-skeptic. One of the sport's greatest experts dismisses fluorocarbon as "a gimmick." Another expert sent me a letter detailing fluorocarbon's shortcomings, concluding with, "I don't use it and see only disadvantages instead of advantages." Between them, these gents have more than a century of fly-fishing experience.

Many anglers handle the knot-strength problem by going up a size. That is, they use 5X fluorocarbon in a situation where they would use 6X nylon. But doesn't that negate some, if not all, of fluorocarbon's visibility advantage? And a hunk of 5X fluorocarbon is much heavier and stiffer than an equal length of 6X nylon. It will sink faster and deeper, which can only bring it closer to the fish's eye level, and its stiffness cannot do anything good for the fly's drift or action.

Knots in Fluorocarbon

If you use fluorocarbon, be fanatically careful about your rigging. If you take a casual approach, you will produce some rigs that an anemic chub can snap.

For leader-to-tippet connections, use only the Bimini tippets described in chapter 4 or the ligature knot from chapter 3. Using anything else is irresponsible. That sounds harsh, but here's why I say it. Fluorocarbon is astonishingly durable stuff. That's one of its selling points—it doesn't have a shelf life; it doesn't "go bad" in a year or two. But that also means that lost fluorocarbon will be around for a long, long time. A fluorocarbon tippet left in a river will still be there after you and I are dust.

The material makes particularly poor line-to-line knots. If you attach a fluorocarbon tippet with a surgeon's knot, Orvis tippet knot, or blood knot, you run a high risk of busting off the entire tippet on a snag or a fish. In tests with one brand of 4X fluorocarbon, seven-turn clinch knots consistently beat Orvis tippet knots; the rigs broke at the tippet knots rather than at the hook knots. Previous tests had shown the Orvis tippet knot to be stronger than the surgeon's or blood knots in this material. More tests with a digital scale showed a roughly 40 percent loss of strength at the tippet knot. Tests with another company's 5X and 6X fluorocarbon showed a roughly 30 percent loss of strength where two pieces were joined with an Orvis tippet knot, which had proved stronger than the blood or surgeon's knots in this material.

Using heavier material doesn't solve the lost-tippet problem; you merely leave behind a larger volume of super-durable plastic trash. If you must fish with this stuff, please use the strongest possible connections between line and leader.

The ligature knot is always stronger than a blood, surgeon's, or Orvis tippet knot in light fluorocarbon. But it's still not particularly strong. In light nylon, the ligature knot often achieves 100 percent efficiency. In one batch of test rigs made with 6X Umpqua nylon, this translated to an average failure strength of 3.33 pounds; with 5X material, the figure was 4.15 pounds. When I repeated the tests with two brands of new and allegedly improved 6X fluorocarbon, the average breaking strengths were 2.4 pounds and 2.59 pounds. In 5X fluorocarbon, ligature knots failed at an average of 3.27 pounds. Fluorocarbon simply doesn't make good line-to-line knots.

With a light nylon tippet, the ligature knot's great strength lets you use any of the extra-strong hook knots—the nonslip loop, the 16-20, or the Orvis knot. But if you use the same junction to attach a 3X or lighter fluorocarbon tippet (the ligature knot is practically impossible to tighten in heavier fluorocarbon), you're still stuck with the plain old clinch knot at the fly, because all the better, stronger hook knots create the lost-tippet problem.

A Bimini tippet will let you use a better knot at the fly, and it's really the only safe way to rig with this material. In most light fluorocarbons, and certainly in 4X and lighter material, the nonslip mono loop beats the other knots I've tried, though it never achieves 100 percent efficiency, as it often does in nylon. I recommend it for all subsurface trout and smallmouth fishing with fluorocarbon. In 4X and 5X fluorocarbon, try making the nonslip loop with eight wraps; in 6X or 7X material, tie it with nine wraps. The extra turn seems to make a difference. Lubricate the wraps before drawing them tight.

Recommending a tight-to-the-eye knot is harder, because test results were less consistent. Across a range of sizes and brands, the top three knots were the Orvis knot, Trilene, and Palomar. If you want to know which is strongest in the brand of fluorocarbon that you use, you will have to sacrifice several spools of material to run your own tests. All three beat the clinch knot practically all the time. Since it doesn't involve passing the tippet through the hook eye twice, the Orvis knot wins for simplicity and with small flies. It seems reliable and reasonably strong in all the 3X and lighter fluorocarbons I've handled. That's hardly a ringing endorsement, but busting more than a quarter of a mile of fluorocarbon tippet material convinced me that there are no truly good knots in the stuff. Except for an occasional Bimini twist, I am unable to find any knot that achieves 100 percent efficiency in fluorocarbon.

So one's choices for most freshwater fishing with fluorocarbon boil down to the nonslip mono loop and the Orvis knot. The Duncan loop performs poorly; the clinch and improved clinch ditto. The Orvis knot is just as quick and easy as the clinch, and always stronger. Remember, though, that if you use anything but a Bimini tippet, then you should use a clinch knot at the fly to avoid breaking off entire tippets.

The 16-20 knot, which performs so reliably in light nylon, seems less consistent in fluorocarbon. Some fluorocarbon materials will not let a 16-20 knot seat properly; no matter what I do, I simply cannot get the knot to click as it tightens. The same thing sometimes happens with the Eugene bend, another knot that clicks to show that it has properly seated. The 16-20 worked reasonably well in a couple brands of light fluorocarbon that I tried, but I'm inclined not to trust it in this material. For trout fishing, I'd rather use an Orvis knot.

Fluorocarbon's abrasion resistance has endeared it to saltwater anglers, but tying good knots in 0.010 inch and heavier fluorocarbon is a miserable chore. Some anglers sidestep the challenge of making efficient knots. A few years ago, a friend and I went striper fishing with a guide in a harbor full of hazards. Our guide inspected my leader at the start of the day and pronounced it unfit. He peeled a couple yards of 25-pound-test fluorocarbon off a spool and tied a loop in one end. After interlocking the loop with the one on the end of my sinking fly line, he attached a fly to the 25-pound-test fluorocarbon with a Homer Rhode loop knot tightened with pliers. It was an ungainly rig that probably had an actual breaking strength of no more than 12 pounds, but that's enough for most striper fishing. The heavy fluorocarbon eliminated worries about abrasion; we could have used that leader to scrape barnacles off rocks. We traded efficiency for bulk and toughness, and in that situation it was a good trade.

A similar trade makes sense in other situations. If you're dealing with saltwater fish that aren't particularly leader shy, consider using a leader that ends with 15- or 16-pound fluorocarbon. Attach the fly with a five-turn clinch knot. Even if the tippet is only 70 percent efficient at either end, it's still strong enough to let you pull very hard with a fly rod; 70 percent of 15 is 10.5 pounds, which is more force than an average person can generate with anything lighter than a specially made billfish fly rod. And you won't have to worry about abrasion.

If saltwater fishing calls for a thinner, more flexible tippet, you face two challenges: making a good connection to the main leader and tying a fairly efficient knot at the hook. A Bimini tippet is the solution to the first challenge. If the tippet material is, say, 0.010- or 0.011-inch fluorocarbon, use a main leader that ends with at least 0.019-inch material. Loop the 0.010- or 0.011-inch Bimini tippet to that. At the business end, attach the fly with a nonslip mono loop or a Trilene knot. You still won't have as much strength as you would with a nylon tippet of the same diameter, but you'll probably have enough, and you'll have greater abrasion resistance. If you can't tighten the Trilene knot, use a five-turn clinch. Practice at home before going fishing, because saltwater-weight fluorocarbon is hard to work with.

Fluorocarbon lines will almost certainly become better as manufacturers tinker with the formulas. I hope so. For now, my solution is to avoid the stuff except in very special circumstances. I'll cheerfully change my mind if line manufacturers can make fluorocarbon more pliable, more elastic, and easier to tie high-strength knots with.

Does the final knot in your system really require this much neurotic attention? With a 10-inch trout or bass, no. But why rig for small fish? Four-pound trout turn up in unexpected places, and I've caught some long, fat largemouths on little flies intended for panfish. Big stripers often feed beneath a school of their adolescent relatives.

You never know. That's half the fun of fishing. And because I never know what might happen next, I want the final link to be as strong as I can make it. Yes, the tippet-to-fly knot is worth a lot of thought.

TYING THE NONSLIP MONO LOOP

Photographing hands tying a knot with light monofilament is practically impossible, at least for me. Using colored wire seems the best way to produce comprehensible illustrations, so that's how I did it. The following photos might not be elegant, but they'll let you follow the path of the line.

The biggest variable in tying the nonslip mono loop is the number of wraps made with the tag end around the standing line. Five wraps usually suffice with most materials from 0.009- (2X) to 0.012-inch. With most 3X materials, make six wraps. With 4X, make seven wraps. With 5X and 6X, make eight wraps (this is one more than Lefty Kreh and Mark Sosin recommend). If you want to tie nonslip loop knots in 7X tippets, make them with eight or nine wraps.

The second variable is the length of the finished loop. After some practice, you'll see that you can make the loop smaller by doing two things before you wrap the tag end around the standing line. First, pull gently on the standing line to make the overhand knot smaller. Then pull gently on the tag end to shorten the loop, bringing the hook closer to the overhand knot. After doing these two things to adjust the size of the loop, you can make the wraps around the standing line.

In the following photos, the wire colored black represents the standing line; the white wire is the tag end. Try learning the knot with 3X material and a big hook.

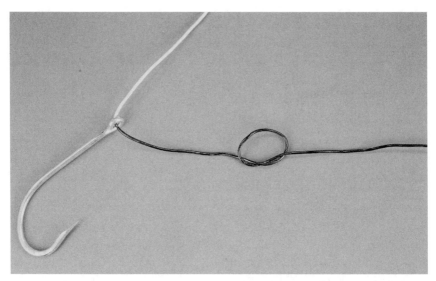

Tie an overhand knot about 6 inches from the end of the line. With practice, you'll be able to use less line; for now, though, give yourself plenty to work with. Thread the tag end through the hook eye, and slide the hook close to the overhand knot.

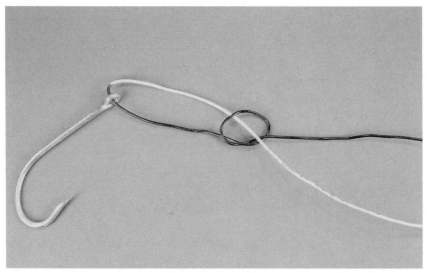

Bring the tag end (the white wire in the photo) through the overhand knot. Note that the line reenters the overhand knot on the same side from which it exited. This is very important.

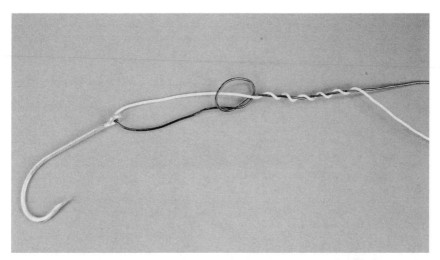

Make the required number of wraps with the tag end around the standing line. In this case, we've made five complete wraps. You'll probably find the wraps easiest to make if you hold the knot by pinching the loop and the overhand knot between your thumb and forefinger.

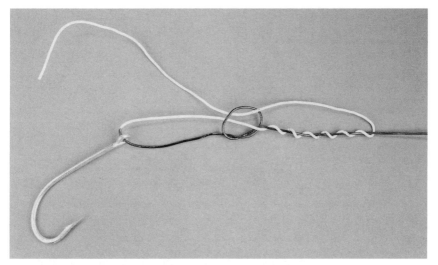

Pass the tag end back through the overhand knot. Again, note that the line reenters the overhand knot on the same side from which it exited. In other words, the white line is on top of the black line when it leaves the overhand knot, and it's again on top of the black line as it reenters the overhand knot.

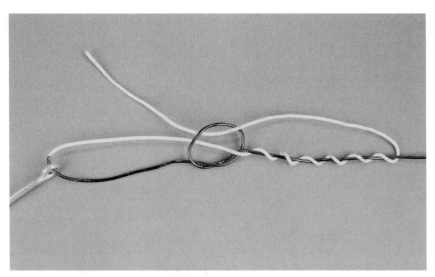

Here's a closer view showing how the line travels. At this point, hook the fly on something, keep moderate tension on the standing line, and pull on the tag end to tighten the wraps and draw them against the overhand knot.

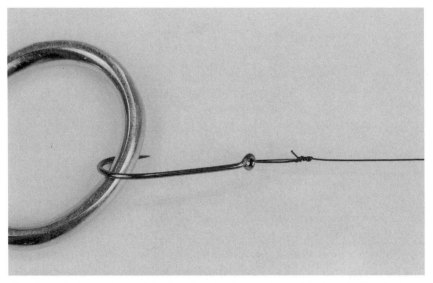

After tightening the wraps, pull hard on the standing line to seat the knot. Pull against something solid such as a finger loop on your forceps. Trim the tag end, leaving a short stub.

TYING THE 16-20 KNOT

Remember that the 16-20 is, for the most part, a knot for 3X and lighter nylon. In those materials, however, it makes a very strong, tight-to-the-eye knot. The 16-20 knot will probably feel awkward at first, but with a little practice, you will be able to tie it more easily than a clinch knot.

Like the preceding sequence, most of the following one was shot using an immense hook and colored doorbell wire. The wire colored black is the standing line; the white wire is the tag end.

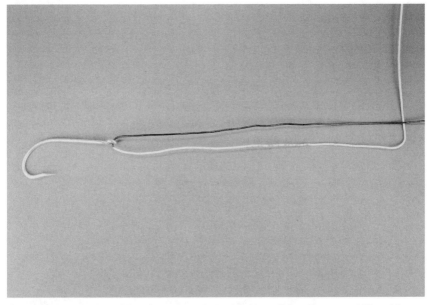

Thread about 8 inches of line down through the hook eye. Bring the tag end (the white wire in this photo) up behind the standing line.

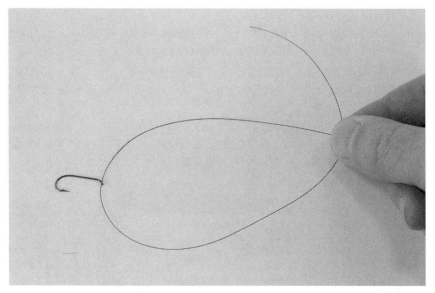

Here's how to hold the line while tying the 16-20 knot. Pinch the cross made by the tag end and standing line between your right thumb and forefinger. Let the hook dangle while your left hand manipulates the tag end of the line.

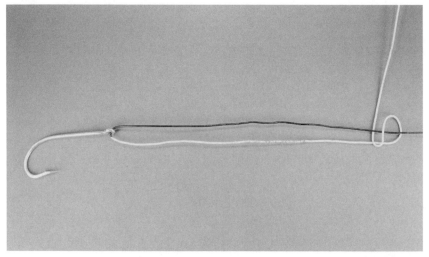

Back to our wire model. Make one complete wrap with the tag end, so that it is pointing up again.

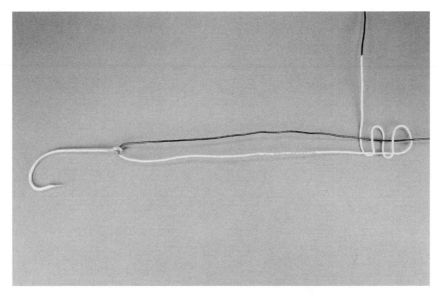

Make a second complete wrap with the tag end. At the end of the wrap, the tag end is again behind the standing line and pointing up.

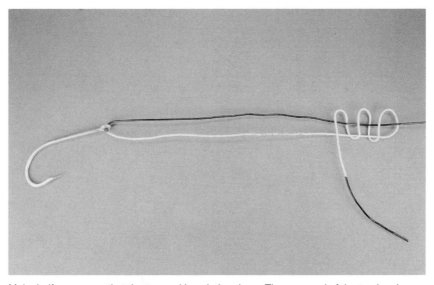

Make half a wrap, so that the tag end is pointing down. The very end of the tag has been colored black to make the next step easier to follow.

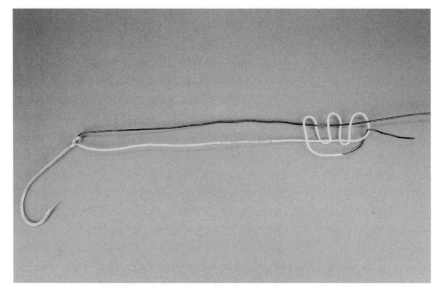

Bring the tag end up and tuck it through the bottom of the first wrap as shown, entering the loop from the back.

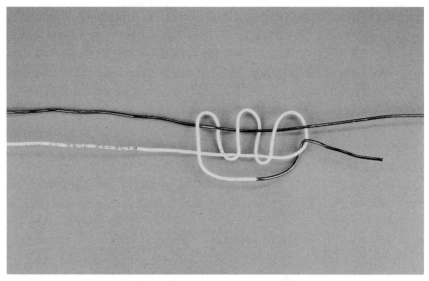

Here's a closer view. Note that the black tag end enters the knot from the back side. This is critically important. Tied this way, the knot can achieve 100 percent efficiency. But if the tag end enters from the front side, the knot will snap before it tightens.

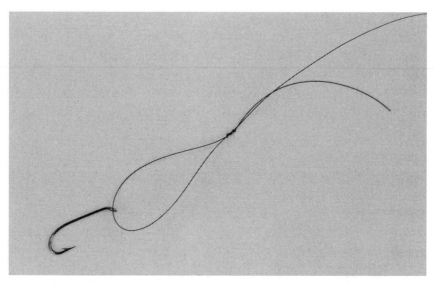

The wire model wouldn't serve for this photo and the next one, so I switched to dyed-black monofilament. Pull gently on the tag end to compact the wraps. Don't pull too hard—make the wraps snug, but not really tight.

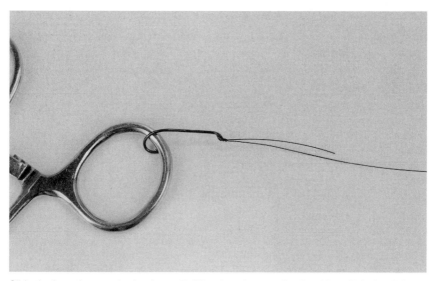

Slide the knot down to the hook eye. Pull hard on the standing line. You will feel a click as the knot seats. Note that the tag end now comes out of the front of the knot, virtually parallel with the standing line. You must feel the click and see the tag end in this position.

TYING THE ORVIS KNOT

This is among the easiest knots to tie and the strongest. In the following photos, the black part of the wire represents the standing line; the white wire is the tippet's tag end. "The come-from-behind knot" would be another good name for this connection. Every time the tag end begins an operation with another part of the line, it starts from behind.

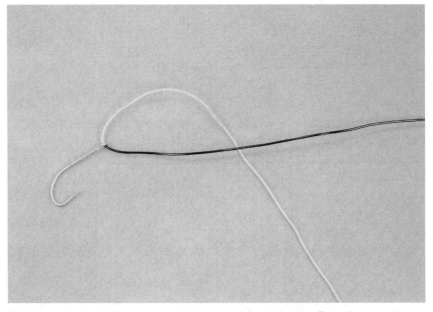

Slide about 6 inches of line through the hook eye from the bottom. Bring the tag end (white) down behind the standing line (black).

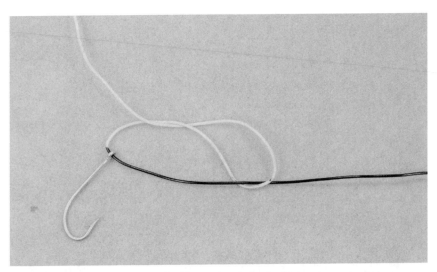

Bring the tag end under the standing line and up in front of it, forming a closed loop.
Insert the tag end through the closed loop from the back to make a second closed loop.
Remember: Come from behind every time.

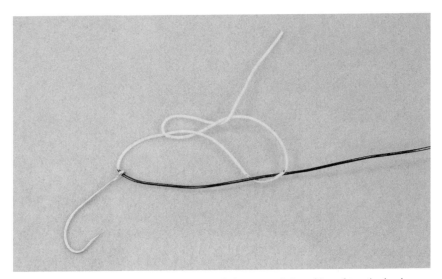

Bend the tag end forward and insert it through the second closed loop from the back
side. Lift the tag end as shown. You now have three closed loops, each created by bringing the tag end behind the line.

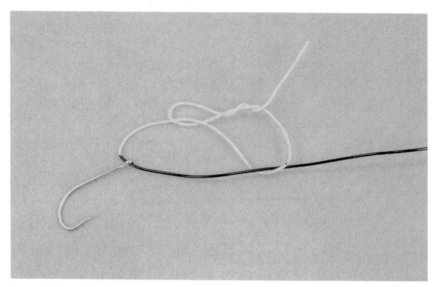

Make one more complete wrap with the tag end around the top of the closed loop. The knot seems too simple to work, but it does.

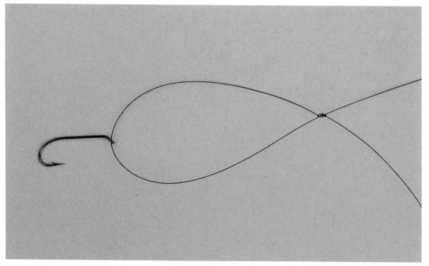

Tightening a knot in electrical wire is impossible, so it's time to switch to dyed monofilament. Pull on the tag end to close up the loops and wraps. You end up with something that looks like a tiny bow tie on the standing line.

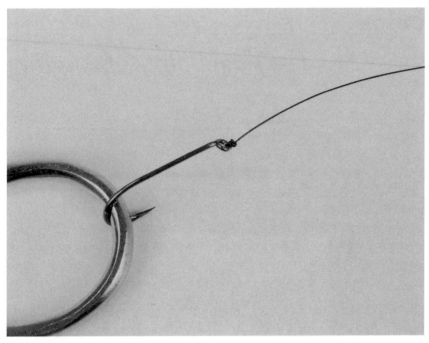

Slide the knot down to the hook eye. Pull on the standing line to tighten and seat the knot. Clip the leftover tag end.

6

The Fine Points of Angling

"So sharp that just *looking* at them makes your eyes bleed." That's how a friend describes the hooks of his bass bugs. It's the only smart way to think about hooks.

Years ago, fly-tying instructions often began with a command to sharpen the hook. I will bet the price of a dozen top-quality nightcrawlers that you will find no such instructions in this year's magazines. Fly hooks have become better over the years: They're made of stiffer, stronger wire, their points are pointier, and their barbs are smaller. Many saltwater fly fishers still spend time filing hook points, particularly those of tarpon and billfish flies, but most trout anglers rarely think about hooks these days. Right out of the box, modern fly hooks are, to use the New England vernacular, some wicked sharp.

The improvement comes from advances in manufacturing technology. We modern anglers take good hooks for granted; we can buy a superb dry-fly hook for about the price of a stick of chewing gum. Once upon a time, when they were made one at a time and by hand, good fishhooks were precious items. Individual craftsmen made livings as hook makers, and some authors of fishing books made a point of recommending hooks produced not by big companies (of which there were none in the fishing business), but by cottage industries.

If you've ever watched a craftsman make a hook by hand, you know that shaping and honing the point takes a lot of time and a deft touch. The latter stages of the industrial revolution brought grinders and polishers powered by electric motors, precisely regulated tempering ovens, and a certain amount of automation to the hook business, but putting a sharp, straight, precise point on a piece of thin wire still slowed down the hook-making process. Some hooks had cut points, others had ground points, and some had points that were cut and then ground. Many old hooks had excellent points, but many others didn't. Until relatively recently, most fly hooks required some sharpening. Big hooks, particularly those for bass and saltwater fish, generally needed serious work with a fine file.

These days, most premium hooks have chemically sharpened points. As I understand the process, the point is ground to shape and then dipped in an acid that removes a thin layer of metal. The process results in hooks with frighteningly sharp, consistently good points.

Chemical sharpening has also resulted in a generation of fishermen and fly tiers who have rarely sharpened a fly hook. But it's a mistake never to think about hook points, especially for an angler who buys his flies. Not all mass-produced flies are tied on premium hooks, and even the best hook cannot remain sharp indefinitely. The hook, after all, is what defines the sport; indeed, the word "angler" comes from an old word for hook, as in *The Treatyse of Fysshynge wyth an Angle,* printed in 1496. An angler who pays attention to hook points and takes the time to maintain or improve them will catch more fish than one who doesn't.

Fly fishers can do several things to make sure that their hooks perform as well as possible. Keeping hooks as good as new—and making some better than new—doesn't require great skill or a heavy investment in tools.

DOWN WITH BARBS

I knew about barbless (or at least debarbed) hooks for a long time before I started using them. Fish seemed too rare and valuable to risk losing even one. It's not that I killed everything I caught; but I needed to land each fish, to possess it at least temporarily. In time, I got over that silliness and started flattening the barbs on some flies, and then on all flies and lures. I've been fishing entirely barbless for more than a decade now, and I catch more fish because of it. Yes, every now and then a bass will throw a barbless plug or buzzbait (so what?), but fish rarely come unstuck from debarbed flies. And I'm convinced that using barbless flies translates into missing fewer strikes. A hook with a mashed-down barb penetrates more easily than one with an intact barb.

Obviously, barbless or debarbed hooks make catch-and-release angling easier and more consistently successful. They can also improve your hookup percentage; a thinner object is simply easier than a thicker object to drive into a fish's jaw. And perhaps most important, hooks without barbs greatly lessen the chance of serious injury to yourself or a fishing partner. So the first way to improve your hooks is to pinch down their barbs with smooth-jawed pliers.

FREQUENT CHECKUPS

Fishing is rough on flies. Stone is harder than steel, and nymphs, streamers, bucktails, and wet flies have many opportunities to bounce off underwater rocks. Nymphs in particular make frequent contact with riverbeds. Dry flies and topwater bugs aren't immune: Everyone occasionally drops a backcast onto a gravel bar or bounces a fly off a rock. Even relatively soft substances such as wood or a fish's jaw can dull a hook's point.

Don't assume that a needle-sharp hook will stay that way for long. Check hook points frequently while you fish. When a nymph or streamer hangs up on the bottom for a moment, strip it in and make sure that the point is still pointy. If you drop a backcast onto a bar or the shoreline, don't fish out the forward cast; bring the fly in and check its point. Test the hook point after releasing a fish or pulling a fly off a snag. Every time you change flies, check the point of the new one before knotting it to your tippet. Strikes do not come so frequently that an angler can afford to miss some because of dull or bent hooks.

The thumbnail test remains the standard way to check a hook point. With the point at about a 45-degree angle, try pulling the hook across your thumbnail. Don't jam the hook into your nail; just drag it across with barely any pressure. If the point doesn't dig into your nail *instantly*, the hook is too dull to use. Replace the fly or sharpen the hook. To do the latter, you need a tool.

TOUCH-UPS IN THE FIELD

Fly shops and catalog outfits sell a variety of pocket-size hones and files. For touching up the points of trout flies, you want a very fine file or a hone. Besides the tools sold by tackle shops, the tiny files carried by hardware and hobby stores do a good job with the points of size 12 and larger hooks. The type of sharpener you carry—ceramic, diamond coated, or steel—doesn't much matter; all of them work well enough, though ceramic and diamond-coated hones are easier to use than files. Some diamond-coated tools, such as those sold by Dr. Slick, have a coarse side, a fine side, and a groove on each side so that you can sharpen nearly any type of hook. What matters most is that you always have a sharpener in your fishing vest, belt pack, or tackle bag.

Tiny hooks, say from size 18 down, are difficult or impossible to sharpen, at least in the field. When the point of a size 18 hook becomes dull or gets damaged, I generally say bye-bye to the fly. From size 16 up, fly hooks are easy to sharpen in the field. File into the point—toward the bend, that is. Hone the left and right sides of the point, and then the outside. If a fly is large enough to give you some working room, clamp the upper part of the bend in your hemostats so that you have a solid grip on the hook. In any case, don't put a fly back into play unless it passes the thumbnail test.

If you carry a lot of flies, you might find it easier simply to replace a dull or damaged one. Put flies with blunted points in a separate container (I often carry a 35-millimeter film canister for this

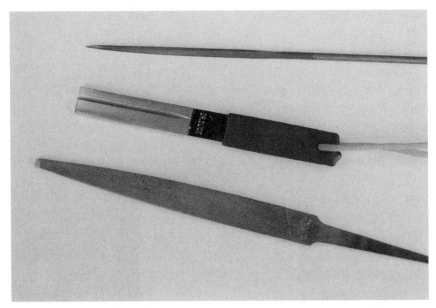

Small, fine files work well for sharpening large- and medium-size hooks. A two-sided, diamond-coated hook hone like the Dr. Slick model in the center does an excellent job of sharpening or touching up nearly any hook. Always carry a sharpener; streams and rivers are full of things that can blunt the point of a hook.

purpose) or in a designated corner of a fly box, and then resharpen them at home, where you can do a better job.

SHARPENING AT HOME

Even if you never plan to tie a fly, you will find a sturdy, inexpensive fly-tying vise a worthwhile investment. A vise holds a hook rock-steady while you sharpen the point, and it lets you use both hands to guide the sharpening tool. Working indoors also gives you the benefit of good light.

To sharpen dry flies, wets, and most nymphs, use the same sort of hone or tiny file that you'd use in the field. For larger nymphs and most streamers, try a diamond-coated sharpener, a small triangular file 6 to 8 inches long (hardware stores call these slim taper files), or even a 6-inch flat file. Avoid cheap, imported files; fish-hooks wear them out almost immediately. If you need to buy files, go to a good hardware store and get the Nicholson Black Diamond brand.

Most modern, chemically sharpened trout-fly hooks have conical points. Many larger hooks and some older designs (such as Mustad's standard models) have cut or ground points with triangular or square cross sections. Generally, it's a good idea to try to maintain the shape of a hook point when you file or hone it, though I often file a triangulated tip on an originally conical point. File into the point. Filing the other way, toward the front of the hook, will make the tip roll to the side, and the hook will never become truly sharp. Sharpening a hook is much like sharpening a knife, except that you work on more than two planes. Use light pressure; you're not grinding the edge of a 12-pound maul.

Don't remove any more metal than necessary, and try not to drastically alter the angle of the point. A long, skinny point with a

A fly-tying vise is a good investment even if you never tie flies. By holding a hook securely, a vise simplifies sharpening the point and makes for a better result. File into the point, toward the hook's bend.

shallow taper will bend easily, and a short, steeply tapered point might have trouble penetrating a fish's mouth, though if I had to pick one or the other, I'd take a shorter, steeper point because it's more rugged.

A big streamer or bass-fly hook might need a two-stage treatment, especially if it's really dull or damaged. Start with a slim taper file, and then finish with a fine ceramic or diamond hone.

I'm fond of points with triangular cross sections because they have three cutting edges. Such a point penetrates very easily. For that reason, I still use a lot of older, less expensive hook models, which I sharpen with fine files. But I learned a long time ago not to triangulate the entire point of a freshwater hook. That type of sharpening works well on a tarpon hook, which needs to penetrate a yap about as hard as a fiberglass boat hull. A fully triangulated trout-fly hook, however, tends to penetrate instantly and then cut its way out almost as quickly. On a freshwater hook, triangulating just the tip of the point works better.

PREVENTIVE CARE

Even a thin film of rust makes a hook less sharp and less likely to penetrate. When you get home from fishing, bring your fly boxes indoors and open them so that the contents can dry. If you leave a few soggy flies inside a plastic box that's in a zippered pocket of a vest left in the trunk of your car for a week, you might find three dozen badly rusted flies the next time you go fishing. Flies last longer when they're stored indoors.

Entomology, streamcraft, and skillful casting don't catch fish. Those things might help you get a bite, but *hooks* are what catch fish. Sharp hooks catch more of them. Don't take good points for granted.

7

Positive Buoyancy

One late-spring day many years ago, I popped into a shop where I occasionally bought fly-tying materials. The proprietor was out, toiling at his part-time day job, and he'd left the store in the hands of his mother, a loquacious lady about a decade past retirement age. She had no interest in angling, but seemed to enjoy chatting with men who wore funny-looking vests and goofy hats. I think she regarded the lot of us as nice dolts enjoying a harmless amusement that kept us away from horse tracks and saloons.

We got to talking—with her, one had no choice—and she told me about a grumpy gent who had come into the shop and scrutinized the fly bins in silence for ten minutes. Finally, he looked up.

"Do you have any wet flies?" he demanded.

The old gal had never paid much attention to subtleties of fly design. But she hated to lose a sale.

"Wet flies? Well, I'm not sure," she said. "But we have a sink in the back, and if you see some flies you like, I'd be glad to moisten them."

The grump got a laugh out of that, she told me, and left the shop half an hour later with a hefty assortment of merchandise. She knew more about fishermen than she let on.

Her story has practical applications. Get a typical dry fly suffi-ciently moist, and it's no longer dry in either condition or function. Standard dry flies do not really float as a cork does; that is, they do not weigh less than the volume of water that they displace. A Light Cahill, Hendrickson, or Adams perches on top of the water, sup-ported on the surface tension by the tips of its hackle fibers and tails. Only flies made with closed-cell foam, balsa, or cork are buoy-ant in the strict sense of the term. Hold a conventional dry fly beneath the surface until it soaks up some water, and it stays there.

A dry fly can turn wet in a disheartening hurry, but you can do a number of things to help your cause.

MATCH THE WATER

One of the first things a fly fisher learns is the importance of choos-ing a fly that looks like whatever variety of bug the trout are eat-ing. But think about the type of water, too. Dry flies don't all float equally well, and some stretches of a stream are harder than others on buoyancy.

Rough, high-gradient water knocks a fly around. Strong, con-flicting currents, like those formed where a stream flows around rocks, can pull on the leader and drag a fly beneath the surface. In such situations, you want a fly that resists sinking and will pop back up if it goes under for a second.

A bushy, heavily hackled fly is one answer to rough water. An Elk Hair Caddis with a full wing and plenty of hackle will bounce down a riffle that would sink a spare, slender pattern. When an Elk Hair Caddis does go under for second, it generally comes back up, thanks to the buoyancy of the wing material and the tiny air bub-bles trapped by the hackle. A traditional, sparsely tied Light Cahill floats fine on slow and moderately choppy stretches, but a bushy, hair-tailed White Wulff is more likely to remain afloat on rough pocket water.

A fly's body material and construction can make a difference. As any boater knows, polypropylene ropes float. Polypropylene dubbing not only weighs less than water, but it's also nonab-

Part of dry-fly fishing is matching the fly to the water. With its sparse, trimmed hackle, the low-riding caddis pattern *(left)* is best suited to slow, flat water. Thanks to its deer-hair body and bushy hackle, the black Goddard Caddis *(right)* will stay afloat on the roughest, fastest stream. Trout like both styles—but the sparse, slender pattern quickly becomes a wet fly when it's cast on choppy water.

sorbent, and a body made with poly dubbing will not become waterlogged. Most fly tiers reflexively give their dry flies smooth, neat bodies, but several great tiers have pointed out to me that a rough-dubbed, shaggy body often floats better, particularly if it's treated with waterproofing. The fibers sticking out of a rough body increase the area that contacts the surface film, and they'll hold tiny air bubbles if the fly takes a dunking.

Deer-hair patterns such as the Goddard Caddis and Irresistible hold a lot of air in their bodies and will float where most other flies can't. They'll also float longer than most other flies. I'd tied these patterns for years, but I never really appreciated them until I moved to South Carolina and began fishing Appalachian trout streams. In this part of the country, most good trout water is high-gradient stuff—very high gradient. Some of our mountain streams consist of plunge pools connected by cascades and stretches of violent pocket water. The jungle that covers the southern mountains and hangs over every stream often makes a backcast impossible. It's the most physically demanding trout fishing I've ever done. But the plunge pools and pockets are full of trout that love to rise to dry flies. With a well-greased Irresistible or Goddard Caddis, I can make ten or twelve roll-cast presentations to a spot or even drive the fly into the base of a waterfall. The deer-hair flies keep floating. On many of these streams, my elegant Catskill-style flies are useless; in some places, not even an Elk Hair Caddis will stay afloat for long.

Flies made with closed-cell foam can save you some time and trouble when you fish a rough, fast stream. A mountain brook full of rapids, cascades, plunge pools, and powerful eddies will eventually drown even an Irresistible. But a foam-bodied fly will pop back up every time it goes under, and you'll have to change flies less often. That's why I'm fond of foam ants, crickets, and inchworms, and why I continue to experiment with foam-bodied caddisflies; such flies let me spend time reading water and casting instead of replacing waterlogged lures.

Let the stream guide you. In slow, flat water, you can use sparse or no-hackle patterns. Where the stream wants to play rough, tie on a bushier dressing, a deer-hair pattern, or a fly made with closed-cell foam.

WATER RESISTANCE

The more water-resistant you make your flies, the longer they'll float. Any floatant provides some degree of protection, but a dab of goo applied just before you start casting might not protect the entire fly. I treat many dry flies at home, giving whatever product I use time to soak into the materials. I'll add a little floatant in the field, but I like a fly to be as waterproof as possible before it gets tied to my tippet.

Anglers have used all sorts of things to waterproof flies. Many pioneer dry-fly fishermen anointed each fly with a drop of kerosene. That's actually a good dressing, though hardly environmentally correct. I've read about old dry-fly dressings made with deer tallow and other animal fats.

One excellent dry-fly treatment is a product called Water Shed. This isn't a streamside dressing, but rather a waterproofing agent applied at least twenty-four hours before a fly is used. It works very well, sealing the fibers and materials against water.

Many dry-fly sprays also work fine as waterproofing agents. Dump a bunch of flies into a coffee can and give them a spritz of silicone spray. Shake the flies around, spray them again (not too heavily), and let the can sit for a while with the lid on. Then put the flies back in your box. It's politically incorrect to say so, but I've had good results using hardware-store products such as CRC Heavy Duty Silicone Spray to pretreat flies.

Some anglers try water-repellent fabric sprays such as Scotchgard. These can work, but they can also leave a powdery residue on your flies, particularly if you apply too much. Go easy with such products, and test them on just a few flies until you learn that they work. While Scotchgard and similar products work well on my winter coats and felt hats, they don't seem to do as good a job waterproofing trout flies.

ANOINT YOUR OFFERINGS

Even if you treat flies with a water repellent a day or two before going fishing, you'll still want to apply some sort of liquid or goo before putting a fly into play. Most floatants work at least pretty well, but they don't all work with all flies.

Be careful with thick greases or pastes. They provide good flotation and water resistance, but they can also mat a fly's fibers together. Daub a Hendrickson with heavy grease and you'll turn its elegant wings into tan sticks and change the tail fibers into a single rod sticking out of the fly's butt. That actually impairs the fly's ability to float, not to mention spoiling its looks.

You can use a paste on a standard dry fly as long as you apply it sparingly. Pick up a tiny bit of the stuff on a fingertip, and apply it to the body, tails, and hackle collar. Try not to get any on the wings. A few false casts will separate any fibers that the grease

Match the floatant to the fly. Liquid floatants work well on flies with delicate hackles and tails, but they're not a good choice for big hoppers or deer-hair bugs. Thick pastes and greases are good for hair bugs and some hairwing caddisflies, but they can mat the wings, hackles, and tails of traditional drys. An ointment with the viscosity of skin lotion, such as the inexpensive brand on the left, works well with a wide range of flies. It's wise to carry two types of floatants.

stuck together. On a big fly such as a grasshopper or cricket, a paste floatant provides excellent flotation. Grease works very well on the deer-hair bodies of Irresistibles and Goddard Caddis.

Note, though, that some paste floatants seem to harden or congeal over time. While rummaging through a bin of fishing stuff, I came across some old hairwing caddis patterns that I'd dressed with paste floatant about two years earlier. I could even remember the afternoon on which I'd used a couple of the flies on the headwaters of the Walloomsac River in Vermont. The paste had shrunk and hardened, and the flies' wings had become solid lumps that looked like slivers of wood. A paste might make a fly float well, but it can also mat the materials and ruin them. Don't apply such a floatant to a fly until you need to.

A liquid floatant, such as a silicone-based spray, is easier to use on small or delicate flies. Again, go easy with the stuff. Make a few false casts to blow any excess floatant off the fly before dropping it in front of a fish. Some liquids leave a tiny oil slick the first time a fly hits the water. If your floatant does that, make a couple of short drifts to let excess oil leave the fly before casting it to the target. Real bugs don't make oil slicks.

Some floatants feel like gels or lotions, thicker than silicone spray, but thinner than paste. These work very well on most types of flies. Gehrke's Gink is probably the best-known product of this type. As with a paste, don't slather too much of the goo all over a fly.

In cool weather, a gel floatant might assume the consistency of axle grease and become difficult to apply. For that reason, I sometimes carry floatant in a shirt pocket rather than in my vest, so that my body heat can keep it warm. In a pinch, you can hold a bottle of floatant in your armpit to warm it up.

BUOYANCY BUSTERS

If you've ever accidentally spilled a bunch of dry flies onto a stream, you might have observed through your tears that they all floated beautifully as they drifted downstream. That's because nothing but their own inconsequential weight was trying to make them sink.

A leader can do bad things to a dry fly. Fluorocarbon has certain virtues, such as good abrasion resistance, but it's denser than nylon monofilament. Indeed, a fluorocarbon tippet can be heavy enough to pull a sparsely tied, barely afloat dry fly under the surface. I might use fluorocarbon with nymphs, but I stick with nylon for dry-fly work.

Even with nylon, use the lightest tippet you can. The less mass attached to a dry fly's nose, the better it will drift and the longer it will float. Conventional wisdom might suggest using a 4X tippet with a size 12 Adams, but try 5X or even 6X; the fly will float better.

Once the butt of a nylon leader absorbs some water, it becomes an anchor, dragging the tip of the fly line and your dry fly down with it. It pays to grease the first few feet of a leader's butt to keep it from sinking, particularly in choppy water. Don't grease the whole leader; a tippet perched atop the surface film looks like a hawser to a trout viewing it from below. The faster and rougher the water, the more of the leader you can rub with floatant.

You might want to grease the first 2 or 3 feet of your fly line, too. The buoyant coating on the tip of a fly line is very thin, and it barely keeps the line afloat. A bit of dry-fly dressing keeps a floating line from turning into a sinking tip that pulls the leader below the surface and eventually drowns your fly.

BLOW-DRY YOUR FLY
Minimal false casting is the sign of efficiency. A good caster doesn't make eight false casts for each presentation; he'll pick up 30 feet of line and leader and develop enough speed with a single false-cast cycle to drop the fly 50 feet away.

With a nymph or streamer, that's great. Learn to make your subsurface deliveries with as few false casts as possible. With a dry fly, however, an extra false cast is not wasted effort, because it helps blow-dry the fly. You can often get another half dozen drifts out of a soggy fly simply by adding an extra false cast to each delivery. When the current or a submerged leader drags a dry fly beneath the surface, try not to let it stay submerged too long. Get it up in the air and use a false cast or two to dry it off.

Watch where you make false casts. Line flashing back and forth over a trout will spook the fish. Water spraying off the line and leader can do the same thing. Keep your extra false casts short and off to the side of the target, and then lengthen the line and change direction to hit the target.

I'VE BEEN SLIMED
A well-tied, well-anointed dry fly will float through many casts. But you hope that the thing ends up in a fish's yap as soon as possible. When that happens, the fly not only gets submerged, it also gets covered with fish slime, and slime has exactly the opposite effect of floatant. Indeed, I've used fish slime to help a leader sink

when fishing a nymph. I'll catch a chub, get my mitts good and slimy handling the fish, and then rub the slime on the leader. It then slices right through the surface film.

That's not what you want a dry fly to do. And so we have desiccants, powders that absorb water and slime and make a bedraggled fly buoyant again. These products are fine powders that come in little plastic tubs. When a fly becomes waterlogged or gets slimed by a fish, you put it (still tied to the tippet) in the container of desiccant, close the lid, and shake the tub. Remove the fly from the tub and blow off the loose powder. Resume fishing. Desiccants are good things to have if changing flies is troublesome for you.

Eventually a fly simply refuses to float any longer. That's why you carry more than one. But no one complains when a fly becomes too slimy to float. Those rare days when we run out of dry flies are the stuff of memories.

8

Not-So-Blind Casting

We make a big deal out of dry-fly fishing, don't we? For more than a century, the mystique of casting dry flies to trout has dominated the sport. We take it on faith that dry-fly fishing is harder, more challenging, more intellectual, more rewarding than other sorts of angling. To many anglers, matching a hatch is the whole point of fishing with a fly rod; to have done so is to have reached the zenith of skill and accomplishment.

Catching any kind of fish on the surface is loads of fun, and fishing dry flies well takes more than a spoonful of brains. But maybe we shouldn't make quite such a fuss over matching hatches and casting flies that float. After all, a dry-fly angler begins with a number of clues. A trout rises to take a bug, then rises again and again in roughly the same spot and at more or less regular intervals to eat more bugs. The angler has a target. He knows where a fish is, knows that it's eating, and knows where it's eating. That's half the battle. Now the angler has to figure out what the fish is eating (sometimes an easy task, sometimes not) and choose a pattern that resembles the real insects. If he succeeds there, his next step is to make a good presentation. If the good presentation doesn't work, the angler has to reconsider his choice of fly or the size of his tippet or the angle of his cast.

Sure, dry-fly fishing can get tricky. Therein lies much of its charm. But while the fly fisher sorts through the variables, his target remains in the same place unless he does something clumsy to frighten it. The fisherman can use a bunch of clues to solve the puzzle and can often take his time doing it. It's all great fun, but it's not on the same intellectual plane as the space program.

And maybe we miss some fun by elevating dry-fly angling to such a level. Consider the language that we use. We talk about sight fishing and hatch matching and technical angling. Noble, lofty pursuits, all of them. And then there's "blind casting." It sounds like random, desperate flailing by which a yokel sometimes snags a fish through dumb luck.

There's really no such thing as blind casting unless you pick a fly with your eyes closed and then stumble around slinging line in any direction and hoping that your fly collides with a fish. Even when a stream seems asleep, a good angler can find clues. For many fishermen, and I'm one, this sort of puzzle solving is every bit as much fun as finding the right fly to feed a rising trout.

Besides, hatches and spinner falls don't happen all the time and with equal regularity in all places. Some spring creeks produce clouds of mayflies with all the predictability of Old Faithful. In June, a heavy hatch of *Ephemera ittybittius* comes off between 2:00 and 3:00 every afternoon. The trout chow down and spend the rest of the day burping, and an angler who wants to catch them had better be on the water at 2:00 with an assortment of upholstered hooks that look like *E. ittybittius* emergers and duns. But many freestone streams operate differently. Emergence periods are spread out or downright diffuse. Water levels and temperatures fluctuate from week to week, often from day to day. From midspring until late summer, the best aquatic-insect activity on some streams begins shortly before dusk, leaving the daytime hours quiet. On many streams, hatches are so sparse and sporadic that one wonders how the bugs manage to continue their species. The fish work hard to scratch out a living.

Yet many waters that don't have heavy, predictable, glamorous hatches still support a lot of life. Their total biomass is huge; it's just not unionized. Fish at the top of the aquatic food chain—trout, bass, sunfish, or whatever—nibble at a light buffet all day. I've lived near this sort of water all my life, in the mid-Atlantic region, in New England, and now in the South. Yes, I've enjoyed some fine hatches and evening spinner falls (the best, believe it or not, on a New Jersey stream that I would name only after prolonged torture), but I've enjoyed many more days of good fishing and progressively less blind casting on rivers that would strike some anglers as almost lifeless. They are, however, very lively places indeed. And they'll tell you how to fish if you pay attention to the clues.

UP OR DOWN?

When you see lots of insects and riseforms on the surface, you know how you're going to fish: upstream, with an emerger or a dry fly. When you see neither bugs nor the rings made by rising fish, you have to make some decisions. The first is whether to fish upstream or down.

It's okay to indulge a whim when you have a choice. If you just plain feel like fishing downstream today, tie on a wet fly or streamer and go to it. Angling doesn't always have to involve careful analysis of all known variables followed by rational selection of strategies and tactics most likely to produce success. You're allowed to do something just for the hell of it.

Often, though, the environment will nudge you in one direction. If the riverbed has more than a tiny amount of silt, you should fish upstream. Wading through pockets of silt produces plumes of mud that put fish on the alert and might even make them flee. If you work upstream, you can kick up silt without alarming the fish to which you're casting.

A small, rough stream with lots of rocks, pocket water, and plunge pools is more easily and productively fished upstream. Casting upstream, you can drop a nymph or dry fly onto small targets, let the fly drift a yard or two, and then roll-cast the line into the air to begin the next cast. It's a fast, *flick-flick-flick* style of angling, and it works because it lets you hit all the washtub-size spots that might hold a fish. Making a good downstream presentation in this kind of water is often difficult or impossible.

No hatch? No rising trout? No idea what to do? If you have enough room, try Grandpa's method: swim a wet fly, a Muddler, or a small bucktail downstream and across. This old-fashioned approach lets you prospect a lot of water, and it shows the fish a fly that looks like everyday food. The simplest solution often works best.

Fishing in any direction can be tough on a brook hemmed in by shrubbery. The trees and bushes won't permit the backcasts that let you throw your line across the current. If you want to put the line in the air, you have to keep it more or less parallel with the banks. That seems to mandate upstream fishing. You can, however, roll-cast your way down a small, brushy creek, swinging an old-fashioned wet fly or a midget streamer on a short line, and this kind of fishing can be very pleasant if you have a rod that roll-casts well.

Fishing downstream makes a lot of sense on any river where you have room to cast diagonally across the current. Nowadays, relatively few anglers fish this way; we've been trained to turn upstream as soon as we enter a river. But casting across the flow and swinging the fly through an arc lets you cover a lot of water. The flies that lend themselves to across-and-down fishing—streamers and wet flies—represent creatures that trout, bass, and panfish like to eat. A hungry fish rarely turns down a chance to put a minnow into its stomach. Soft-hackled patterns, the Leadwing Coachman, the Breadcrust, and many other old wet flies mimic emerging caddis pupae or diving female caddisflies that have returned to the water to lay their eggs. Caddisflies, like midges, are among the bugs that fish see day after day, and a good wet-fly angler is simply playing the percentages.

Deciding whether to fish upstream or down doesn't commit you to fishing in only one direction. You can use both approaches, switching from one to the other as conditions indicate. You might start by casting upstream, but then, an hour later, come to a long run that looks perfect for a streamer. Or you might start with a wet fly and come to a spot that looks ideal for some work with a floating ant or cricket.

Look at the water and the surroundings and ask yourself, "Can I fish this hunk of river better by working downstream or upstream?" That question should be on your mind all day. If you've never done much downstream angling—and a lot of younger fly fishers haven't—then stock a fly box with streamers and wet flies and give it a try. Swinging a wet fly or a baitfish imitation might at first seem like blind casting, but it's not. It's an excellent way to show the fish lures that resemble some of their staple foods.

GEOLOGY IS DESTINY

The notion of "reading the water" ignores at least half of the story. We need to read not only the fluid that has no choice but to flow downhill, but also the earth through and over which the fluid moves. The riverbed, the banks, and the general topography can provide lots of clues.

A high-gradient stream that bounces down the side of a mountain can support a fair number of trout and a few surprisingly big fish, but much of the water is too violent or shallow to hold trout. This kind of stream forces most of the fish into small areas: plunge pools, deeper runs between rapids or waterfalls, depressions in the bed, and eddies and deep holes where the stream turns. Finding a

Trout in rocky, high-gradient streams have to find places where they can escape the fast currents. Fishing upstream or up and across works best in this kind of water. Expect to make a lot of short casts to small targets. You might not need to match hatches, but you will need dry flies that float uncommonly well and nymphs that sink very quickly.

refuge from the raging currents is a fish's first job—and yours. Look for the spots where trout can find a break from the current.

Its setting makes high-gradient water a tough neighborhood. It generally lacks a good nutrient base. Heavy rain can quickly turn a pleasant brook into a dangerous torrent, but after a storm passes, the water drops as quickly as it rose. The stream's elevation exposes it to the most extreme winter weather. Yet these little streams often hold an amazing variety of life. Just don't expect to see a lot of heavy, predictable daytime hatches. A brook crashing down the flanks of a mountain might harbor many species of aquatic insects—often more than spring creeks and tailwaters hold—but it probably doesn't grow many individuals of each species. Hatches are sparse flurries rather than blizzards.

Fishing a high-gradient stream requires stamina, accuracy, and good line-management skills, but it rarely demands a huge assortment of flies. Most of the time, the trout eat whatever's on the plate; they can't afford to be snooty. Dry flies for this kind of water usually don't need to replicate specific insects, but they do need to float very well. A size 14 or 16 Goddard Caddis is tough to beat; it floats like a cork popper and looks like insects that the trout eat day in, day out. An Irresistible is another good choice; trout like it and you can see it on fast water. If you run into an honest-to-goodness hatch, you might need to match it, but a few Goddard Caddis and Irresistibles will take care of most blind casting with dry flies on high-gradient water.

Most mayfly nymphs in high-country streams belong to the clinger and crawler groups. They're wide, squat, flattened insects with broad heads and heavy-duty legs, and their colors roughly match those of the stream's bottom. Weighted, size 12 through 16 Gold-Ribbed Hare's Ears tied slightly darker than usual (mix a little dark brown or black fur into the dubbing blend) are reliable nymph patterns. The main requirement is that they sink quickly.

Since its cold water contains a lot of dissolved oxygen, a high-gradient stream usually has a population of stoneflies. I've seen some immense stoneflies come out of little streams in the Green Mountains of Vermont and in the southern Appalachians. Remember, though, that stoneflies have two-year life cycles, which means that you don't have to cast a huge, unwieldy imitation of a full-grown nymph. A size 10 or 12 black stonefly pattern represents a younger nymph, and it will catch mountain trout every day. It's also easy to cast accurately with small-stream tackle.

Those four types of flies will catch trout in nearly any small, high-gradient stream. It's not complicated: The habitat tells you how to fish and what to cast. You know that you want flies for upstream fishing because downstream angling is difficult to impossible in a fast, rough headwater full of boulders. You know that fish can't hold in the cascades and ankle-deep rapids; they have to live where they can get a break from the most violent currents. Since high-country fish work hard for a meager living, they're rarely as selective as trout in more fertile water, so you don't need eight fly boxes crammed with different fly patterns. To fish on top, though,

Here are two of the safe bets in high-gradient water. Cold, rocky, well-oxygenated streams typically have good populations of stoneflies. A medium-size stonefly pattern *(left)* looks like common food, and it's easier than a bigger, much heavier nymph to cast accurately on a short line. A squat, generic mayfly nymph pattern *(right)* represents any of the wide, flat, clinging mayflies that live in fast water.

you do need dry flies with exceptional buoyancy; Goddard Caddis and Irresistibles will float practically anywhere. A mountain stream almost certainly holds wide, flattened, midsize mayfly nymphs and stoneflies. It holds many other insects, of course, but size 10 stonefly nymphs and size 12 or 14 mayfly-nymph patterns have enough mass to sink quickly and enough bulk to catch a trout's attention.

The geology of a high-gradient stream creates a harsh habitat that gives the fish relatively few choices. You, then, need relatively few flies, as long as they're suited to fast, turbulent water. To the basic selection of Goddard Caddis, Irresistibles, stonefly nymphs, and weighted, generic mayfly nymphs, I'd add small Brassies for wintertime fishing (they represent midge larvae) and a cricket or inchworm for surface fishing in high summer.

If you live in the East, pay particular attention to the bed of a high-gradient stream. Because they flow down the sides of ancient mountains (the oldest on the planet, I've read), some of these little rivers have carved their channels all the way to solid bedrock. There's a pretty creek in upstate South Carolina that flows for long stretches—hundreds of yards in some places—over smooth, solid, barren rock that harbors practically no fish food, and therefore no fish. When you run into a stretch of solid bedrock, keep moving until you find a better substrate. Rivers at lower elevations might flow over bedrock in places, but they also carry more sediments and nutrients that settle to the bottom and support life. In a small, fast stream, bedrock is continuously scoured clean.

A larger river's bed can also tell you a lot. A long stretch of smooth, uniform bottom composed of sand and a little gravel isn't much better than bedrock. It supports relatively few invertebrates that fish can catch (nymphs that burrow into a sandy bottom are rarely available to trout) and gives the fish nowhere to hide from the current. A flat, sandy bottom makes for easy wading, but it probably won't make for good fishing. Move quickly through such areas, but keep an eye peeled for isolated features—a fallen tree, a clump of rocks, a patch of weeds—that might hold a fish or two.

The more surface area and variety a riverbed has, the more life it can support. A mix of coarse gravel, pebbles, assorted rocks, and large stones has millions of nooks and crannies where insect larvae, crayfish, and small fish hide and feed. Because it's uneven, such a bottom creates many pockets of slow or slack water where trout, bass, or panfish can hold. There seems to be a correlation between the quality of the fishing and the beating that a riverbed inflicts on one's feet and ankles. The places that hold the most fish food and gamefish are also those that make my feet most sore.

Even the slipperiness of the riverbed makes a difference. The brooks that I used to fish in Vermont are nightmares to wade. Their uneven bottoms are covered with algae on which felt-soled boots slip and slide; every step is an adventure. But those streams also support a respectable quantity and variety of insects, and some of them produce pretty good hatches. The southern Appalachian streams where I fish these days are not nearly so slippery; they lack the nutrients that let algae thrive. In the warm months, I often leave the felt-soled boots home and fish in a pair of cheap cross-training

A mixed, uneven bottom composed of coarse gravel and a lot of rocks will beat up your ankles, but it supports a lot of fish food. Sculpins, crayfish, and a huge variety of insect larvae populate this type of riverbed, making it a well-stocked grocery store for trout, bass, and panfish. Take your time in water like this; a mixed bottom generally provides much better fishing than bedrock, sand, or mud does.

shoes. By and large, though, these southern streams grow fewer bugs than those in New England.

Don't complain too much about tough wading. The more your feet slip and the more your ankles hurt, the more likely you are to find fish and the things they eat.

Because a mixed, rough, and slippery bottom supports a good variety and quantity of aquatic insects, it's likely to produce reliable hatches and more of them. Or, to state the obvious, classic water is where you're most likely to enjoy classic, hatch-matching angling. But no river provides continuous dry-fly or emerger fishing. If the bottom has a lot of gravel and cobble, it probably has a good population of sculpins or darters, too. That makes one of the many varieties of Muddlers a good choice between hatches. Fish that live in a rich habitat get plenty to eat, but some of them will always chase a plump sculpin. A baitfish imitation lets you cover a lot of territory, increasing the likelihood that at least one cooperative fish will see the fly. When you're not sure what to cast in a freestone river, you can do much worse than to fish downstream with some type of Muddler. Trout and bass both love these flies.

If you'd rather fish upstream with a nymph, start by studying the colors of the bottom. Prey creatures generally match their surroundings. Matching the bottom might seem a simplistic approach, but it has served me well for a long time. When I blind-cast with a nymph for trout, I generally start with a size 14 fly that's roughly the color of the riverbed. Chances are that the fly resembles something that lives in the stream and often ends up in the drift, and it's big enough to catch a trout's eye from a few feet away. It's a reasonably good generic lure that will probably catch a fish or two while I look for clues that will help me refine my approach.

Among those clues are stonefly husks on exposed rocks. When you see a lot of empty husks, you can assume that stoneflies have been emerging in the evening and at night. To do that, they have to crawl across the bottom and climb up the rocks, activities that expose them to fish. Try a black or dark brown nymph about the same size as one of the empty skins, and fish it deep. Concentrate on the heads of pools and deep runs below stretches of fast, rough water. On a summer afternoon, you can often catch several fish with a stonefly nymph while waiting for an evening rise.

If the riverbed has sandy or muddy areas between stretches of harder bottom, it probably contains some burrowing mayfly nymphs such as green drakes, brown drakes, or yellow drakes. Since these large nymphs spend much of their lives in the bottom rather than on it, fish don't see them very often. In late spring and early summer, however, the nymphs of big drakes become more active as emergence time approaches. If a river has the right habitat for green, brown, or yellow drakes, you can do pretty well with an appropriate nymph pattern in the late afternoon and early evening.

Look for patches of soft bottom along the edges of a stream, too. Some rivers scour their beds from bank to bank, keeping the bottom clear of silt and trash, while the banks of others have many

Many rivers have large pockets of slack water along their banks, where dead leaves and other trash can settle and decay. Such detritus is where dragonfly nymphs live, and fish like to eat them. If the streams that you fish have this kind of habitat along their banks, carry a few flies that look like dragonfly nymphs; simple patterns like these will catch trout, bass, and panfish.

places where dead leaves settle to the bottom and decay. Eddies and calm spots full of rotting leaves and silt are where dragonflies come from; their nymphs live and hunt in the detritus, and fish eat them. Dragonfly-nymph patterns aren't everyday flies on most trout and smallmouth streams, but they come in handy on rivers that have the right habitat. A real dragonfly nymph can shoot forward by squirting a jet of water out of its abdomen. When you fish an imitation in a soft-bottomed eddy or hole paved with decaying leaves, punctuate the drift with an occasional short, quick strip.

The angle of a stream's banks can also tell you how to fish. Steep banks usually drop off into relatively deep water, and they often have vegetation growing down to the edge of the river. Fish like deep water along a riverbank. The vegetation shades the water during part of the day, and irregularities in the bank give fish hiding spots out of the main current. Terrestrial insects fall from the land and from overhanging branches. Floods undermine the banks and topple trees into the river, where they become habitat for fish.

Trout or bass could be anywhere in water that runs between steep banks, but the odds are good that many of them will live in the luxury housing along the edges. If you want to fish on the surface between hatches, look for steep shorelines, ideally those with trees, brush, or grass. In a warmwater stream, slap a popper, a grasshopper pattern, or a big cricket against the bank. In trout water, try a beetle, ant, cricket, or, in late summer, a hopper. During the afternoon, you're more likely to find fish willing to rise along the shaded bank.

Gently sloping banks let a river spread out during high water. At its normal level, the stream might have long, wide stretches of exposed gravel and sand along its edges. Generally, the water next to these gravel beaches is shallow, often only a few inches deep. At

Steep banks often create luxury housing for fish. This short piece of river has a pocket of calm, fairly deep water against the bank, a nearby current that carries food, several nooks and crannies where a fish can escape the midday sun, fallen trees that provide hiding spots from which to ambush prey, and a good supply of terrestrial insects, thanks to the trees and bushes crowding the edge of the water. Trout and river bass gravitate toward places like this.

night, trout or smallmouths might come to the edge of the shallow water to hunt stonefly nymphs, hellgrammites, or minnows. During the day, though, shallow water flanked by low, gradually sloping banks holds few fish. You can wade on the gravel-bottomed shallows, but cast toward the channel in the middle of the stream. Here the topography steers you toward the center rather than the edges. Since the water in the middle of the stream receives little or no shade for much of the day, the fish living out there probably congregate in the deepest spots from midmorning until early evening. Throw a weighted nymph or streamer at them.

Geology and topography shape a river and, in the absence of runoff and other human contributions, determine its fertility. Read the water by studying the land and the riverbed. Some of the clues will tell you where not to fish; others will suggest which flies to use.

WEED BEDS

Aquatic weeds support a different mix of fish food than bare gravel or rocks do. The plants also create shade and give fish places to hide. A tuft of weeds surrounded by bare riverbed might not seem important, but it matters to fish—or at least to one fish. Over the years, I've spooked dozens of smallmouths and trout from clumps of weeds that didn't look big enough to hide a small sunfish. Those fish were probably resting in the shade, and the odds are that I couldn't have caught them no matter what I did. Still, they were missed opportunities.

Don't assume that an isolated patch of grass or weeds doesn't hold a fish just because you can't see one. In a trout stream, drift a small nymph past the weeds. Make several presentations, because the weeds might obscure the fly from the fish's view. In a warmwater stream, try a medium-size nymph (size 10, say) or a small popper or slider. Don't animate the popper; drop it softly about 2 feet upstream of the weeds, and then let it drift, fishing it like a dry fly.

A weed bed the size of a car constitutes a microhabitat. It probably harbors a school of minnows plus assorted fry. Damselfly and

Weed beds harbor different types of fish food than rocky bottoms do. Among the flies you'll want for prospecting weeds are scuds *(top);* damselfly nymphs *(middle),* which catch both trout and bass; and imitations of slender, swimming mayfly nymphs such as *Baetis (bottom).* Fish weed beds slowly and carefully; they usually contain fish that you can't see.

dragonfly nymphs live in weed beds, as do the nymphs of *Baetis* and other swimming mayflies. If a stream contains many weed beds, it might also have a lot of scuds, particularly if the water is slightly alkaline.

A trout or bass can lie anywhere inside a weed bed. Fish will also hold just downstream of the weeds, waiting for nymphs or scuds to drift to them. If you're working upstream, look first for fish at the bottom end of the bed. You don't want to spook a fish that will alarm all the others.

A size 16 or 18 Pheasant Tail or an olive Hare's Ear is usually a safe bet in a trout stream. In the summer and early autumn, an olive damselfly nymph is also a good choice for fishing weed beds. Cast to the downstream end first, then work your way up one side of the bed by lengthening your casts. Keep the fly close to the edge of the weeds. You might even try a few casts over the top of the vegetation if you think that the water is deep enough.

Use larger flies in a warmwater stream. On a clear day, fish a light-colored streamer or bucktail along the edges and over the top of each weed bed. Cast from above or one side of the bed, keep the fly close to the weeds as long as you can, and then strip it away at a good clip. On an overcast day, make the same presentation with a darker streamer such as a Woolly Bugger or the Jonah Fly described in the next chapter.

A popper or slider will often pull smallmouths out of weed beds. The fly doesn't have to be very big; something a bit larger than a bream bug will do. Cast from below or alongside the weeds and fish the bug slowly, giving it an occasional twitch and letting it drift between twitches. If you don't get any action in a spot that you're sure holds a fish, add a dropper to the surface bug. Tie 12 to 16 inches of tippet material to the bug's hook bend, and attach a nymph to the dropper. Fish the rig a little more aggressively, giving the bug frequent twitches. A bass will notice the commotion that the popper or slider makes, swim over to investigate, and take the nymph drifting beneath the bug. It's an old trick, but fish don't know that.

TIME OF DAY

Cold-blooded creatures such as fish are most comfortable and active within a certain temperature range. (So are some warm-blooded creatures, such as me.) A fish can't change the temperature of its environment, but it can move around to find the most comfortable spots. If you move to the same spots, you'll catch more fish.

In the spring and fall, when the water is cooler than it is in midsummer, the best fishing usually doesn't start until at least a few hours after sunrise. There's not much point in getting up before dawn to fish in a river full of early spring snowmelt or one chilled by a week of frosty October nights. If you're on the river early in the morning, work the slower, calmer water with a nymph or midge larva, and keep the fly close to the bottom. Cold, sluggish fish don't like to fight strong currents, and they won't expend much energy to take a fly. As the sun warms the stream, the fish spread out, and more of the river comes alive. By lunchtime, you can start to catch fish in riffles, runs, and the downstream ends of pools.

In hot weather, the middle of the day is usually the slowest time on a trout stream. Smallmouth bass can remain frisky in surprisingly warm water, but even they tend to shut down during the middle of a sweltering August day. Remember, too, that fish don't have sunglasses and can't squint; they avoid the midday summer sun. Work the shady side of the river, and look for trees and bridges that throw shadows on the water. In the middle of a hot day, you

From midmorning to late afternoon on a sunny day, pay attention to shaded spots. Since fish have fixed pupils and can't squint, dark places provide the only relief from the sun that their eyes get. In the summer, shade becomes particularly important to fish.

will generally find the most cooperative trout and river bass at the lower ends of riffles, the heads of pools below riffles, and the middles of the deepest pools. Flat water that's exposed to the sun will hold fewer fish. Floating ants, beetles, inchworms, and hoppers work well in water that's no more than a few feet deep. In a deep pool, try drifting a heavy stonefly nymph or casting a weighted streamer upcurrent and stripping it back along the bottom.

Even in moderate weather, fish move to different areas at different times of the day. Many anglers assume that "insect activity" refers only to hatches, but aquatic insects also engage in less obvious activities. One of these is something that entomologists call the drift. At dawn and dusk, larvae move around more than they do during the middle of the day. Some of them deliberately let go of the streambed and drift downstream for varying distances; others lose their footing and become captives of the current for a little while. What all this activity means to fish is that the larvae of mayflies, caddisflies, stoneflies, and midges become more visible and available early in the morning and again in the evening. In part, the drift explains why we often enjoy the best fishing early and late in the day: There's more going on underwater, even if we don't see it.

The challenge is figuring out which nymph or larva pattern to cast during these drift periods. Only local knowledge can provide an exact answer, because the mix of insects varies from river to river, but we can make some educated guesses. Entomologists tell us that nearly every healthy trout stream contains a sizable (if mostly invisible) population of the larvae of midges, caddisflies, and small olive mayflies. That suggests certain fly patterns: midge larvae, caddis larvae, and little olive or Pheasant Tail nymphs. But the larger mayflies and stoneflies also are more active in the morning and evening. More often than not, several fly patterns will work more or less equally well during the drift periods.

You still need to choose a fly. What to do? One solution is to pick one according to conditions—that is, to match the water. Very clear, relatively quiet water calls for thin tippets and delicate presentations. Try a midge larva or a size 18 Pheasant Tail or olive Hare's

Ear on a 7X tippet. In faster, rougher water or a stream that has a bit of color, tie on a caddis larva pattern or a generic mayfly nymph such as a size 14 Gold-Ribbed Hare's Ear. If you're fishing good stonefly habitat—a fast, rocky stream with cold, well-oxygenated water—cast a medium-size stonefly pattern. If the bottom has lots of soft areas, a fly that resembles the nymph of a green, brown, or yellow drake is a good choice, particularly in the evening.

Another answer to the "Which fly?" question is to pitch more than one. Although I'm not crazy about two-fly rigs, because they can tangle (when cast by me, at any rate), a dropper rig does let you make two presentations with each cast, and giving the fish a choice improves the likelihood of showing them something that they'll eat. You can easily make a two-fly rig by using a Palomar knot with a long tag end to attach a size 12 or 14 nymph to your tippet. Tie a midge larva or caddis larva pattern to the tag. Don't try any casting heroics with such an arrangement. Cast a moderate length of line, open the loop a little, use a slower, longer stroke, and you'll avoid most tangles.

During the morning and evening drift periods, you'll probably find the best fishing in riffles, pools below riffles, and downstream of weed beds. Riffles and weeds are rich habitats that contribute many insects to the drift.

Since insect larvae are less active during the middle of the day, fish see fewer of them. And since the riverbed is producing less food, fish tend to spread out and move into their daytime resting spots. Look for places where a trout or smallmouth can find shade and a break from the current. Ants and beetles fished on fine tippets will take trout holding in shallow, shaded water during the middle of the day. Small poppers and large terrestrials will appeal to resting smallmouths. The stretch from late morning until late afternoon is also a particularly good time to cover a lot of water and explore deep holes with a streamer.

THE WEATHER

"Bright day, bright fly; dark day, dark fly." That old adage is at least half true. Dark streamers and wet flies almost always work as searching patterns, but light-colored flies work less well on overcast days and in dark water. It's a question of visibility: Fish can see a black Woolly Bugger or nymph against nearly any background, but they might not spot a pale streamer on a gloomy day or in a stained stream.

Clear, bright days with high barometric pressure seem to affect bass more than trout, but they push almost all fly-rod fish toward shade and into deeper water. Perfect picnic weather also makes fish grumpy. Although you can't expect nonstop action in this kind of weather, you can still catch a few fish. Whether you cast a nymph or a streamer, concentrate on deep water and on weed beds or fallen timber where fish can hide, use a long leader and a fine tippet, and fish slowly. Keep the fly deep, and make more than your usual number of presentations to each spot. Under a postcard-perfect sky, fish often need some coaxing.

A warming trend in the spring or fall usually produces good angling, particularly if it ends with an overcast day before the arrival of rain and a cold front. Fish seem to lose some of their caution on a dark day, and they'll often spread out into shallower water along the edges of a river, where you can go after them with floating terrestrial patterns or, in a warmwater stream, poppers and sliders. This is also one of my favorite times to cast a black or brown streamer or a chunky baitfish imitation such as a Marabou Deceiver.

A cloudburst or thunderstorm can improve the fishing or shut it down. Obviously, you shouldn't stand in a river and wave a long tube of highly conductive carbon fibers during a lightning storm. Take shelter and wait it out. Once the storm has passed, you might have some good fun along the edges of the stream. The rain will have knocked many terrestrial insects off trees and bushes on the banks, and the runoff, which continues after the rain stops, will carry in more bugs. Flies that look like ants, beetles, crickets, inchworms, and grasshoppers are all good choices.

A cloudburst also washes soil into a river. How much depends on the surrounding countryside and the intensity of the rain. A little runoff that creates narrow strips of muddy water along the banks isn't a big problem. You might even find some fish hunting along the edges of the dirty water. But if you notice broad bands of mud forming along the banks, knock off for the day. You don't want to get caught in a flash flood or trapped on a gravel bar by rising water. Besides, you're not going to catch much as the entire river turns brown.

FLIES FOR NOT-SO-BLIND CASTING

Every angler has his own assortment of fallback flies, and smart anglers know that the tastes of fish vary considerably from place to place. The following list reflects my own fishing preferences, but the flies it contains have proved themselves in many streams.

1. Black streamers, Muddlerish patterns that look like sculpins, and white or light gray streamers that mimic shiners or chubs. A few of each will do. Sizes 6 and 8 for trout, 4 and 6 for bass. I like blind casting with a streamer because it's an active style of fishing that covers a lot of water. It's a good way to hook a big fish, too.

2. Gold-Ribbed Hare's Ears or similar nymphs in sizes 12 through 16. There's always something crawling around on the riverbed that these can imitate. Early and late in the day, a generic, size 14 nymph is a good searching pattern in nearly any trout stream.

3. Dark gray nymphs, also in sizes 12 through 16, for fishing over dark bottoms. If you tie flies, you can simply copy the Hare's Ear style and substitute a few different materials: black thread, dark grizzly fibers for the tails, and gray squirrel-fur dubbing for the abdomen and thorax. If you want a very dark nymph, replace the shiny rib with heavy black thread. I've caught a lot of trout on these flies.

4. Olive Hare's Ear or Pheasant Tail nymphs, sizes 16 and 18. The larvae of *Baetis* (blue-winged olive) mayflies are among the most numerous insects in many trout streams. These patterns are particularly good in low, clear water, where you want a smaller fly and fine tippet; in the fall, when many streams have hatches of olives; and near weed beds, which often contain lots of *Baetis* nymphs.

5. Olive damselfly nymphs tied on sizes 8 and 10 long-shank hooks. In streams that have weed beds, these are useful from mid-summer through early autumn, and they'll catch trout or bass.

6. Black stonefly nymphs in sizes 6 through 10. Fish can't miss a big, black nymph as it tumbles down a riffle or into the head of a pool. In a trout stream, cast these in fast, rough water and in pools below riffles. In a warmwater river, use them anywhere; I suspect that bass and sunfish often pick them up as immature hellgrammites.

7. Floating ants or beetles in sizes 12 through 18. These will catch fish from midspring until after the first couple of frosts. Ants are primarily trout flies, but I've caught some good smallmouths and a few largemouths on size 12 pismires.

8. Crickets and hoppers. Both appeal to trout and bass, and both are big enough to pull a fish up through several feet of water. Use crickets from spring through fall, hoppers from mid-summer on.

9. Floating caddisflies in several colors and styles, sizes 12 through 18. The sheer abundance of the insects makes these reliable searching flies. When I want to fish a dry fly even though I haven't seen a trout rise in more than an hour, I cast a caddis in choppy water or an ant in a gentler flow.

10. Popping bugs or sliders small enough to be cast comfortably with a 6-weight or lighter outfit. These, naturally, are for bass and sunfish, though I've also caught a few trout on small, yellow bream bugs.

That's a sparse assortment of flies, but it will get the job done on most freestone streams. Many anglers would add some caddis larva patterns and soft-hackled wet flies, and some folks blind-cast with midge larvae or pupae. Most fly fishers also carry local or regional favorites, and everyone makes seasonal adjustments in his assortment. In the Southeast, yellow-bodied dry flies catch a lot of trout, though most fly fishers in the rest of the country have never heard of flies such as the Yellarhammer, Jim Charley, and Adams Variant. An angler who fishes in alkaline streams that have lush weed beds always has a box of scuds and cress bugs. I've seen outlandishly big, garish nymphs and ghastly things tied with purple plastic chenille catch wild trout that wouldn't touch other flies. Some flies work in some waters for reasons known only to the fish.

Part of casting not-so-blindly is learning local tricks. Much of it, though, is learning how to look at the banks and the riverbed, watching the angle of the sun and the shadows it casts, changing your fly or leader or tactics according to the time of day, the season, and the weather.

I know a guide in Virginia who inspects the undersides of leaves during the summer. He's looking for the egg clusters of dobsonflies. When he starts finding the white patches of eggs stuck to the bottoms of leaves near the river, he knows that the hellgrammites have been emerging at night. The smallmouths know it, too, and they're looking for big, black, horrible nymphs creeping toward shore. Guess what kind of flies the guide gives his clients when he starts finding dobsonfly eggs on leaves?

A few years ago, a friend and I fished a big river with a great smallmouth bass guide. Late in the afternoon, and for no immediately apparent reason, the guide told us to replace our streamers with topwater flies while he ran the boat upstream. We'd been looking at the water, but he'd been looking up at some high-tension wires covered—absolutely covered—with hundreds of birds. "We'll have a white-fly hatch at dusk," he said. "Somehow, the birds know. Tie on a popper and we'll catch some bass on top as it gets dark." We did, too, because the white flies seemed to draw every fish in the river to the surface. Even the walleyes came up and ate poppers.

Such anglers never cast blindly. Sure, they know their home waters the way a good shortstop knows how to judge a hop on his home infield. But they've also learned to read all the signs. It's called streamcraft. The same signs are there for the rest of us.

9

Meat Hooks

[A] large Trout will come as fiercely at a Minnow, as the highest mettled hawk doth seize on a partridge, or a greyhound on a hare.

—Izaak Walton

Only the stench of the skunk marred an otherwise perfect spring morning full of sunshine and birdsong. I'd even spent a few minutes admiring an honest-to-goodness bluebird. One could hardly imagine a better time for traipsing around a trout stream with a fly rod. But no one had told the fish to celebrate the day, and after three hours I hadn't hooked one.

As I slogged upstream casting a nymph, I spotted an angler above me. He was fishing downstream, casting across the current and letting his line swing, occasionally stripping to give his fly a little action. I found a comfortable-looking stump on the bank and sat down to wait for the other guy to fish his way down to me.

He eventually came over for the usual chat between anglers. I admitted that my morning had consisted of casting practice and bird-watching. When I asked about his luck, the other guy said that he'd caught two trout, upstream where he'd started. I asked what he'd caught them on, noticing that he'd palmed his fly to hide it.

"Streamers," he said, "so it's not like they really count. I don't know why there's nothing hatching. Christ, I *hate* fishing streamers."

I looked for words of sympathy, but not very hard, and found none. He'd caught two trout. I hadn't. Yet he seemed less happy than I because he'd stooped to catching trout with streamers.

It's an attitude that I didn't and don't understand. I like streamer fishing in rivers. Sometimes I like the dry-fly work more, and nothing beats fishing a popper on a warmwater stream, but casting a streamer never strikes me as second-rate fly fishing. Streamers and bucktails catch a lot of fish, sometimes the biggest ones and often when nothing else works. They let me deal with spots that I can't fish effectively with an upstream, dead-drift presentation. Throwing a baitfish imitation gives me a chance to stretch out some line and make long casts, or to fish lazily, letting the line and fly trail in the current while I enjoy the scenery. The solid *thump* of a trout or smallmouth whacking a fly as it swings on a tight line thrills me, and I get an immense kick out of firing a cast

Although it affords no opportunities to recite the Latin names of bugs, swinging a streamer across the current is a fine way to find fish, particularly in water that you don't know well. As the line swings directly downstream, let the fly hang in the current for a minute. For reasons of its own, a fish will sometimes watch a streamer for a little while before deciding to kill it.

to a small target and provoking a fish to bite. A fish hooked on a downstream cast almost always feels bigger than it really is, and that, too, pleases me.

No, I cannot weep for a guy who grumbles about having to catch trout with streamers. He inflicts his own suffering. And misses a lot of fun.

Most anglers know that streamers have a powerful appeal to game fish and often take fish that won't move for other flies. Yet a lot of fly fishers don't act on the knowledge. They have a few Woolly Buggers (two black, one olive) and a couple of Muddler Minnows (with loose, overly large heads) in their fly boxes, and every now and then they throw one around when the water is high and dirty or the fish seem inactive. But they're looking for an excuse to clip the streamer from the leader and go back to a dry fly or a nymph. Or maybe a fly fisher casts streamers from a drift boat during a fishing trip but rarely tries them on his home waters. Some guys fish streamers only at the beginning of the trout season, before the good hatches start, or only in late autumn, figuring that brown trout preparing to spawn are the only good targets for streamer flies.

The truth is that streamers and bucktails will catch trout year-round and smallmouths from the time they become active in the spring until the cold weather shuts them down. A fly fisher who takes streamers seriously, and learns to fish them well and often, will catch more fish. He'll have more fun, too, and isn't that the point?

STREAMER WATER

Although a streamer can work just about anywhere, it works better, or at least more easily, in some places than in others. Fast, rough water with standing waves is tough to fish with a streamer unless you use a very heavy fly and a fast-sinking line. The standing waves knock around a floating line and create so much slack that you can't control the fly or feel a strike, and the fast current makes all but the heaviest streamers race downriver only a few inches under the surface. In this kind of water, your best option is probably to use a heavy nymph with split shot on the tippet and a big strike indicator on the leader, lobbing the rig into the waves and keeping the rod tip high as the indicator bounces downstream.

Trout in pocket water full of boulders will clobber streamers, but you have to make a lot of short, very accurate casts to cover pocket water effectively. Since the fly doesn't travel far before you pick it up for another cast, it needs to sink very quickly, which means that it needs to be dense and heavy. But a heavy fly doesn't lend itself to lots of short, accurate casts. In most pocket water, I'd rather work upstream, casting a dry fly or nymph on a short line.

Slow, glass-flat water is hard to fish by any method. The fish see and feel you coming a mile away, the fly line suddenly seems four weights heavier, and the leader that seemed delicate enough in the riffles now looks like a hunk of clothesline. Yet you can catch flat-water fish with a streamer, particularly if the water is deep. And what are the alternatives? Dry flies and emergers look even more fake than usual on flat water, and your leader, no matter how long and fine, seems as visible as a length of 30-pound-test backing. In deep, slow, calm water, one of those spots that seem like a pond within a river, a streamer sometimes wins by default. Switch to a longer leader (from 9 feet to 11 or 12, say), make a long cast with a lightly weighted fly, and drop the fly well above the target area. Let the feeble current carry the streamer to the spot that you want to fish, and then begin your retrieve.

Runs and long stretches of water with moderate currents are ideal for prospecting with a streamer. The classic across-stream-and-down swing lets you cover a lot of water in a series of overlapping triangles. If you can wade more or less down the middle of a 100-foot-wide river, you can use a streamer to cover all the water from bank to bank, casting to one side and then to the other. This is a good way to check out a stream that you're fishing for the first time.

Streamers work beautifully in pools, particularly deep ones. A fish in the middle of a deep pool might not want to rise for a dry fly; the meal doesn't justify the effort. You could go after the fish

Here's a lovely piece of streamer water. The broken surface downstream of me marks a ledge with a trough that nearly always holds a couple of trout. A big eddy swirls beneath the fallen tree on the far bank, and a smaller eddy lies directly to my right. This is a tricky place to fish upstream; the various currents make a drag-free drift very hard to achieve. With a streamer, though, I can slosh down the edge of the bar and swim a good-looking specimen of fish food wherever I want.

with a nymph, and that's often the right tactic, but getting a good drift can be tricky if you have to cast from the faster water of the tailout to the slower water in the middle of the pool. From upstream, you can swing a weighted streamer right across the fish's nose. Deep pools often hold big fish that would rather eat a hunk of meat than a tiny bug. At the head and tail of a pool, a streamer solves the problem of currents that complicate dead-drifting a dry fly or nymph.

Solving problems is perhaps what streamers do best. We all know the frustration of failing to make a drag-free presentation in a swirling eddy or a spot where seventeen different currents clash with one another, and we've all snagged blowdowns by trying to cast a dry fly just a little farther into a tangle of limbs that we just *knew* held a fish. But a streamer isn't supposed to drift passively. It

Streamers come in handy for hitting targets and solving certain problems. The tributary behind me has carved a long, deep trough in the riverbed; note the darker water to my right. Several waterlogged trees lie on the bottom of the trough, making the spot prime habitat for trout during the cool months and redeye bass in the summer. But the water's depth precludes an upstream approach, and the midstream current complicates casting across the flow. A weighted Jonah Fly let me remain in a safe, comfortable spot, cover all the water through a 90-degree arc, and hook a small trout at the edge of the trough.

represents a mobile creature that can swim against or across the current. It obviates the drag-free drift.

When you can't make a good dry-fly or nymph presentation in an eddy, move above or across from it and throw a streamer into the swirling water. If tangled currents snatch your line and make a strike indicator look like it's water-skiing, strip a streamer through that spot. From upstream, you can swing a streamer into a blow-down and then let some line slide through the guides so that the fly swims beneath the obstruction. When you strip the fly away from the fallen tree, a fish might grab it.

A streamer solves so many problems and covers water so well that it's often my first choice. I've spent entire days fishing almost nothing but streamers, switching to other flies only if fish began rising or a particular spot struck me as perfect for a bit of dry-fly or popper fishing.

GOOD TIMES TO FISH STREAMERS

Trout-fishing lore recommends casting streamers early in the spring, before the good hatches commence, and again in the fall, as insect activity declines and brown trout start thinking about spawning. That's good advice, but it's not the whole truth. Trout will eat streamers year-round, except when extra-cold winter temperatures discourage them from eating much of anything. Small-mouths and other river bass will attack streamers as long as the fish are warm enough to bother eating at all.

Given a choice, most anglers prefer to fish on top of the water, and I'm no different. We are visual creatures. Often, though, fishing on top means a great deal of casting with very little catching. When the fish don't want to come up, a streamer will work at least as well as anything else, and often better.

A fine time to fish a streamer is the first two hours of daylight on a summer morning. Perhaps the trout enjoyed a good feed during a hatch or spinner fall the previous evening, but they're hungry again by the time the sun rises. Big browns that do much of their feeding at night are still on the lookout for one more meal before retiring to deep, shaded holes for the day. Smallmouth bass aren't very active in the dark, and they're ravenous by sunup.

On a morning without a hatch, fish could be anywhere in a river. Trout and bass generally avoid shallow places during the middle of a sunny day, but at sunrise they like to hunt minnows in shin-deep water. Fish the banks hard in the morning, and don't neglect the shallow side of the river. Look for targets along the edges of the stream: an old log lying in a foot and a half of water, the exposed roots of a big tree that the next flood will topple, the remains of old fish weirs or stone walls, the mouth of a small feeder creek, a patch of weeds on the bottom, and even, heaven help us, car tires and rims that slobs threw in the stream years ago.

As the sun rises higher and the light grows more intense, game fish usually move to deeper spots or into their daytime stations, where they can rest or eat whatever sort of bug is hatching. If you're lucky, you can spend the hours from midmorning until late afternoon casting dry flies, emergers, terrestrials, or, on a warm-water stream, poppers. If your luck holds, you'll run into another good hatch or spinner fall in the evening.

But if the topwater action never materializes, you can often do as well during the middle of the day with a streamer as you could with a nymph or wet fly. Concentrate on pools and on deep runs along the banks or next to gravel bars, and look for holes surrounded by shallower water. I'll never forget a 13-inch Vermont brook trout that came out of a depression in the middle of a little river to attack a bunny-fur Muddler. The bathtub-length dent in the riverbed created only a few extra inches of depth, and I didn't spot the trout until he shot up from the bottom and hit the fly like he meant to break it in half. He was a patriarch among backwoods brookies, old and dark and fat, with a long scar on one side.

An evening hatch or spinner fall often produces the best dry-fly fishing of the day, but a streamer can take an extra fish or two at the end of the rise. Some of the trout are still hungry, and they'll snap at a streamer fly swinging across the current. Loads of insects on the surface bring up not only the trout, but also chubs and other minnows. The bigger trout know this, and they come out to hunt as twilight falls.

Years ago, I met a gent who loved to fish the evening rise on the little river that we sometimes shared. But he never used a dry fly or even a fly rod. He'd wade along the bank upstream of the feeding fish and use a soft, ultralight spinning rod to toss a floating-diving plug, making gentle sidearm casts that dropped the lure with no more splash than a trout makes eating a mayfly. Then he'd let the plug drift on the surface until it took up all the slack in the line. As the line came tight, the little balsa crankbait would dive a few inches and begin to wobble. He'd let the lure hang in the current for half a minute, and then slowly steer the plug across the stream. Sometimes he'd open the bail of his tiny reel and let the plug dead drift another few yards before beginning a slow retrieve.

I'm not sure who caught more trout during the evening rise, but I know that my friend with the spinning rod caught the biggest fish. One evening, I watched him land two browns that must have weighed 3 pounds apiece while I netted a few 10-inchers. He never intruded on my fly-casting space and, indeed, sometimes sat on a log and smoked a cigarette while watching me fish our favorite pool. After I'd finished, he'd put his little crankbait to work and catch a good trout that I hadn't even suspected was there.

"The chubs come up to eat them bugs," he once explained, "and the trout come up to eat the chubs."

His success didn't persuade me to give up dry-fly fishing in the evening, but it did make me think that a few casts with a streamer might be a good way to wrap up the day. And it is. After you've had some fun on the surface, swap your dry fly for a dark streamer as the light fades. Cast at an angle across the current, let the fly swing on a tight line, and then pump it back toward you. In the gloaming, when you fish as much by feel as by sight, every strike is doubly exciting.

Streamers also work well on dark, drizzly days. Fish are often very active when a low-pressure system produces a soft, misty, off-and-on rain, and I think that they feel safer and more confident in the dimmer light that accompanies such weather. The next time you fish on such a day, tie a streamer to your tippet and cover all the water you can, paying special attention to targets along the banks.

A big, black streamer is often the best choice after heavy or prolonged rain raises a river a few inches and discolors the water. Although the fish are probably eating lots of dislodged larvae and terrestrial bugs, they can see a large, dark streamer more easily than a nymph or caddis grub pattern. In off-color water, throwing something that the fish can see usually matters more than casting a perfect replica of an insect. My favorite color scheme for stained or dirty water is black with gold Flashabou or Krystal Flash. In high water, of course, you should pound the banks, looking for spots where trout or smallmouths can escape the main current. Drive your streamer into every dent, pocket, and eddy along the shore. When a river is running high, a hole in the bank no bigger than a turkey platter can hold a good fish.

TYPES OF STREAMERS

Izaak Walton mentions an artificial minnow constructed of silk, silver thread, and quills ("made by a handsome woman, that had a fine hand," he says in *The Compleat Angler*, ". . . and all of it so curiously wrought . . . that it would beguile any sharp-sighted Trout in a swift stream"), but bucktails and streamers are relatively modern developments. Flies that we would recognize as bucktails seem to have become popular (or at least widely so) well after the Civil War, and featherwing streamers date from about the turn of the twentieth century. Dry flies, often regarded as the zenith of fly development, actually predate good baitfish patterns.

Once they arrived, streamers and bucktails caught on in a big way, and fly tiers have devised thousands of patterns over the past hundred years. Some rival fancy-dress salmon flies for elegance and complexity; others consist of plastic hair hot-glued to hooks. As far as I know, no species of game fish has not been caught with some type of streamer or bucktail; and as far as I know, the same cannot be said of any other type of fly.

Entire books—big ones, too—have been devoted to streamers, but practical folk like us can divide the lot into three broad categories: the dark uglies, patterns that try to mimic real baitfish, and gaudy flies.

Dark Uglies

You'd think that a meticulously crafted replica of a minnow would always prove the best streamer fly, but it doesn't. Fish often climb all over a dark, simple, ugly, and even crude streamer. Over the past decade or so, I've probably caught more trout, panfish, and bass with black or brown streamers than with lifelike baitfish patterns.

Visibility is probably the main reason that dark flies work so well. In almost any conditions, fish can see a black or dark brown streamer. In poor light or in stained water, black is often the easiest color for fish to see. This isn't a complicated process for the fish. A moving object equals something alive equals protein—might as well eat it. The easier the object is to see, the more likely it is to get eaten.

Black Woolly Buggers are the most popular of the dark uglies, and they've caught millions of fish over the past several decades. A

Although it couldn't win a beauty contest judged by its own mother, a Jonah Fly is perhaps the most reliable streamer I tie. Jonahs and other dark uglies work in all conditions, and they're often the only flies that work in stained water or dim light. Tied on a weighted, size 6 or 8, 3XL hook, a Jonah Fly consists of a tuft of black or brown marabou, a few pieces of gold Flashabou, black or dark brown yarn or dubbing, and a laid-back collar made with a webby, black or dark brown hackle.

simple black marabou streamer works nearly as well. These days, I favor a streamer that I call a Jonah Fly, an acronym for Junk on a Hook. It's hardly the sort of pattern that lets a fly tier show off, but it catches lots of fish. A Jonah Fly begins with a heavily weighted, 3XL size 6 or 8 hook. Its tail is a tuft of black marabou with two or three pieces of gold Flashabou on each side. The body is black dubbing or fuzzy yarn. At the front, three wraps of a folded, black saddle hackle with long, webby fibers form a collar that lies back and shrouds the body. In the water, this ugly mess has a streamlined, fishy silhouette and loads of movement.

Though it's simple to the point of crudity, a Jonah Fly has all the necessary characteristics of a dark ugly: enough weight, a bold profile, a little flash, and lively action. That combination makes for a very effective lure.

Depending on how they're tied, Muddlers straddle the line between dark uglies and baitfish imitations. Some Muddler-style flies represent sculpins, darters, and other bottom-hugging forage fish; others look like shiners or chubs. A black Marabou Muddler, though, is hardly a model of a minnow; it's a big, dark lure, and a very good one.

Jonah Flies, Woolly Buggers, and other dark uglies work year-round and in all types of water, but they're particularly good in stained or dirty water, on overcast days, and at dawn and dusk. If you have the nerve to wade a river at night, you can catch some big fish with a black streamer. Black has always been one of the best colors for largemouth bass fishing in the twilight or at night.

Baitfish Imitations

The dark uglies catch fish despite having no resemblance to real food, except perhaps leeches. More realistic streamers catch fish precisely because they look like food. Flies that mimic minnows and fry are at their best in clear water and on sunny days. They'll catch fish in other situations, of course, but lifelike flies work particularly well when fish can get a good look at them. A trout or smallmouth bass enjoying the day in a clear, well-lit place can turn very picky, refusing flies that don't look like real food.

Forage fish come in many varieties, but let's divide them into two groups: those that spend their lives on the bottom (sculpins, darters, and such) and those that roam up and down through the water column (chubs, shiners, dace, and other minnows). The bottom dwellers generally have mottled color schemes that blend with the gravel and cobble bottoms that they inhabit. Free-ranging minnows vary in color, but most have pale bellies, dark backs, and sides that reflect at least a little light.

Conventional wisdom says that the Muddler Minnow and its many progeny mimic sculpins, darters, and other small fish that live on the bottom. Well, okay, but if you've ever watched darters and sculpins, you know that they do indeed live *on* the bottom. They find comfortable spots in the gravel or between stones and hold on with their big, powerful pectoral fins. When they move, they stay right on the riverbed, darting a few inches to a couple feet at a time, often swimming so fast that they're hard to follow with your eyes. To truly imitate one of these fish with a Muddler Minnow, you'd have to snag the fly on the bottom and let it sit there awhile, then yank it loose, then let it snag another rock, and so on. Generally, though, we fish Muddler-style flies by swimming them across the stream a few inches to a foot or more above the bottom, a height that few sculpins or darters ever achieve. Sculpin imitations hardly ever imitate a sculpin's behavior. But they still catch lots of trout and bass. They work even better the closer to the bottom they swim.

Rock, gravel, and cobble bottoms are all good places to fish a Muddler. If the fly doesn't get deep enough on its own, clamp a small split shot on the tippet at the fly's nose. It also helps to cast across the current or even slightly upstream rather than down and across. As your Muddler drifts downstream, mend your line to keep the current from putting a big belly in it. During the first half of the presentation, you want the fly to drift at about the same speed as the current and just above the riverbed. After mending your line once or twice, follow the fly's drift with the rod tip, let the line come tight in the current, and swim the Muddler across the stream until it's directly below you. Let the fly hang in the current for half a minute, make a few strips, and then pick up the line for another cast. A fish might take the fly at any time during the presentation.

Imitations of chubs, shiners, and dace generally don't need as much weight as sculpin or darter patterns. For one thing, these types of baitfish don't spend their lives clinging to the riverbed. They also live in a great variety of habitats, including the slow or weedy stretches of a river where every cast with a heavily weighted fly results in a snag.

A good generic minnow pattern will catch nearly any type of fish in any water—it's the fly fisher's equivalent of a small Rapala crankbait—and fly tiers have created thousands of these flies. Many trout and smallmouth anglers, however, overlook an especially good group of baitfish imitations: saltwater patterns. A small, marabou-tailed Lefty's Deceiver looks and acts more like a minnow than any traditional freshwater bucktail or streamer does, and it's among the most reliable flies you can cast in a trout stream or warm-water river. Henry Cowen created his Albie Anchovy for false albacore and bonito, but freshwater fish also love it. Saltwater anglers know how to design fake baitfish. They have to: Saltwater angling revolves around bait.

Cowen's Albie Anchovy and similar flies for false albacore, bonito, and Spanish mackerel are available in sizes 4 and 6, small enough for trout and smallmouth bass fishing. They make excellent imitations of shiners, chubs, and other freshwater minnows. Marabou Deceivers tied on size 4, 6, and 8 hooks are harder to find; as far as I know, none of the major fly manufacturers makes them. If you can't tie your own, it's worth going to considerable trouble to find a custom tier to make some for you. Here's a basic recipe for a Marabou Deceiver.

> **Hook:** Any standard-length, heavy-wire O'Shaughnessy model in size 4 or 6. A Mustad 3407 (tinned) or 3406 (bronze finish) works fine.
>
> **Thread:** Brown or olive.

Many saltwater designs translate very well to fresh water. This size 4 Marabou Deceiver is a fine imitation of a shiner or chub. Minnow imitations like this work best in clear water, where they appeal to all species of trout and bass.

Tail: White marabou with a few pieces of pearlescent or silver Flashabou on each side.

Body: Silver tinsel or braid.

Collar: Sparse white calf tail on the sides and bottom; on the top, a sparse clump of natural or dyed-olive squirrel tail. After tying in all the hair, add a few pieces of pearlescent Krystal Flash on each side.

Throat (optional): A small tuft of red bunny fur, red craft fur, or anything similar.

Eyes: Coat the nose and the very front of the collar with Softex or something similar. Household Goop thinned with toluene makes an excellent head coating. After the stuff dries, apply prismatic stick-on eyes. Protect the eyes with another coat of Softex or a homemade equivalent.

Marabou Deceivers and black Jonah Flies might be the best all-around freshwater flies that you can have. I'd give up all my nymphs and wet flies before I'd part with these two streamers—they're that good.

Another type of streamer worth carrying, particularly if you fish for river bass, is an unweighted or lightly weighted Muddler tied to represent a shiner, creek chub, or baby fallfish. I call it a Shiner Muddler. This style differs from the more common versions in two ways. First, since it mimics a shiny baitfish, its wing consists of white or pale gray marabou or arctic fox tail with several pieces of silver or pearlescent Flashabou on each side. Second, the deer-

Standard Muddlers represent dark, bottom-dwelling forage fish such as sculpins, but this Shiner Muddler mimics any of the bright minnows that roam throughout the water column. The fly's tall deer-hair head is shaved flat on the sides to make a foundation for large, stick-on eyes covered with a flexible coating made of Household Goop thinned with toluene (Softex and epoxy work just as well). Since it sinks slowly, a Shiner Muddler works best in slow water and above weed beds. It's primarily a warmwater fly, though it also appeals to brown trout.

hair head isn't trimmed into a broad cone or wedge shape like that of a standard Muddler Minnow. Instead, the hair is trimmed flat along the sides with a razor blade, creating a tall, narrow head on which you can glue big prismatic eyes.

Since it sinks slowly, a Shiner Muddler is perfect for fishing over the top of a weed bed in slow water. It also does a fine job of imitating a sick or crippled minnow struggling against the current as it drifts downstream a few inches below the surface. Smallmouths in rivers are particularly fond of this fly, but trout also take it.

Finally, you'll want some quick-sinking minnow flies for deep or fast water. Bob Clouser's Deep Minnow is hard to beat for this

Many freshwater anglers labor under the delusion that a Clouser Deep Minnow has to be big, very heavy, and bright chartreuse. This trout-size version is tied on a size 8 nymph hook and with a tiny dumbbell. Its belly is fine white bucktail, and its back is a clump of squirrel tail. Although it sinks quickly, a baby Clouser Minnow is easy to cast with a trout outfit. And since the fly resists snagging, you can pitch it upstream into a deep pool and strip it back along the bottom.

purpose. Many freshwater anglers, particularly trout fishermen, seem to believe that a Clouser Minnow always has to be big, very heavy, and chartreuse. Not so. You can tie Clouser Minnows on size 8 nymph hooks, with small bead-chain eyes and sparse, 2-inch-long clumps of calf tail, flash material, and squirrel tail. That's a good trout fly, and one that you can throw all day with a 5-weight outfit. With an assortment of bead chain and small metal dumbbells, a fly tier can make Clouser Minnows for everything from panfish to the largest brown trout.

What about bucktails such as the Black-Nosed Dace, feather-wing streamers such as the Black Ghost, Matukas, Zonkers, and other standard, well-known baitfish patterns? They're not bad flies, but I no longer carry any of them. My fly boxes have only so much room, and Jonah Flies, Marabou Deceivers, Clouser Minnows, and a couple varieties of Muddlers make most other streamers super-fluous. I tie some bucktails and marabou flies, but even they look like small saltwater patterns. I appreciate the elegance and history of classic American streamers and admire the skill that goes into tying them, but other designs are better fishing lures.

Gaudy Flies

In the late 1990s, I fished a beautiful warmwater stream in the Ozarks with the man who owned part of it. This creek is so clear and yet so fertile that it makes some blue-ribbon trout rivers look like urban drainage ditches. It's full of largemouth, smallmouth, and Kentucky spotted bass, plus sundry panfish and more min-nows than I've ever seen anywhere else.

My host fished with a fly rod and an assortment of poppers and streamers. I used my lightest levelwind outfit to throw various surface plugs and crankbaits. Between the two of us, we had the fish pretty much surrounded. But river bass aren't dumb, and after several hours we had two fish to our credit: a small bass that I'd caught on a bottom-scraping plastic crayfish, and a sunfish that ate one of Jim's poppers. We could see bass everywhere, we could see the various prey creatures that they ate, but we couldn't get the fish to bite.

We eventually came to a long, deep trough against the bottom of a bluff. Several trees had fallen from the top of the bluff and turned the spot into luxury apartments for bass. Standing on the shallow side of the stream, Jim and I could see dozens of fish holding in the 8-foot-deep water along the base of the bluff.

Jim tried half a dozen different flies, and I went through several crankbaits. Everything we cast into that astonishingly clear water looked fake and clumsy, and not a single bass so much as turned its head.

"Hell, Art, I don't know what to do," Jim said as we stood on the sandbar and looked at the fish we couldn't catch. "Y'all got any spinnerbaits?"

I had a few ⅛-ounce spinnerbaits, none of which I'd used because they seemed ridiculous lures for bass in such clear water. Spinnerbaits are deadly in many situations, but no one would accuse them of realism.

Jim inspected my trio of spinnerbaits and said, "If I were you, I'd try that little fire-tiger one there." For purists unfamiliar with such heathen implements, the fire-tiger color pattern consists of bright orange on the bottom, chartreuse on the sides, and darker chartreuse with black bands on the top. Besides a fat silicone-rubber skirt sporting those unlikely colors, the lure had a nickel-plated, size 2 Colorado spinner blade attached to an offset wire arm. Dry-fly purists can barely imagine a more loathsome contraption.

I tied the fire-tiger spinnerbait to my line and made a soft sidearm cast, thumbing the spool so that the lure dropped into the water about a foot from the bluff. We could see the shiny blade twinkling as the lure sank. Then I began a slow retrieve. The spinnerbait swam across the bottom, its blade thumping and the gaudy silicone-rubber skirt fluttering and pulsing.

The lure made it about halfway across the creek before a 15-inch smallmouth bass darted from its holding spot and inhaled the entire skirt and head. When I landed the fish, only part of the spinner-blade arm was outside its mouth, and I had to use long forceps to extract the barbless hook. I returned the bass to the river, and we watched it swim away.

"I figured that fire-tiger pattern would work," Jim said after a minute. "We should head back. It's gettin' late."

I can't explain why such lures sometimes catch fish when more realistic ones fail. But they do, and the phenomenon happens in fly fishing, too. I carry a couple of Mickey Finn bucktails partly out of sentiment—my first successful trout fly was a lopsided Mickey Finn—but also because I know that every now and then the fish will ignore every fly except one that should scare them out of the water.

I don't cast a garish, gaudy fly very often. Dark uglies and life-like baitfish patterns are more reliable. But when reason fails, I'll try a few casts with a bright yellow, orange, or chartreuse bucktail or marabou fly.

The Mickey Finn is the best-known gaudy fly, and it still catches a fair number of trout and bass every year, as do yellow Marabou Muddlers. Bright orange and chartreuse also have their moments. These flies don't have to be fancy; a weighted hook wrapped with silver or gold braid and decorated with a tuft of hair or marabou will do. A few strands of Flashabou on each side never hurt.

Maybe, as many anglers have believed over the centuries, garish colors simply anger fish into striking. But there is one situation in which a bright yellow or chartreuse streamer makes a certain amount of sense. The next time you fish in stained or dirty water on a brilliantly sunny day, tie on a gaudy, fluorescent bucktail or marabou streamer and note how well you can see it in the tinted water. The fish, too, can see it, just as they can find a black streamer in water that has a bit of color.

Mostly, though, gaudy streamers are last-ditch flies, lures that an angler resorts to after the patterns that should have worked didn't. You might use them rarely, but sooner or later you'll be glad to have a couple.

A Good Assortment

Since I trust streamers and enjoy fishing them, I probably carry more of them than many other fly fishers do. Even so, a basic selection doesn't comprise very many flies. Here's what I recommend.

- Dark uglies in sizes 6 and 8 for trout, 4 and 6 for smallmouths and other river bass. Two of each size should get you through a day. Woolly Buggers and Jonah Flies are both good choices; I prefer the Jonahs.

- Muddler Minnows, Marabou Muddlers tied with mottled brown and tan turkey marabou, or some other sculpin pattern in sizes 4 through 8. Fly tiers have created scores of streamers that look like sculpins or darters, and all of them work. Since these flies are heavy and wind-resistant, select sizes that you can cast with your outfit; there's little point in lugging around heavily weighted, size 4 Woolhead Sculpins if you do all your trout fishing with a 2-weight rig.

- White Marabou Deceivers in sizes 4 and 6, or 6 and 8 if you habitually fish with a very light outfit. For river bass, you can go up to size 2. These flies are built on standard-length hooks, and therefore are a bit lighter and easier to cast than a Muddler or Woolly Bugger of the same overall length; a reasonably good caster can throw a 3-inch-long Deceiver with a typical trout outfit. Since they're not especially heavy, Marabou Deceivers work perfectly in moderate to slow currents, weedy sections of a river, and other places where shiners and chubs thrive. To make one swim deeper, use a weighted leader like the one described in chapter 4 or a sinking-tip line. These streamers and black Jonah Flies will probably become your workhorse patterns.

- White or gray Shiner Muddlers in sizes 4 through 8. Again, pick flies that you can deliver with your tackle.

- Clouser Minnows in sizes, colors, and weights appropriate for the fishing that you do. For general trout fishing, try some tied on size 6 and 8 nymph hooks, with brass bead-chain eyes, white bellies, pearl or silver flash, and squirrel-tail backs. Olive over white is another good color scheme for trout fishing. The same patterns with small lead or brass dumbbells instead of bead chain work well in a deep or fast trout stream. For river bass, carry the ubiquitous chartreuse Clouser Minnows and at least one pattern with a darker back (olive, for instance); you'll want them in sizes 2 through 6.

• A couple of gaudy flies such as Mickey Finns or bright yellow Marabou Muddlers tied on size 6 or 8 hooks for trout, 4 or 6 for bass.

You can add a few generic bucktails if you want, but this assortment will catch trout, smallmouth bass, spotted bass, and most other river-dwelling game fish anywhere in the country.

METHODS AND PRESENTATIONS

The classic way to fish a streamer is to cast at an angle across the current and let the fly swing on a tight line. You can catch fish by simply slinging and swinging, but you'll catch more if you add a few tricks. The first is line management. When you cast across a stream, the current quickly puts a curve or belly in the line. As the current pushes the bellied line downstream, the fly moves faster and rises closer to the surface. That's sometimes desirable, but rarely at the beginning of a presentation. If you cast at a 45-degree angle across the current and then do nothing, your streamer barely has time to sink before it starts racing across the stream just a few inches beneath the surface.

You'll get a better, deeper presentation if you mend line. Let's say that you've cast at a 45-degree angle across the current and toward the right-hand bank. A second after the fly hits the water, make an arc or semicircle with the rod tip—draw the letter C in the air, starting from the bottom—to pick up about half of the fly line and flip it toward the bank. The point is to rearrange the line on the water, stacking it upstream of the fly. Doing this creates some slack and delays the moment when the current bellies the line and begins dragging the fly through the water. Mending the line—picking up some of it and tossing it directly upstream of the fly—lets your streamer drift straight downstream and gives it time to sink.

After mending the line, follow it with the rod tip as it travels downstream. Eventually, the current removes all the slack and starts to push another belly into the line. When that happens, your streamer changes direction, begins to accelerate, and starts to rise through the water. Follow the fly with the rod tip as it swings across the stream. Often a fish strikes as the fly begins to swing.

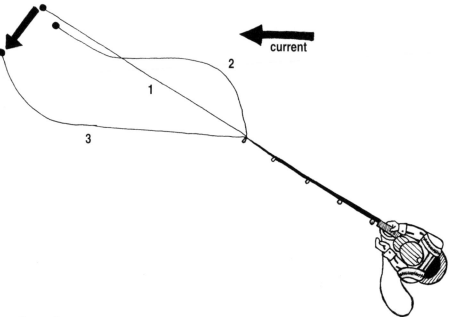

current

2

1

3

Proper line management lets a streamer sink deeper and delays the moment when it begins to accelerate across the current. Cast at an angle across the current *(1)*, and then immediately pick up some of the fly line and flip it upstream and toward the far bank *(2)*. By rearranging the line on the water—mending it, in other words—you give the fly time to sink and postpone its rapid movement across the stream. While the current pushes the line downstream and more or less straightens it *(3)*, the fly drifts freely and sinks deep. Eventually, the streamer will accelerate, rise through the water, and swim across the current. By then, however, the fly is deep enough to catch the attention of a fish.

If nothing happens, let the fly hang in the current when the line straightens out below you. Just let the fly sit there for a minute; the current will give it plenty of motion. Then make a few foot-long strips. Wait a few seconds, and then let the line slide back out through the guides. Angle the rod to one side to make the streamer swim a foot or two across the flow. Make another few strips, wait, and angle the rod to the other side as you let the line slide back out through your fingers and the guides. What you're doing with all this business is teasing the fish. A trout or bass will watch a streamer moving back and forth, up and down through a small area until it just can't stand the provocation any longer.

If the teasing routine doesn't produce a strike, strip in some line and make another cast. After two or three presentations through the same area, take a few steps downstream and begin working a fresh piece of water.

Those are the basics of streamer fishing. How often and how vigorously you need to mend line depend on the length of the cast, the angle of the cast to the current, and the speed of the flow. If you cast 60 feet of line almost perpendicular to the direction of a strong current, you might need to throw several big mends to keep your streamer deep as it travels downstream. A 30-foot cast at a 45-degree angle across a slow stream might require only one mend, or none at all.

After rearranging some of the line to stack it upstream of the fly, you can also let additional line slide through the guides. This trick extends the streamer's downstream drift. By feeding line into the drift and mending as necessary, you can let the current carry your fly into a spot that you can't reach by casting—under overhanging brush, for instance, or beneath a fallen tree. Let the fly slide down into the target area, and then let the current put a belly in the line and swim the fly away from the spot. Fish hate to see a potential meal get away.

In very slow water, the current can do most of the work of making the fly look alive. Cast at an angle to the weak flow, let the current belly the line downstream—or even throw a downstream mend to create a belly of line—and then just hold on as your streamer swims across the river. After the line straightens out below you, strip the fly upstream before picking it up for another cast.

Sometimes you'll do better by hitting specific targets. An otherwise featureless stretch of river has a midstream boulder with a cushion of slack water where smallmouth can hold. A rock ledge creates an abrupt change of depth. A divot in the bank forms an eddy where a fish can hide from the current. For three hours in the afternoon, a bridge casts a shadow on a deep hole. A small, spring-fed feeder stream makes a pocket of cooler water in a river warmed by August's heat. A fallen tree gives a brown trout a hiding spot from which to ambush prey in a nearby weed bed. All of these are targets, and you can fish them by target-shooting with a streamer.

Target shooting tries to provoke something that bass-tournament anglers call a reaction strike. The principle is simple: Show the food to the fish and then take it away. Don't give the fish time to make up its mind. Cast a foot or two above the target, give the fly just a second or two to sink, and start stripping. Jonah Flies and Marabou Deceivers both work well for this type of fishing. From the fish's perspective, something that's clearly alive and probably food suddenly appears and immediately starts to run away. A trout or bass has to react, lest its rivermates drum it out of the predators' union.

Although I greatly enjoy this kind of angling—after popper fishing, it's the most fun I have with a fly rod—I don't step into a river with the intention of firing fast, accurate casts to small targets all day. For one thing, every stream has a mix of good-looking, clearly identifiable targets and longer stretches of water better suited to fishing a streamer on the swing. And target shooting can quickly get tiring, physically and mentally. So I mix methods, looking for small targets while I cast and mend to swing a fly. Most streamer fishing is a pleasant, leisurely, rhythmic business. Shooting a cast to a particular spot and immediately beginning a retrieve adds some variety and intensity to the day. When a good smallmouth or trout wallops a streamer that I'm stripping fast, the day gets very intense in a hurry.

Fishing a streamer upstream is an uncommon method and a tiring one, but it can work very well. Tie on a weighted Muddler, add a small split shot at the fly's nose, and sling it upstream into a run or the head of a pool. Strip fast enough to maintain contact with the fly as it scoots along the bottom. In fast water, you'll probably have to raise the rod to keep a tight line. As the fly passes you, lower the rod, throw an upstream mend, and fish the fly on the swing below you. This is energetic fishing, since it entails making lots of casts with a big, heavy fly and constantly turning to face first upstream, then downstream. It's like nymphing, but magnified, and it can produce some good fish. Don't worry about detecting the strike; you'll feel it just fine.

That's one of the great pleasures of streamer fishing: feeling the strike. A trout will indeed "come as fiercely at a Minnow, as the highest mettled hawk doth seize on a partridge." If Walton had known about bass, he'd have included them. But he didn't, poor guy.

10

Degrees of Nymphing

I can't recall seeing many nymph fishermen when I was a kid. If my dad ever cast a nymph upstream, I don't remember seeing him do it. Every now and then, on one of our trips to the Musconetcong River or the Flat Brook, Dad would point out someone making short upstream casts and carefully following the drift of the line with his rod. "That guy's *nymphing*," Dad would say. I got the impression that it was a form of conjuring. Dry flies and wet flies and bucktails I understood. Nymphing was a big mystery to me. It was to a lot of grown-up anglers, too.

We all knew that trout ate insect larvae, and flies that resembled nymphs and caddis grubs had been around for a long time. We'd all heard about nymph anglers who used their strange powers to outfish everyone else. General theory wasn't the problem; application was. How did you know which nymph to use? How could you have any idea what the fly was doing? How could you tell when you had a bite? What kind of person had the patience and fiendish concentration to fish that way for hours on end? Such information as I heard and read in the late 1960s and early 1970s seemed to suggest that a good nympher had simply achieved a Zen state beyond the ken of rubes, oafs, and adolescent anglers.

Things have changed—perhaps too much. These days, it often seems that every second fly fisher is watching a big strike indicator with a beadhead fly or a Copper John under it. Guides set up novice anglers with weighted nymphs and indicators, teach them the rudiments of high sticking, and turn them loose. The method works so well that some new fly fishers never learn to use wet flies and streamers well. Some of them also never learn all the possibilities of nymphs.

We might as well get it out in the open: I'm not a big fan of extra-heavy nymphs, strike indicators, and casts that could be accomplished with a $3 cane pole. That's not a snooty value judgment on the propriety of casting a sinker and bobber with a fly rod. I'm no purist. My collection of spinnerbaits, plugs, crankbaits, and buzzbaits numbers in the high hundreds. I'll cheerfully watch a red and white float while waiting for a pickerel to come along and eat my minnow. High-sticking a weighted rig and a big bobber simply gives me less pleasure than other kinds of fly fishing, so I don't go out of my way to do it. Since catching beats merely casting, I'll cane-pole the heaviest nymph and biggest strike indicator I own when doing so seems the only way to hook a trout. But I'm glad to change methods when the opportunity comes. It's a personal and aesthetic thing, like one's taste in food, and about as meaningful.

Besides, short-line indicator fishing is just one of many tricks. You can use a nymph in other ways, some of which don't involve a float.

THE NAKED LEADER

I didn't start tying and fishing nymphs seriously until the late 1980s. With only a vague idea of how to go about it, I tied some lightly weighted flies and pitched them more or less straight upstream, using my regular dry-fly leader and watching for the end of my line to jump when a fish took the fly. I didn't know how quickly or slowly the flies sank, and the only time I knew how deep one had sunk was when it snagged something. My first year of nymphing was about as blind as blind casting can be.

Many anglers reflexively use strike indicators every time they fish nymphs, but a naked leader often works better in gentle water like this. Grease the end of the fly line so that it floats high, and let the tip of the line serve as the indicator. In a slow current, you will sometimes see the flash as a trout moves to take the nymph.

But I caught trout right from the get-go. Encouraged, I began turning over rocks and rooting around in riffles to learn more about the shapes and colors of real nymphs (and learned that simple flies dubbed with bunny or squirrel fur are actually pretty good imitations). My technique remained simple: Tie on a fly that had a bit of lead wire under the body, throw it upstream, strip line to keep up with the speed of the drift, and wait for the end of the fly line to twitch or pause. I hooked a fair number of rocks, but I also hooked a lot of fish.

Not having expert instruction during my first couple years of nymph fishing was probably a lucky break. I learned how to fish a nymph on a naked leader, gained confidence in lightly and moderately weighted flies, and began to develop the indescribable sense that tells an angler, "Lift the rod and set the hook now."

Nymphing doesn't have to involve casting a lot of weight and a float. In some situations, a plain leader and relatively light fly make the best combination. By "relatively light," I mean something like a size 14 Gold-Ribbed Hare's Ear with a piece of fine lead wire bound to each side of the shank, or a similar pattern with a very small metal bead at its nose. If you're aware of a fly's weight when you cast, then it's not relatively light.

With that kind of fly and a plain old 9-foot, 6X trout leader, you can make accurate, delicate, and effortless casts all day long. Sinkers and floats, though sometimes necessary, inevitably change your casting and make a bigger commotion hitting the water and coming back out of it. In slow or moderate currents, a naked leader and lightly weighted fly are more sneaky and subtle. You can cast a plain leader farther and more accurately than you can throw a split-shot-and-indicator rig, which lets you keep your distance from the fish. And the current can bat a light nymph around just as it does a real insect.

Getting a lightly to moderately weighted nymph deep enough is not as hard as some anglers think. In the first place, "deep enough" doesn't necessarily mean right on the bottom. Trout are built to look and feed upward, and they'll come a foot or more off the bottom to take a fly. In thigh-deep water moving at a moderate clip, a lightly weighted size 14 nymph usually sinks far enough, particularly if you use the right tippet and make the right cast.

The longer, finer, and more supple the tippet, the easier a nymph can sink and the more movement it will have. With size 10 and smaller nymphs, there's really no reason to go heavier than 6X; with larger flies, you can go up to 5X. Use at least 2 feet of tippet; 3 feet is better, and 4 feet is not too long. A long, fine tippet allows the fly more freedom of movement, helping create the illusion that the nymph is drifting freely, unattached to anything. Don't worry about getting the tippet to turn over. Because it's dense and stream-lined, a nymph sails very well—once it's moving, it has plenty of momentum and requires little help from the tippet.

A nymph sinks more quickly on a slack leader than on a straight, tight line, so try to make the leader hit the water with some slack in it. One way to do this is to cast with a little more zip than is required to shoot all the line that's off the reel. If you have, say, 6 feet of slack fly line as you make the final delivery, cast with enough oomph to shoot 10 feet. The cast pulls all the extra fly line through the rod guides, but then stops short. By stopping the cast abruptly, you make the leader straighten forcefully and then bounce back a couple of feet, and it lands with S-curves in it. Thanks to the slack line, the fly can sink quickly. This trick goes by various names; I call it a bounce cast.

It's also possible to create slack by throwing a cast that collapses before it straightens. Called a pile cast, this trick consists of making a soft, high forward cast, as if you were aiming at a spot 8 feet above the stream, and then lowering the rod as the cast rolls out. Dropping the rod tip robs the cast of its last bit of energy, causing the tippet to collapse—to pile up—before it straightens.

Anglers have devised all sorts of ways to throw some slack into a leader. It rarely matters whether you use a bounce cast, a pile cast, a tuck cast, a deliberately underpowered cast, or a snap of the rod that throws a shock wave down the line. Find some way to manipulate the rod and line so that the leader hits the water in a shape other than a straight line, and don't worry about technical-sounding names.

Back when I started fishing with nymphs, I'd cast straight upstream and let the fly drift back toward me, stripping just fast enough to keep up with the current. I caught a lot of trout, but heaven only knows how many more I spooked by dropping the fly line right on top of them. A cast angled a little to either side works better when you're prospecting with a nymph. You don't need much of an angle; 10 or 15 degrees from parallel with the current is enough. You'll still be able to manage the line easily, but you'll scare fewer fish.

When you cast a naked leader, the fly line serves as the strike indicator. The higher the tip of the line floats, the easier it is for you to watch. The nail-knot loop described in chapter 4 floats well and helps keep the tip of the line on the surface. A bit of paste or gel dry-fly floatant rubbed on the first 5 or 6 feet of fly line also helps; I always grease the end of the line when fishing a nymph.

Sometimes a fish makes things easy by taking your nymph at a gallop. The fly line darts upstream or to one side, and you have no doubt about what you need to do. More often, the line twitches or stops or merely slows down. Sometimes the line just looks a little different—an S-curve of slack becomes less pronounced, a little curl at the tip of the line straightens halfway. It's subtle stuff, and with experience you'll begin hooking fish in response to clues that you can't explain afterward. You just knew. Naturally, you'll also hook some rocks and sticks and weeds on which your fly dragged.

When your fly line does something—jumps, stops, slides sideways, hesitates, changes shape on the water—strike, but strike with measured force. You're trying to twitch a small, very sharp, and ideally barbless hook into the jaw of a trout or smallmouth; you're not trying to drive a size 3/0 saltwater iron into the rock-hard cartilage of a tarpon's yap. Lift the rod smoothly to take the slack out of the line, and simultaneously make a foot-long strip with your line hand. That's usually all it takes. Yanking the rod up and back accomplishes nothing except to exceed the tippet's shock load.

In slow to moderately fast water, you don't always have to dead drift a nymph and rely on watching the line to detect the take. If you make a 35- or 40-foot cast and then strip fast enough to keep up with the current, so that you keep the line more or less tight between you and the leader, you can often feel a fish take the fly. Since the line is already tight, a gentle strike, no more than a soft lift of the rod, will set the hook.

Casting upstream and swimming the nymph downstream violates the rule that says that an imitation of an aquatic insect must always drift freely, but it works. What happens, I think, is that each strip animates the fly for a second and makes it rise a few inches. When you reach forward to begin the next strip, the line goes slack and the fly drops again. Trout, and particularly warmwater fish, often respond to this action, perhaps because it makes the lure look alive. Swimming a fly on a tight line doesn't replace dead drifting a nymph, but it's a good trick to know.

In all but the slowest currents, use a roll-cast pickup to lift the leader from the water and straighten the line for your first back-

Dead drifting is the standard way to fish a nymph, but sometimes it pays to break the rules and fish a nymph actively. In a slow or moderate current, try casting upstream and then stripping fast enough to keep the line more or less tight. The nymph will rise and fall, dart and pause as it swims downstream, and the movement often appeals to fish.

cast. When you dead drift a nymph, the fly line and the submerged leader usually have some slack in them, and the fly might be 3 feet beneath the surface. If you begin a normal backcast, you will use up half or more of the casting stroke just removing slack from the line. Then you'll try to lift the fly line, the sunken leader, and the fly using the tip of the rod and a short stroke. It doesn't work. Better to draw the rod back to take up most of the slack, and then make a good roll cast to straighten the line and leader. Direct the cast at a spot above the water, and begin your backcast as the leader rolls out. If you roll-cast well enough, you can pop the entire leader right out of the water and start the backcast with a tight, airborne line that instantly loads the rod. As we all know, a good first backcast is the key to everything in fly fishing.

LITTLE FLOATS

For me, casting a naked leader and barely weighted fly is the most pleasant way to fish a nymph, but alas, it's not often the most effective way. In most trout water, the fly needs a bit more weight to get deep enough, and I need a bobber to know what's going on under the surface. I resisted using strike indicators for a long time, but I learned how much a bobber helps.

Obviously, a strike indicator lets you know that a fish has taken your nymph, but it does more than that. It can suspend a weighted fly at the right depth, reducing the frequency of snags and the number of nymphs that you leave on the riverbed. A float also lets you see how the drift is going. If the indicator starts skating across the stream, you know that it's time to mend the fly line to remove the belly that the current has pushed into it. When you mend line, the indicator can serve as a reference mark on the stream's surface; rearrange enough of the line to correct the drift, but do it without jerking the float.

Using an indicator doesn't have to mean heaving three split shot and a bobber big enough for live-bait fishing. In many situations, a small indicator and a moderate amount of weight suffice. And since you can truly cast such a rig rather than merely lob it on a short line, a small indicator lets you cover more water with less effort.

Let's consider the fly and the cast first. The nymph needs to sink near (but not necessarily to) the bottom, and it needs to get there reasonably quickly. A long, fine, supple tippet helps. So does a cast that puts some slack in the line and leader. A yard of 6X nylon and a good slack-line cast can reduce the amount of weight that you need to throw. In moderately fast water that's no more than waist deep, you can generally get by with a medium-size beadhead pattern or a nymph tied with three strips of lead wire—one on each side of the hook, and a flattened piece bound to the underside of the shank. A very small pattern might need the help of a tiny split shot on the tippet. Beadhead flies have largely supplanted nymphs weighted with lead, because they're fast and easy to make (and therefore loved by manufacturers) and because some jurisdictions have banned lead weights.

A weighted fly doesn't sink straight down in a stream. Except in very slow, shallow water, the presentation doesn't begin when the fly hits the stream; the nymph might travel a couple yards before it reaches fishing depth. Keep this in mind as you cast. Your casting target—the spot where the fly enters the water—is always above the presentation target. If you want to drift a nymph through a spot that you suspect holds a fish, you need to drop the fly slightly upstream of that spot.

Pay attention to the currents—note the plural—as you fish, because the fly, strike indicator, and fly line often begin moving at different speeds the instant they hit the water. If the nymph plops down on the slower side of a current seam and the fly line lands on water that's moving considerably faster, the line will race downstream, dragging the fly and keeping it near the surface. Every cast with a nymph requires you to consider the relative speeds of the

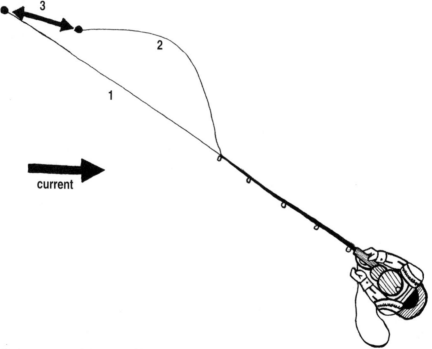

If you cast a straight line up and across the current *(1)* and then do nothing, the current quickly pushes a downstream belly into the line *(2)*. Instead of drifting freely with the current, the strike indicator travels at an angle across the stream *(3)* and moves faster and faster, dragging the nymph behind it. Real insect larvae don't behave this way, and this presentation is unlikely to draw a strike.

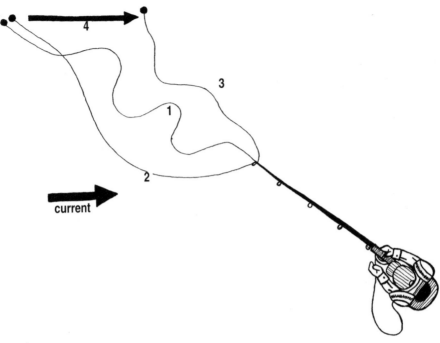

By delaying the onset of drag, a slack-line cast gives the nymph more time to sink and gives you a second or two in which to rearrange the fly line on the water. One of the simplest ways to throw slack into a cast is to wiggle or shake the rod so that the line falls with a series of S-curves in it *(1)*. Before the current has time to remove the curves and push a downstream belly into the line, pick up most of the slack line and toss it upstream *(2)*, mending the line to create an upstream curve in it. By the time the current removes most of the upstream curve from the line *(3)*, the nymph will have drifted freely and more or less straight downstream *(4)*. At this point, you can mend the line again to extend the drift farther, or pick up the line to make another presentation.

line, indicator, and fly. Sometimes you can avoid having the bobber or line drag the fly by carefully choosing the spot from which you cast. If a 30-foot cast made at a 45-degree angle across the stream will drop the fly line on very fast water and the fly in a much slower current, try to move so that you can make a shorter cast and reduce the angle between the current and the line.

Often, though, you have to perform tricks with the line to give the nymph time to sink and to avoid having the fly line or indicator drag it through the water. The first goal is to throw some slack

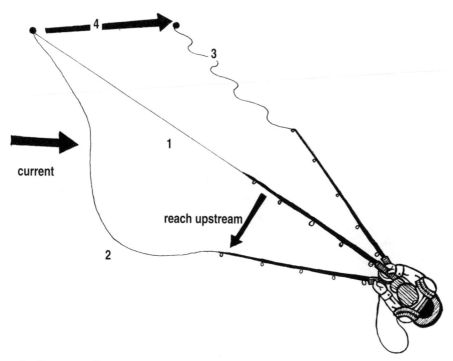

Another way to throw slack is to mend the line while it's still in the air. The reach cast is one example. A standard cast would fall across the water in a straight line *(1)*, and the strike indicator would immediately begin to drag. To throw a reach cast, make your normal casting stroke and stop the rod. As the line rolls out, tip the rod and reach upstream. The line will fall to the water with an upstream curve in it *(2)*. By the time the current pushes the line downstream and removes the curve *(3)*, the strike indicator and nymph will have drifted freely and in a more or less straight line *(4)*.

into the cast. Sometimes it's enough to wiggle or shake the rod as the line rolls out toward the target. This produces S-curves of slack in the line as it falls to the water. The current still snatches the line and pulls it downstream, but you have a short grace period before all the curves in the line disappear and the fly begins to accelerate through the water. During that second or two of grace, the nymph can sink and you can prepare to throw an upstream mend to put some slack back in the fly line.

You can also use a reach cast or aerial mend to make the line hit the water with an upstream belly of slack. This trick takes some practice, but its importance justifies the effort of learning it. As the

Dr. Bill Chiles fishes a nymph on a southern Appalachian trout stream. Note the curves of slack in Bill's line. A good nymph fisherman throws some slack into nearly every cast; without it, the fly can't drift passively and naturally.

cast sails toward the target, tip the rod to the side and reach upstream. Essentially, you're throwing the fly and indicator at one spot, and then, before the cast hits the water, tossing some of the fly line upstream of that spot. The fly line comes down with an upstream curve in it, and you will have a few seconds of grace before the current pushes the line far enough downstream to begin dragging the fly.

Throwing slack into a cast isn't hard. The tricky part is making an *accurate* slack-line cast. Remember that the forward casting stroke and the maneuver that produces slack are two motions. That is, don't wiggle the rod or swing it upstream during the forward stroke. Make the forward cast, stop the rod dead as you always should, and then, a split second later, perform the trick that throws slack or a curve into the line. Stroke, dead stop, throw slack—that's the sequence.

No matter what sort of gymnastics you perform while the line is in the air, you almost always have to mend line on the water to let a nymph remain deep and drift more or less freely. There's no mystery to mending; it consists simply of picking up some of the fly line and tossing it to a new position on the water. If you've had trouble grasping the concept, here's an easy way to understand and practice mending. Use a white or yellow bream bug that's easy to see on the water. Cast a straight line directly across a moderate current. Then do nothing; freeze at the end of the cast and watch what happens. You'll see that the straight fly line quickly develops a downstream curve or belly. One end of the curve is the tip of your fly rod; the other end is the bream bug. As the line bellies downstream, the bream bug will begin to move faster and at an angle across the current, kicking up a tiny wake. That's what we mean by drag, and we want to prevent it.

Make another straight cast perpendicular to the current. As the downstream belly begins to form in the line, raise the rod a little to pick up some of the line, and then flip that portion of the line upstream. That's mending—you've repositioned line to get rid of the downstream belly that causes drag. When you do it, you'll see that the bream bug stops dragging and drifts more or less straight downstream for a few feet. Then another belly forms and the bug starts to drag again.

Repeat the exercise a few times, and then cast at an upstream angle across the current. As the line rolls out, wiggle the rod a little to put some S-curves in the line. You now have some slack between the rod tip and the bream bug. As the belly begins to form in the line, but before the bug starts to skate across the water, pick up some of the fly line and toss it upstream. Try to mend the line without moving the bream bug. This takes a little practice—the timing and force of the mend have to be just right—but you'll get it. Let the bug drift. As another belly begins to form in the line, throw another upstream mend, again without moving the bream bug. If that bug were a strike indicator with a nymph beneath it, you'd be nymphing as skillfully as a professional guide. And you'd be catching fish.

As you get the hang of mending, start practicing the reach cast. Make a normal cast, but right before the end of the fly line begins to turn over, reach upstream with the rod. You'll see that the line falls with an upstream curve or belly in it, and that the bream bug floats freely, with no drag. Soon enough, the current will reverse the direction of the curve, pushing a downstream belly into the line. Before the bug starts to drag, mend the line—pick it up and flip it back upstream. Try to do it without moving the popper. An accomplished mender can drop a strike indicator into the barely moving water of an eddy and keep it there by repeatedly rearranging the line between his rod and the float.

Once you know the rudiments of S-casts, reach casts, and mending line, you become a very dangerous person with a nymph. If you can manage the fly line so that your strike indicator drifts without dragging and without jumping 3 feet across the current every time you mend, you will have little trouble keeping a moderately weighted nymph (a standard beadhead pattern, say) at a good fishing depth. In all but the fastest or deepest water, you will not need to add a ton of extra weight to the tippet, though you might need to pinch a tiny split shot above a midge larva or similarly small fly. Trout and river bass will grow to hate you.

Strike indicators come in many varieties, all of which work. Many anglers use polypropylene yarn treated with floatant, but my favorite indicator is a small bait-rig float pegged in place with part of a toothpick. Used by walleye and panfish anglers to suspend baits off the bottom, these hard-foam floats look like medicine capsules—they're cylinders with rounded ends. They come in several colors, including blaze orange, which I find easy to see on the water, and they cost pennies apiece in Jann's Netcraft and other catalogs. The two sizes suited to most nymph fishing are $\frac{1}{4}$ and $\frac{5}{16}$ inch.

To turn bait-rig floats into strike indicators for fly fishing, I first enlarge their holes by running a $\frac{5}{64}$-inch drill bit through them. Then I sand round toothpicks with 400-grit paper to make them very smooth and a tad thinner. The toothpicks get a coat of nail polish or varnish (anything will do) to keep them from absorbing

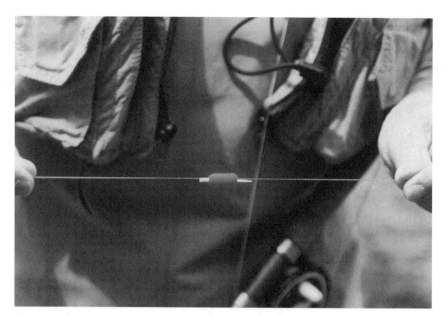

Why struggle to cast a big float if you don't need to? Unless you're throwing an extremely heavy nymph or a couple of split shot, a small indicator will suffice. This is a little bait-rig float pegged to the leader butt with a piece of toothpick. It has practically no effect on my casting; I barely know it's there.

water; once the finish has dried, I cut the toothpicks to size and seal the cut ends with varnish or nail polish. When I need an indicator, I slide one of my little orange floats into position on the leader butt and secure it by jamming a toothpick into the front end (the end nearer the fly), pinning the leader butt between the hardwood toothpick and the inside of the hard-foam float. It's just like pegging a weight for a Texas-rigged plastic worm.

Installing one of these floats is quick and easy—nothing to cut or trim, and no need to tie extra knots in the leader or mess around with floatant. Moving it up or down the leader is just as easy. Thanks to their shape and density, bait-rig floats cast nicely; the ¼-inch size is barely noticeable. When I'm done nymphing, the float and its peg rejoin a bunch of others in a small plastic bag. The fly-fishing trade sells several equivalent products that work just as well, but homemade indicators appeal to the tightwad in me.

A long, fine tippet lets a moderately weighted fly sink fast enough and deep enough in many situations, and a moderately weighted fly does not require a huge bobber above it. This combination—small indicator, supple tippet, and a nymph that's not very heavy—lets you make longer, effortless casts, which in turn let you stay farther away from your target and lessen the chance of spooking a fish.

In slow currents, put a strike indicator about one and a half times the depth of the water above the fly. In faster water, leave more room between the bobber and the fly; twice the depth of the stream is a good starting point. The location of a strike indicator on the leader is always a juggling act. You don't want the float to hold the fly too far off the bottom, but you don't want every cast to snag the riverbed. You're in pretty good shape if the fly ticks a rock every now and then; losing a few flies is the price of nymphing. Naturally, you'll have to adjust the position of the indicator (or the length of the tippet, if you use a float that's difficult to move) as the depth of the water changes.

Picking up a strike indicator and a weighted nymph is harder than beginning a backcast with a dry fly. For starters, you've deliberately put slack in the fly line, and the backcast can't really begin until all the slack is gone. By the time you remove the slack, you've probably run out of casting stroke. And a float with a weighted nymph 4 or 5 feet below it is an ungainly rig to get airborne, even when you do everything right.

Your position in the stream makes a difference in how easily you can pick up the line. Whenever possible, wade so that you can fish on the same side as your rod arm. That is, if you're right-handed, try to keep the fly line and indicator somewhere to the right of an imaginary line running straight upstream from your position. With the line on the same side as your rod arm, you can begin the next cast more easily.

If you have at least 10 feet of fly line out of the rod, you can use a roll-cast pickup to hoist an indicator rig out of the water. Bring the rod back smartly to remove as much slack from the line as possible, and immediately go into the forward roll-cast stroke. Direct the cast out or slightly up, not down at the water. You want to lift

Picking up a small bobber and a weighted, deeply submerged fly isn't like sliding a dry fly off the water and into the air. And if you're fishing properly, you almost certainly have some slack in the line. Instead of starting with a normal backcast, bring the rod back and then use a roll-cast pickup to get the rig airborne and straighten the line. This simple trick lets you begin the first backcast with a tight line that instantly loads the rod.

With a very heavy rig—a big stonefly nymph and split shot, say—a water haul often works better than a standard cast. Let the indicator and fly drift all the way downstream, until the line is straight below you. Lower the rod tip almost to the river's surface . . .

. . . and then use a long, smooth stroke to lift the line, float, and fly from the water. Load the midsection and butt of the rod, not the tip. Stop the rod at the end of the casting stroke, then drop the tip to get it out of the way and open the loop. This is more like slinging a sinker than casting a fly; it's not pretty, but it's safer than trying to false-cast a big hook, one or more split shot, and a jumbo strike indicator.

the indicator and the fly from the surface and straighten the line so that you can begin a backcast with some load on the rod.

With a strike indicator and a weighted fly, sometimes it's easier to let the line drift farther downstream and then use a water haul to get the rig airborne. Follow the drift with the rod tip until the fly line, indicator, and fly are directly downstream from you. Reach downstream and lower the rod tip almost to the surface of the water. Then use a long, smooth stroke to lift the line, bobber, and nymph from the stream. You'll see that the rod loads very well and throws the line with considerable zip, probably with enough to let you shoot a little line. Make one backcast and then the delivery cast. Do not make half a dozen false casts with a float on the leader and a weighted nymph at the end of the tippet; it always ends in sorrow.

Nymph fishing with a float requires some special casting and line-handling tricks, but it's still a very pleasant and even graceful way to catch fish. A long, fine tippet and good line management will let you fish most trout and smallmouth water with a moderately weighted fly and a small strike indicator. That sort of rig is both more pleasant and more accurate to cast than a string of split shot and a huge wad of greased poly yarn. With a little practice, you'll be casting your little float 35 or 40 feet with no problem and catching fish that you might have spooked if you had waded closer.

MORE WEIGHT, A BIGGER BOBBER

The summer before I started writing this book, I spent a few days with a group of fellow anglers in Harrisonburg, Virginia. That part of the world is an overlooked gem, with wonderful fishing for trout and smallmouth bass in some of the prettiest settings in America. Naturally, the mere threat of my presence had its usual effect on the weather, and heavy rains had pushed nearly every river out of its banks. Only the brook trout water up in the mountains was in approximately normal condition; every other stream would have scared the guys who wrote the Old Testament.

One morning, several of us accompanied our guide to a lovely, carefully managed private trout stream that flows through Mennonite farmland. The water was frighteningly high and so milky that most flies disappeared after sinking half a foot. Foolishly, I turned down the guide's offer of a huge strike indicator and a heavily weighted size 6 Prince Nymph, and spent the morning throwing around flies that the trout probably never saw. A smarter angler rigged up with one of Billy's heavy nymphs and big bobber, added a BB split shot to his tippet for good measure, and parked himself near the bottom end of some raging water that had foot-high standing waves. For about an hour, he caught fat rainbow trout with revolting ease and regularity, while I had an all-too-familiar visit to Skunk City.

In some places and at certain times, you don't have much choice: Lob a jumbo float and a lot of weight, or go fishless. Of all the things that I can do with a fly rod, this kind of nymphing is among those I enjoy the least. But it works, and I shall not eschew it again when I have to fish in violent water.

The unpleasantness arises from having to deliver a graceless rig consisting of a weighted nymph, one or more split shot on the tippet, and a strike indicator large enough to support all the metal. With a short line, ordinary casting is out of the question: The fly line's mass cannot carry the fly and sinkers while also overcoming the air resistance of the big float. The safest way to make short casts with split shot and a bobber is to use a water haul. Simply drop the whole mess into the drink and let the current carry it downstream until you have 10 or 12 feet of fly line outside the rod. Lower the rod tip to within a few inches of the stream's surface, make sure that the line is straight, and use a long, smooth casting stroke to lift the entire affair off the water and lob it up and across the current. You're throwing the split shot rather than the fly line, so don't try to make a tight casting loop; a big, open loop will work better. As you begin the stroke, keep the rod low to load its midsection rather than the tip. Accelerate smoothly and gently as the strike indicator and fly become airborne, stop the rod for a split second at the end of the stroke, and then drop the tip to get it out of the way and open up the loop.

As the rig hits the water, raise the rod to keep as much line as possible off the stream. This is why it's called high sticking. Even

When you fish a short line in fast, turbulent water, lift the rod to keep as much of the fly line as possible off the surface. If the fly line isn't lying on the water, the current can't grab it, pull it downstream, and drag the nymph.

with little or no fly line on the stream, you still might have to mend, because the water on the surface is moving faster than the water along the streambed. Pushed along by the fast surface current, the indicator will quickly outrun the nymph and begin to drag it up through the water column. So, a second after the leader touches down, mend the line with enough oomph to lift the float and toss it upcurrent a foot or more. Keep the rod high and follow the drifting indicator downstream. Make another mend halfway through the drift. Slowly lower the rod during the second half of the drift, until it's pointing downstream and the tip-top is within inches of the surface. Let the current straighten the line below you, and then use another water haul to make the next cast.

This style of angling isn't pretty or easy, but water hauling and high sticking let you drift a nymph along the bottom of fast, rough, deep water. Trout can find pockets of slack water along the bottom

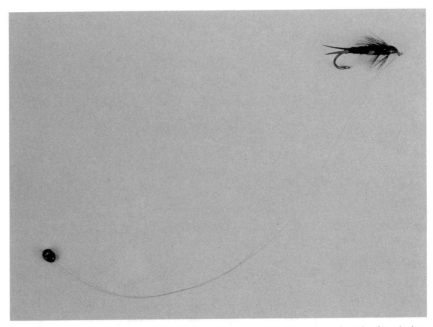

When you fish in fast or deep water and need extra weight, try a drop-shot rig. Attach the fly with a Palomar or Orvis knot, leaving a long tag end. Tie an overhand knot at the end of the long tag, and pinch the shot above the overhand knot. By letting the fly drift a few inches above the bottom, this rig decreases the likelihood of hooking a rock.

of a fast run or in the head of a plunge pool—they'll hold in places that only a fool would try to wade through—and sometimes the only way to put a fly in front of these fish is to lob a couple of split shot and then mend like crazy to keep the strike indicator more or less above the nymph.

When you need to fish this way, put the float one and a half to two times the depth of the water above the fly, and pinch the split shot 8 inches to a foot above the nymph. An alternative method uses a drop-shot arrangement to put the sinker or sinkers below the fly. The advantage of a drop-shot rig is that it reduces the frequency with which your fly snags the bottom. To make such a rig, attach the fly with an Orvis knot or Palomar knot, but deliberately leave a tag end about 6 inches long. Tie an overhand knot as close as possible to the end of the long tag end to make a stop for the split shot, and pinch the shot just above the overhand knot. The split shot will slide over most rocks on the streambed, with the nymph drifting a few inches above it. If the sinker does get stuck between two stones, it generally slides off the end of the tippet when you pull, and you don't lose the fly. Replace the split shot and you're back in business.

NYMPHS FOR PROSPECTING

Local knowledge always wins. The invertebrate community varies from stream to stream, and an angler who knows a little about the local hatches will outfish a stranger who chooses flies randomly. In some streams, fish have definite, albeit inexplicable tastes for flies that an entomologist might not choose. But for prospecting water that you don't know well, you can generally get by with a small assortment of patterns.

Remember that we're talking about fishing between good hatches or spinner falls—educated blind casting, in other words. You probably don't have to cast exactly the right replica of some aquatic bug. The fish might prefer some flies to others, but their between-hatches tastes encompass more than one size of one pattern.

According to entomologists, midges and *Baetis* mayflies (blue-winged olives, broadly speaking) are among the most numerous insects in most trout streams. Midge larvae are available to trout all year, and *Baetis* often hatch several times between spring and late fall, which means that trout can eat the nymphs for most of the fishing season. To cast a midge larva pattern or a small, dark olive nymph is to play the percentages, and I know some anglers who do very well with these little flies, particularly in busy, popular streams. As a lure for blind casting, however, a size 18 nymph or an even smaller midge larva has a couple of drawbacks. Trout are marvelously adept at finding food, but it stands to reason that a fish is less likely to spot a size 20 fly than a size 14 pattern, especially in water that's less than perfectly clear. More important, tiny flies have little room for built-in weight, though wire-bodied patterns such as the Brassie sink quickly enough. Small Brassies and similar flies work fine as midge patterns, and thanks to the variety of colored wires now on the market, we can tie them in black, red, and other midge larva colors.

A midge larva, a small Pheasant Tail, or a small olive nymph with a dubbed body can make a fine fly for prospecting as long as you remember two things. First, the fly needs to sink deep enough and quickly enough. If the fly can't do it on its own, you'll have to add some weight to the leader. Second, fish have to be able to see the fly. If the water has some color, you might do better with a larger, more visible pattern.

From the end of winter until mid-July (roughly speaking), it's hard to go wrong in a freestone stream with a size 12 or 14 generic mayfly nymph. Many species of mayflies are active during this stretch, and a lot of the nymphs become fish food as they drift. A size 14 fly is big enough for fish to see at a fair distance, promises enough nutrition to justify a trout's moving a few feet, and sinks well, thanks to the heavy-wire hook and some added weight in the form of a bead or strips of weighting wire. The Gold-Ribbed Hare's Ear is a good model for this type of nymph. I've long relied on a simple rabbit-fur fly that's essentially a Hare's Ear with a rib made of three or four strands of pearl Krystal Flash twisted together. In sizes 12 through 16, it's taken trout for me from Quill Gordon time until well into autumn.

Perhaps casting a midsize, generic mayfly nymph doesn't count as scientific fishing, but, like casting a midge larva, it does qualify as playing the percentages. All-purpose nymphs such as a Hare's Ear or my version ribbed with Krystal Flash look like a lot of the things that trout eat. Beadhead mayflies—Hare's Ears, Pheasant Tails, or whatever—and such patterns as John Barr's Copper John sink quickly and often obviate extra weight on the leader.

Caddisflies thrive in practically every trout stream and small-mouth river, and many anglers do much of their prospecting with caddis larva and pupa patterns. For irrational reasons, I fish both less often than I should. I have more confidence in a mayfly nymph than a caddis larva because nymphs, many of which are active little creatures, seem more likely than the wormlike caddis larvae to

Not sure what to cast between hatches? Practically every freestone stream contains mayfly nymphs that generic patterns do a reasonably good job of imitating. A size 12 or 14 Hare's Ear or a fly like either of the bottom two can represent many mayfly species that hatch over much of the season. A larger, black nymph can mimic a stonefly or an immature hellgrammite; it will catch fish in cold- and warmwater streams. Besides basic patterns like these, carry some seasonal hatch-matchers (sulfur nymphs in late May and June, for instance) and some midge larvae for clear water and snooty trout.

accidentally or deliberately drift with the current. An entomologist might disagree with that view, and many good fishermen hammer the trout with weighted caddis larva patterns, but it's hard for me to give up my cute bunny-fur nymphs with Krystal Flash ribs.

Caddis pupae often drift with the current, and pupa patterns catch a lot of trout for a lot of anglers, but when I think about subsurface caddis, I think about casting a soft-hackled wet fly and fishing it on the swing. Whether that's a better method than dead drifting a pupa imitation I can't say, but I enjoy the hell out of wet-fly fishing, so I do it.

My reluctance to fish upstream with fake larvae or pupae should be regarded as a personal failing. You should carry and use some weighted, size 12 through 16 caddis larva patterns (cream and green are good colors) and some pupa patterns in various shades of cream, tan, brown, and amber. Local fly shops know which patterns work best in their waters. Brassies and other wire-bodied patterns in sizes 12 through 16 are good larva flies for fishing deep in fast water.

Big, black nymphs work well in rough, rocky streams because they look like stoneflies (which fish love to eat, even if they don't get many of them), they sink quickly in turbulent water, and they're easy for fish to see. A stonefly pattern doesn't have to be complicated or especially realistic to catch fish; a large, black Hare's Ear with a shaggy thorax usually works. Dark nymphs on size 6 and 8 hooks also have a powerful appeal to smallmouths and other river bass, perhaps because they resemble immature hellgrammites. For warmwater fishing, carry a few weighted, size 8 Woolly Worms, too; bass and panfish still love them, even if Woolly Worms have gone out of fashion among sophisticated trout anglers.

Add some local or hatch-matching patterns (March Brown nymphs in the spring, for instance, and big green drake or brown drake nymphs later on), and you're ready to go prospecting. Mostly, though, work on your casting and line-management tricks. Learn when to use a strike indicator, whether to cast a lightly weighted nymph or a heavier one, how to throw some slack into the line, when and how to mend your line, and how to cast and control a float. Use a light, long tippet. The guy catching all the fish sometimes has the magic nymph, but more often, he's making the magic presentation.

11

Low Riders

My dad used to shoot skeet with an accomplished fly fisherman who held a heretic's view of dry flies. This gent tied very neat, elegant dry flies in a bunch of sizes and colors, but each of his mayfly patterns consisted of hackle-fiber tails, a body, and a hackle collar. No wings. Such appendages, he maintained, were put on flies by commerce-minded tiers to make them more appealing to customers. Trout, he insisted, do not care whether a mayfly pattern has wings.

Some high priests of hatchmatchery would punish such apostasy with a quick trip to the stake, where they would chant the Latin names of mayflies while the blasphemer roasted over a slow fire. But my dad's skeet-shooting buddy had caught trout from the Catskills to Montana on his simple, wingless dry flies. Not even a Piscatorial Inquisition would have made him recant.

The orthodox view, of course, is that trout care very much about the wings of floating flies. Let's hope that they do. What a shame it would be if all the styles of wings invented by fly tiers made no impression on fish.

The sheer variety of dry-fly wings shows that they matter to anglers, who, we assure one another, have figured out what matters to trout. But consider this list: Adams, Parachute Adams, Light Cahill, Comparadun, Harrop Hairwing Dun, White Wulff, Blue Quill, Loop Wing Paradun, Swisher/Richards No-Hackle, Usual. That list contains ten different types of wings made of ten different materials. All ten flies catch fish, and each style has devoted advocates.

If dry-fly wings mattered so much to trout, wouldn't one style have emerged as the best under most circumstances?

When it's not flying, a real mayfly dun holds its wings together over its back. The wings slant rearward and look almost like a tiny lateen sail. Except for some cut-wing patterns (which first showed up in the late 1800s) and flies winged with single clumps of material attached to lie back over their bodies (Theodore Gordon tied flies this way a century ago), few dry flies have wings that even approach realism. In the above list, only René Harrop's Hairwing Dun has a wing with approximately the right profile—but the hair doesn't form a vertical plane over the back of the fly, so it doesn't look realistic from the front. None of the other nine flies has wings that look much like those of a real mayfly. Yet all ten styles catch trout.

Here's another list with some of the same names: Comparadun, Parachute Adams, Swisher/Richards No-Hackle, Harrop Hairwing Dun and CDC Tailwater Dun, any of Shane Stalcup's zillion-and-one CDC mayfly patterns, Loop Wing Paradun, RS 2, and my own Spundun flies. The wings of these flies differ greatly from one another, but the designs in this list have one thing in common: All of them ride low on the water, with their bodies touching or awash in the surface film.

That, I think, is the important difference between a standard Adams and the parachute version, or a traditional March Brown and a Spundun tied to represent the same insect. Trout love low-riding drys, perhaps because the body of such a fly looks more like that of a real mayfly (which rides the water with its abdomen touching the surface), or maybe because a low rider has a clear, bold silhouette. Or perhaps many low riders that we regard as dun patterns actually look like emergers to the trout. Many mayflies

Low-riding flies don't have to be poor floaters or hard to see. A Foamback Emerger *(top)* sits very low in the water—it barely floats at all—but a short tuft of Hi-Vis or Metz Wing-brite makes it visible at moderate distances. The same material creates a bright spot on a Beacon Spundun *(middle)*, a low-riding fly that floats very well thanks to its plump deer-hair thorax. A parachute fly tied for choppy water *(bottom)* has two extra turns of hackle and a fan of stiff hackle fibers in place of the more common sparse, forked tails.

hang in the surface film while they transform from nymphs into duns, but relatively few ride the water as winged adults for any length of time. Maybe all of these reasons are true; we can only guess what goes on in a trout's tiny brain. But it's worth noting that most, indeed nearly all, of the successful dry-fly designs hatched in the past thirty years are low riders. Flies that perch on the tips of stiff tails and bushy hackle collars still catch trout, but their popularity shrinks every year.

Besides looking less fake than a fully hackled pattern, a fly that hugs the surface or sags into the film has another advantage: It's easy for a trout to take into its mouth. A bushy, high-floating fly can bounce away as a fish rises to it, pushed aside by the tiny bow wave that the trout creates. We've all missed fish that rose, sometimes with considerable vigor, to conventional dry flies. Trout are built to suck insects from the surface film, and a low rider occupies the same position on the water as a mayfly working to escape from its shuck or a freshly hatched dun waiting for its wings to fill with the insect equivalent of blood so that it can fly.

Fly fishers have known about the value of low-riding drys for a long time. Vince Marinaro trimmed the hackles of his thorax duns so that the flies would sit low on the water. Carl Richards and Doug Swisher started tying No-Hackles in the 1970s. Parachute drys have been around forever. But many anglers who know about low riders use them only in special circumstances because of two perceived problems: flotation and visibility. They believe that low-riding flies can remain afloat only on flat, gentle water—a spring creek, for instance—and that the only way to make a dry fly visible is to equip it with big, upright wings and a dense hackle that holds the front of the fly off the water.

There's no question that rough, fast water quickly turns a Comparadun or No-Hackle into a wet fly. Some other low-riding flies, however, float well enough to work on faster, choppier water. One of the things that excited me when I stumbled onto the Spundun design is that the fly has all the advantages of a Comparadun or Sparkle Dun, but none of the drawbacks. On a Spundun, the wing butts form a deer-hair thorax that surrounds the hook behind the wing. Deer hair contains a lot of air, and a Spundun's thorax keeps it afloat in all but the roughest water.

Many of the cul-de-canard (CDC) patterns on the market look like they'd sink after a second or two, but the fluffy material from a duck's backside provides a surprising degree of buoyancy. A CDC fly might just barely float—its body might even settle to the underside of the surface film—but it generally won't submerge except in choppy, turbulent water. Even then, it often resurfaces, thanks to tiny air bubbles trapped by the hooked barbules on each CDC fiber. Anointing the fly with floatant actually spoils its buoyancy, because dry-fly dressing mats the fibers so that they no longer hold bubbles.

Simple modifications can add buoyancy to some low-riding flies designed for spring creeks and other relatively gentle waters. The Harrop Hairwing Dun style, for instance, usually has forked, realistic tails and a sparse hackle with a broad V trimmed out of the bottom. Tied that way, it's a fine design for flat or slow water, but it might have trouble staying afloat on a rougher stream. More tails and a denser hackle (still with a V trimmed out of the bottom) turn a Hairwing Dun into an excellent fly for fishing a fast mountain stream. The fly retains its convincing shape and low stance, but the extra fibers at the back end and along the sides provide more support on the surface film.

Parachute flies float pretty well, but a fly tier can do several things to make them better suited to fast, tumbling streams. A fan of stiff hackle barbs at the aft end provides more support than sparse, divided tails, and an extra turn or two of hackle gives a rough-water parachute a more solid footprint up front. Waterproof synthetic materials such as Superfine Dry Fly Dubbing or polypropylene dubbing make buoyant bodies. Replacing the conventional wing post with a piece of white closed-cell foam gives a parachute fly an emergency float; if the rest of the fly wants to sink, the foam post will keep the pattern suspended against the bottom of the surface film.

Closed-cell foam also provides buoyancy on a very simple type of super-low-riding fly that I call a Foamback Emerger. It's nothing more than a nymph pattern tied on a light-wire hook and with a strip of brown closed-cell foam in place of the usual wing case. The idea has been around for years. For the rib, I generally use three pieces of pearl Krystal Flash twisted together. This sort of fly floats at an angle with its tails and body in the water—it's more of a "damp" fly than a dry one—and trout love it. A Foamback Emerger can be tied in any size and color to match any hatch, and it always floats, thanks to its bulbous foam wing case and foam head.

But a Foamback Emerger exemplifies the second drawback of some low-riding flies: It's practically impossible to see on the water. With most flies, the solution is to attach a tuft of bright (sometimes garish) synthetic material. These days, fly catalogs contain a raft of patterns made with white, bright yellow, chartreuse, or hot orange posts. These posts don't represent wings; they simply make the flies easier to see at a distance. Polypropylene yarn and products such as Metz Wingbrite and Hi-Vis work well for this purpose. (That trout do not object to a tuft of neon-bright material sprouting from the back of a fly makes me wonder all the more about the importance of lifelike wings; but let it pass.)

Fly tiers can add high-visibility posts to most low-riding patterns, using different colors to make flies for different situations. A short tuft of fluorescent red Wingbrite attached between the wing case and head makes a Foamback Emerger visible in choppy water and at a fair distance. On a similar pattern for flat water populated by judicious trout, a short post of white or gray poly yarn might work better. Adding a sparse clump of yellow or orange Hi-Vis or poly yarn to the front of a Spundun's wing turns the fly into a Beacon Spundun and makes it visible at longer distances or in poor light. The same trick works on Harrop Hairwing Duns and many CDC patterns. Most anglers have little trouble following a parachute with a white wing post, but a fluorescent yellow or orange post stands out better in dim light.

Another way to make a small, low-riding fly easier to see is to attach it to a larger pattern. Some anglers use a bushy, buoyant dry fly as a strike indicator above a small nymph, attaching the nymph to a dropper tied to the hook of the floating pattern. If you have a lot of trouble seeing a low-riding fly on the water, you can use a similar rig to give yourself a reference point on the stream. Tie a visible dry fly to your tippet—anything that you can see easily and cast comfortably will do—and attach a 14- to 16-inch piece of tippet material to the hook bend. Tie the low rider to the dropper. When the rig hits the water, you'll have no trouble following the bigger, more visible fly. The smaller, low-riding pattern, the one on which you expect to catch a fish, is within a foot or so of the "indicator" fly. Since you're looking for the low rider in a small area, you have a better chance of spotting it. If you lose track of the hard-to-see fly a second before a trout sucks it in, the bigger fly will serve as a strike indicator.

A two-fly rig is a desperation tactic, but it can help in poor light or on broken water. It might even produce a few extra strikes: A trout will come up to inspect the bigger fly, reject it, but then notice and eat the low rider. Like any setup that has two hooks, this one necessitates extra care when landing a fish, lest the hook that's not in the fish's mouth wind up in your hand.

Whether they represent emergers or winged adult insects, flies that ride low on the water catch trout during mayfly hatches. Compared with a heavily hackled, high-floating dry fly, a low rider simply looks more like real food. Don't limit your use of low-riding drys to flat water just because many of them were created for calm flows. The right design or a few modifications can make these flies good choices on any stream.

12

Lessons from the Salt

"Let's give you a big-fish fly," Captain Greg said half an hour after we'd launched near the mouth of the Merrimack River. "I want to see you catch a keeper, and that little fly's not gonna do it."

The "little fly" was a size 1 Deceiver with a marabou tail, lifelike eyes, and lots of flash. I liked its looks very much. But I learned long ago that if a guide suggests standing on one foot and whistling selections from *Oklahoma* while you cast, it's best just to do it and find out why later. So I watched as Greg replaced my tippet with stouter stuff and attached something that was clearly not a little-fish fly. He called it a Striper Dragon. Tying instructions would begin with skinning a very large rooster, or maybe two. It was a beautiful fly, all 8 inches of it.

"Strip it *hard*," Greg instructed. "When you do it right, it imitates a Slug-Go. Hard strip, then dead stop."

He was right. When I retrieved the big fly with a series of vigorous yanks, it darted and flopped through the water, looking much like a soft-plastic jerkbait.

"What are these fish eating?" I asked as I practiced the retrieve.

"Sand eels, mostly," Greg replied. "But they like these big flies."

He was right again. Over the next several hours, I caught eight striped bass and missed about that many more. A really big one eluded me, but none of the fish that I brought to the boat was shorter than 2 feet. It was a good morning, even by the standards of the Merrimack. A friend fishing from the other end of the boat did find the big one: 42 inches, according to the tape. One of my own flies, a fat, Muddlerish thing, eventually took a couple of bass later in the morning, but Captain Greg's handiwork produced far more consistent results.

Throwing his big fly also produced a weary casting arm. I managed, most of the time, but casting what amounted to a 10-weight fly with an 8-weight outfit is work. Picking up the immense streamer and my full-sinking line took a lot more oomph than the types of casting I'm used to. The energetic retrieve added to the workout and shortened the rest period between casts. After a couple of hours, I was bushed.

Sometimes, though, that's what you have to deal with in the salt. The fish demand a fly bigger than any you had expected to throw, and they want you to hump it along at a good clip at least a few feet below the surface, which means casting a sinking fly line.

It's not impossibly difficult, but it's nothing like casting to freshwater trout. It's worth learning to do, because the fish are nothing like freshwater trout, either. Besides, knowing how to handle a full-length sinking line and a sizable fly is a valuable, though often overlooked, skill in freshwater angling. A sinking line cuts through the wind better than a floater and lets a fly fisher go down after trout, bass, pickerel, pike, and even panfish that are beyond the reach of a floating line. And "big" is a relative term. On my 8-weight outfit, Captain Greg's 8-inch streamer felt like a very big fly. With a 5- or 6-weight rig, a 3-inch-long bucktail qualifies as big—but it's just the right size for many freshwater fish. A fly fisher who can use a 6-weight sinking line to deliver a 3- or 4-inch fly can have a lot of fun with pickerel, bass, and trout. He'll cover more water and catch fish that he'd never reach with a floating line.

It's a different style of angling, however, and it calls for some mental and physical adjustments.

DELIVERING OVERSIZE PACKAGES

A good deal of inshore fly fishing consists of throwing a sinking line and a fly that's big, heavy, or big and heavy, and doing it over and over and over again. Freshwater anglers can have trouble making the transition. I speak from experience. Learning to cast long with a 9-weight rod was no big deal—on the grass and without a fly. Real saltwater casting, however, remains a challenge. I'm not a gifted fly caster, but I think I've learned a few things that can help fellow trout anglers prepare for fishing the salt or using large baitfish flies in fresh water.

Except in one respect, which we'll get to shortly, the sinking line is not the problem. If you're not used to it, you'll like the way a full-sinking line slices through the air. A sinker does require a slight adjustment in your timing—each cast unrolls and begins to fall more quickly—but it's a pleasant line indeed to throw.

The difficulty arises when you attach a jumbo fly. And sooner or later, you will. Sometimes you have to match unexpectedly large bait. Even when the bait du jour is small, game fish might be more receptive to an oversize fly. You tie on the big fly and discover that your high-performance outfit suddenly feels two weights too light. Each forward cast begins with a jolt and ends in a heap 30 feet short of the target.

Here's the root of the problem: If you turn your head, you'll see that your backcast fails to straighten. When that happens, your forward cast is doomed; nothing you can do will compensate for beginning with a slack line. Your backcast *must* straighten completely and with some authority. That's true of all fly casting, of course, but a light trout outfit and a small dry fly will pardon sins that a heavier rig, sinking line, and bigger fly will not forgive.

Your first instinct, to apply more muscle, will not work. Inevitably, you shock the rod, whip it through a wide arc, or both. You tire quickly, and your casting gets worse and worse.

There isn't one pat, universal answer, though it helps to remember a few general precepts. Accelerate smoothly, not with a jerk, and stop the rod dead at the end of the backcast stroke. While you're learning to cast big flies, watch the rod tip to see if you're forming a good loop. You will find that, up to a point, it's easier to carry a big or heavy fly with a longer line than with a short string, so pay attention to when you pick up the line for the first backcast.

Mostly, though, you learn to cast troublesome flies by casting them and noting when things go right and when they don't. You have to practice. If you can, practice on water rather than grass. If you tie flies, make up a few practice dummies. Lash a wad of long feathers to the rear of a big hook, spin a fat, sloppy deer-hair head on the shank, and cut the hook at the bend. I used such dummies in the late 1980s when I decided that I wanted to learn how to fish with heavier tackle, and they helped a lot.

Don't worry about throwing the whole line. In most situations, a guy who can consistently cast 60 feet is going to catch a lot of fish in fresh or salt water.

When you practice, start with a fixed length of fly line; 35 feet is enough. Turn a little so that you can watch your backcast; that's all you're worried about for now. Are you forming a good loop? Does it roll out with zip? Does the line straighten *completely* before it begins to fall?

If the backcast dies before it goes anywhere, try to figure out why. If you have to, switch to a smaller, lighter fly until you find your rhythm, and then go back to the larger fly. Don't think about fishing; don't worry about throwing a long forward cast. Right now, your job is to make a good, clean, crisp 35-foot cast behind you. It might help to pick a target and pretend that the backcast is actually the presentation cast. (When you fish from a boat, you often have to present the fly with a backcast.)

A longer stroke gives you more distance over which to accelerate and makes it easier to accelerate smoothly. Try hard to start each backcast with your arm at least partly extended and the rod pointing down the line. You cannot succeed if you begin the cast with your elbow tucked into your side and the rod pointing upward at a 45-degree angle to the line. Long, smooth strokes are one key to better backcasts.

You might find that you do better casting nearly sidearm. I noticed this about my own casting years ago; I could more easily throw a long line and big fly sidearm than I could with an overhead cast. With the rod angled to the side—not horizontal, but beyond the 45-degree mark—I had little trouble making good loops and throwing long, accurate casts, particularly with a heavy line or a large fly. Then a couple of experts told me that I was doing it all wrong and would, for reasons never made clear, burn in hell if I persisted in casting that way. I took experts more seriously in those days, when I knew fewer of them, so I gave up on the sidearm business. Years later, when I had the pleasure of editing his casting articles for *Saltwater Fly Fishing*, Ed Jaworowski set me straight. Ed is probably the best fly-casting teacher on the planet, and he assured me that throwing more or less sidearm is not only okay, but often a good thing, especially as a training device. Try it.

Stick with 30 to 35 feet of line for a while, until your backcast rolls out smartly and neatly. Once you've mastered a 30-foot backcast with a big fly, you'll find the next 10 feet of line fairly easy to add. And once you can carry 40 feet of sinking fly line, you'll have little trouble shooting to a target 60 feet away.

Since a sinking line travels through the air faster than a floater (because it's thinner) and falls more quickly (because it's denser), you have to adjust your timing. You can begin each casting stroke earlier than you do with a floating line. Don't wait to feel a tug as the backcast straightens before beginning the forward stroke. By the time you feel the tug and react to it, a sinking line will have fallen to the water behind you. During your first several practice sessions with a sinking line, watch each backcast, and learn to begin the forward stroke just before the line straightens completely.

You need to develop considerable rod and line speed to throw a streamer or bucktail that really belongs on an outfit two weights heavier. Smooth acceleration and a relatively long stroke get the job done. You want your hand moving fastest at the *end* of each stroke, a nanosecond before it stops the rod dead.

Practice diligently but not to exhaustion, and relax. Nobody masters this right away. Heaven knows I'm still learning, and I've had help from more great casters than most anglers ever meet.

I wish that I had a universal answer, some easy and infallible trick for casting oversize or overweight flies. All I can do is note that nearly all of my own casting problems, and most of those I've observed in other fly fishers, begin with failed backcasts. Get that backcast to roll out with a big streamer on the leader, and your forward cast's problems will mostly disappear.

You will generally use a shorter leader with a sinking line than with a floater. You might use a 9-foot leader to fish a streamer with a 6-weight floating line. With a sinking line the same weight, you can use a leader half that length or even less. The short leader helps you throw a larger fly.

Remember that a sinking line, even a slow-sinking model, pulls the fly down. Since you can rely on the line's density to get the fly deep, you can cast a lighter fly. With a floating line, you'd need a heavily weighted fly to reach the top of a weed bed 4 feet below the surface. With a sinking line, you can cast an unweighted fly and let the line provide the depth. A fly with little or no extra weight, a short leader (3 feet is often enough), and a relatively dense line that slices through the air add up to the ability to throw a big fly long distances. That's the beauty of sinking fly lines.

GETTING AIRBORNE

Earlier, I mentioned that many of us have a common problem with sinking lines. Actually, it's less a problem than an adjustment.

You can't pick up a sinking line, particularly one with a big fly tied to the leader, as you pick up a floater. Even if the line is only a foot beneath the surface, you run out of casting stroke before you get the string in the air. You could strip the fly almost to the rod tip, but then you have to carry a big fly with only a few feet of line that doesn't weigh enough to load the rod. Lotsa luck.

Better to use a roll cast to get the line to the surface. This is why you want to practice on water and with a fly, so that you can get a feel for how much line you can hoist to the surface with a strong roll cast.

Bring the rod back pretty far to begin the roll cast, and direct the loop out and up, never down at the water. The point is to lift the submerged line to the surface. As the line rolls out, lower the rod until it's horizontal. The instant the roll cast ends, start the backcast. This is much easier than trying to drag 20 feet of sunken

Don't try to hoist a sinking line from the water as you would a floater—it won't work. Bring the line to the surface with a strong roll cast, as outdoor writer King Montgomery is doing here, and then make your first backcast. Direct the roll cast forward and slightly upward, not down at the water. Marking the pickup point of a sinking line lets you know when to begin the roll cast.

line and a hefty fly up through a yard of water, or beginning with only 10 feet of line and leader between the rod tip and the fly. Mastering the roll-cast pickup will help all of your fishing; I use it all the time with weighted nymphs.

Consistency helps in any type of casting, and many anglers mark the pickup point of a sinking line so that they can begin each cast with the same load. A mark on the line keeps you from trying to start a cast with more line than you can get out of the water or with too little mass to bend the rod. It's an excellent trick. Once you've determined the comfortable pickup point, you can use a permanent marker to color a few inches of the line. Or you can tie a couple of nail knots around the line with 6- or 8-pound-test monofilament and coat the knots with Pliobond, Knot Sense, or whatever. A lot of anglers prefer the nail-knot method because they can hear the knots hitting the guides or feel them passing over their fingers. No matter how you make the mark, begin your roll-cast pickup when you see or hear it enter the top of the rod.

PICK IT UP AND THROW IT

Through pure serendipity, my first few saltwater fly-fishing excursions happened in Florida. One of them involved flogging the mangroves at the western edge of the Everglades for snook. I didn't catch a snook, but I did get a useful, if somewhat curt, casting lesson.

My host watched me wave a very strong 8-weight rod back and forth for half an hour, making five or six false casts before each delivery, working out line a couple yards at a time as if I were casting a Royal Coachman with an antique cane rod and double-taper line. He finally had all he could stand.

"Goddammit, Art, I *know* that you can do this," he barked. "Just pick up the friggin' line and throw it. It'll go. *Don't* false cast. I'm getting' tired just watching you."

He was right. As long as I made a decent pickup, my first forward cast with the powerful, fast-action rod would shoot enough of the saltwater-taper line to reach the mangroves.

Most fly fishers, including me, make too many false casts. That's a bad habit in any type of fly fishing, but it's a recipe for disaster with an extra-large fly and a sinking line.

Get in the habit of limiting your false casts. Use a roll-cast pickup to get the line in the air. Make your first backcast a good one. Shoot some line on the forward cast, make another strong backcast, and then shoot the delivery cast. That's your range. Don't fool yourself into thinking that another false cast (or two or three) will extend your distance with a big fly. It might, but it's more likely to cause trouble. And any extra line that you *hope* you can throw inevitably winds up underfoot or snagged on something.

Restricting yourself to two backcasts might seem to put a severe limit on your distance. Yes and no. You're not going to make many 80-foot presentations after a single false-cast cycle; I can't, though the really good saltwater casters can. But if you work at the roll-cast pickup and your backcast, you'll soon be able to throw a big fly 50 feet with just a pair of backcasts. It's not world-class casting, but it puts you in the game. Concentrate on making consistently good casts within your comfortable range, and you *will* catch fish. Your comfortable range will increase as you gain experience.

Does a freshwater angler need to know how to cast sinking lines and big flies? Sooner or later, yes. Midway through this book, I spent two days with outdoor writer King Montgomery at a fishing club to which he belongs. It's a lovely spot in eastern Virginia with three ponds full of bass, pickerel, and assorted panfish, and we looked forward to some good fishing. The front arrived about the same time I did. On the first morning, the thermometer on the clubhouse porch read 30 degrees—in April in Virginia—and a howling wind was pushing whitecaps across the ponds. We caught a few pickerel on spinnerbaits that afternoon, drained King's trolling-motor battery fighting the wind, and returned to the clubhouse chilled to the marrow. Our fly rods spent the day in their cases.

The wind had weakened by the next morning, but the porch thermometer read 26 degrees. Our cars still had frost on them at

9:00. We loaded the boat with the recharged battery and a spare, sundry levelwind and spinning outfits, and since the wind had lost some force, my 6-weight rod rigged with a slow-sinking fly line. We were counting on the spinnerbaits, though.

The temperature skyrocketed into the 40s by midafternoon, the wind quit, and the April sun made the day seem warmer than it was. But several days of frigid weather had chilled the water, and a combination of high pressure and a cloudless sky had had its usual effect on the bass and bream, driving them deep and giving them lockjaw. We gave thanks for chain pickerel, whose mean disposition rarely changes.

Late in the afternoon, I picked up the fly rod and began throwing around various streamers and bucktails. Not surprisingly in a pond full of pickerel, yellow proved the magic color, and I caught a couple of the slimy, toothy characters on a big bucktail tied bend-back style on a long-shank, size 4 Gamakatsu saltwater hook. It would have been a handful to cast with a floating 6-weight line and a long leader, but throwing it with the sinking line and short leader was effortless.

Then we found the crappies. King caught the first one, on a tiny jig with a soft-plastic tail. They're called panfish for a reason, and we needed dinner, so the crappie went into the cooler.

"Throw that bucktail in there," King said. "Just cast and let it sink. Barely move it. That fish was pretty deep."

A crappie ate the big yellow bucktail on my first cast. King was right: They were holding deep, well below the range of a floating fly line. I caught another, then a third. For more than an hour, we traded the fly rod and spinning outfit back and forth as we moved down the shoreline. Our technique consisted of throwing medium to long casts, letting the fly line sink almost to the bottom, and then crawling the fly back toward the boat. A single presentation took a couple of minutes. We put enough crappies into the cooler for a splendid dinner of deep-fried fillets, and all but one fell for the yellow bucktail fished deep and slow. The big yellow fly caught a few more pickerel, too, which we released.

You never know when or where a sinking line will come in handy. Driven deep by several days of exceptionally cold, blustery springtime weather, this crappie and a dozen of its mates were beyond the reach of floating fly lines. A sinking line and short leader let King Montgomery and me take turns casting a big, bright yellow bucktail that the crappies could see in the murky water. They made a fine dinner.

If I'd brought a floating line rather than a sinking one, I believe that King and I wouldn't have caught those fish. Even with a weighted fly, we wouldn't have been fishing deep enough. And the crappies wanted a big lure that day; only a couple showed any interest in the little jigs that we cast. The 3-inch bucktail also appealed to half a dozen pickerel, which we greatly enjoyed catching on a light fly rod.

It wasn't saltwater fishing, but it used skills that we'd learned from saltwater anglers. Sinking lines and big flies have many uses in fresh water. And if you can throw a sizable fly with a relatively light outfit, whether it's a 7-inch streamer on an 8-weight or a 3-inch bucktail on a trout rod, you'll have more fun with the fish you hook.

13

Help with Tiny Flies

"I swear that they're making these damn hook eyes smaller," your buddy says as he fails, again, to poke a 7X tippet through the eye of a midge larva pattern.

"Quit your blubbering," you reply. "You're just gettin' older."

Your statement is undeniably correct. But your buddy might also have spoken truth. The hooks you're using might indeed have smaller eyes than those of the hooks that you used years ago. It's not the result of a conspiracy among hook makers growing rich on kickbacks from optometrists, but an outcome of how hooks are made and packaged.

The barbs of newer, premium fly hooks are much smaller than the barbs of older designs. That's swell for anglers and fish, but tiny barbs can give manufacturers a headache. If the point of one hook, including the barb, can pass completely through the eye of an identical hook, then the one can catch the other. In a pile of ten thousand such hooks, hundreds, perhaps thousands of them will catch others, creating a tangled mess that someone has sort out by hand. That costs money. But if hooks are made so that they can't catch one another, then counting or weighing quantities and putting them in packages goes more smoothly.

When was the last time you opened a box of a hundred fly hooks and found half of them hooked together? I'd guess that your answer is never. I can't recall ever having to pick apart such a mess, and I've gone through quite a few boxes of hooks. That's because the designers make the eye of each hook too small for the barb of an identical hook to pass through. The smaller the barb, the smaller the eye has to be to prevent horrible tangles in the factory. Compare the barb of an older design such as a Mustad 94840 to the barb of, say, a Tiemco TMC 101 the same nominal size. Then compare the diameters of the eyes. You'll see a perfect correlation: The TMC 101's tiny barb is matched by a smaller eye. If you want one, you have to take the other.

Yeah, you're getting older. But depending on whose hooks you use, maybe you're also poking tippets through smaller holes than you were twenty years ago. We should all take comfort in this knowledge.

Understanding the link between barbs and hook eyes doesn't make tiny flies easier to handle. You can, however, do several things to keep exasperation and profanity to a minimum when you have to fish with itty-bitty bugs.

Check the eyes of small flies at home, under a good light and with a magnifier if necessary. It doesn't take much to block the eye of a size 20 fly—a few errant wraps of thread, a tiny bit of misplaced head cement, the butt ends of materials that weren't trimmed perfectly. An angler who ties his own flies generally knows when he's fouled something up, but someone who buys flies probably won't discover a blocked or cemented hook eye until he can't attach the fly to his tippet.

Try to thread each of your small flies onto a piece of 5X tippet at home. If you find any blocked eyes, use a fine needle or a piece of stiff wire (No. 2 leader wire, for instance) to clear them. If an eye is blocked by imperfectly trimmed materials, such as the butts of a wing or a hackle stem that should have been clipped closer, try heating the wire with a cigarette lighter and then poking the hot wire through the hook eye. An eye blocked by wraps of thread (and this happens on some mass-produced flies) can't be fixed; discard the fly or return it to wherever you bought it.

Pack tiny flies carefully. Brassies, midge larvae, and most nymphs can go in ripple foam boxes. You won't hurt such flies by squeezing them as you remove them from ripple foam. Boxes with compartments make better homes for dry flies; ripple foam can distort the hackle or tails of a small dry fly, and it increases the likelihood that you'll crush a fly by pinching it to remove it from the foam.

Don't put too many flies in each compartment. If you cram a dozen size 20 Blue-Winged Olives into an inch-square compartment, you'll have a hard time removing only one. How often have you really *needed* a dozen copies of a particular pattern in an afternoon? Carry as many flies as you realistically expect to use, and store the spares in other boxes at home or in your tackle bag.

Packing dry flies and subsurface patterns in separate boxes lets you pretreat the floating flies without any fear that they'll contaminate the sinking flies with floatant. If you anoint your tiny dry flies at home, you eliminate the need to apply floatant in the field, where you might overload a size 20 or 22 pattern with too much goo. Liquid floatants work fine with little drys. Put a bunch of them in a small jar or can, give them a spray of silicone, dump the flies onto a paper towel, wait a minute for the paper towel to absorb the excess floatant, and stow the flies in a box divided into small compartments.

Some fly tiers use electronic test clips sold by Radio Shack and similar stores as hackle pliers. I don't like test clips for that purpose, but these spring-loaded, plunger-style gadgets make good holders for tiny flies. Drill a $1/16$-inch hole through the base of a test clip so that you can carry it on a retractor or a big snap swivel attached to your vest with a piece of old fly-line backing. When you need to tie a small fly to your tippet, use the test clip to hold it by the bend of the hook. This way, you can't drop the fly or crush any of its parts, and you can easily turn it to have the best view of the hook eye. After forming the knot, hook the fly on the snap swivel so that you can seat the knot firmly. Even in 7X material, knots need to be tightened all the way, but getting a good grip on a size 22 fly is nearly impossible. Pulling against something solid, such as the snap swivel at the base of your test-clip fly holder,

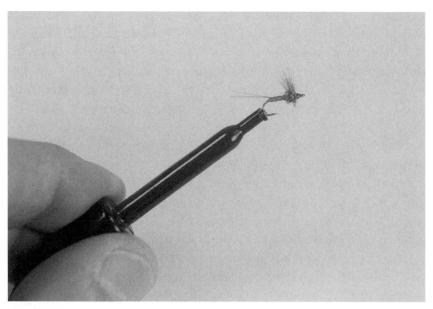

It's hard to hold a fly like this size 18 Spundun without bending the tails or squashing part of the wing. An electronics test clip makes a good handle that lets you turn the fly to get the best view of its tiny eye. Since it wasn't crushed between your fingertips, the little fly will float better.

ensures that every knot will tighten properly. (If you don't yet have trouble handling tiny flies and threading the eyes of their hooks, be patient; middle age is coming.)

Very sharp nippers can make a difference when you fish with small flies. Cheap nail clippers with crude edges flatten monofilament as they cut it, creating a lump on the end of your tippet that you then have to shove through a tiny hook eye. Razor-sharp nippers make a clean cut and don't deform the end of the mono. Trimming the end of the tippet at an angle makes it a little easier to poke through a tiny ring.

For many anglers, seeing a small fly on the water remains the greatest challenge. Flies with bright posts help, but a size 20 or 22 pattern has room for only so much fluorescent fuzz. In a pinch, you can try a two-fly rig like the one described in chapter 11, letting a larger, more visible fly guide your vision to within a foot of the tiny one. Even if you completely lose track of the smaller fly, the larger pattern will serve as a strike indicator.

Sometimes you have to do the best you can without seeing the fly. When I lived in New England, I spent many happy evenings on a boisterous little stream full of trout that loved foam-rubber ants. More than once, I caught a score of the rascals without changing flies, retying the tippet knot after every third or fourth fish. Fishing inside a tunnel of greenery, I could see the little black ant on the dark water about a third of the time. I'd spot the fly for a split second as the cast reached the target, then keep one eye on a bubble bouncing downstream or the tip of my fly line to have some idea where the ant was. When I lifted the line for the next cast, I'd see if I had accurately guessed the path of the fly's drift. After a while, I became pretty good at estimating a fly's position. And of course, I struck (gently) whenever I thought a fish had taken my ant. Sometimes I struck at phantom trout, but not often.

Occasionally casting a fly that you can't see on the water, or at least can't see all the time, is part of fly fishing. It's unavoidable, so don't let it rattle you. You can, however, make tiny flies less exasperating to handle and thread onto tippets. Let's just hope that hook makers don't keep making the eyes smaller.

14

Appropriate Force

"Keep his head up!"

"Give him the butt!"

"Put the wood to him!"

The sport's lingo drips with clichés referring to the ways in which we demoralize and defeat fish. We speak of fighting them and wrestling with them and ripping lips. No self-respecting author merely tugs on a good trout until it gets tuckered out and gives up; he wages an epic battle, the sweat of fear glistening on his brow as he strains his tackle to the very limit of its strength. Or he hangs on—grimly, more often than not—and listens to his reel's drag howl and screech as the fish races downstream, its powerful progress beyond the angler's ability to stop. And so on.

Phooey. By and large, freshwater fly fishers don't fight fish. We play them, or more accurately, play with them. When an angler does need to fight a big fish, he probably doesn't know how, probably doesn't realize what a piddling amount of force his doubled-over fly rod exerts on the creature with the hook in its yap. Freshwater fly fishers rarely think about this part of the game.

I've told the following story elsewhere, but it's worth repeating. About fifteen years ago, I had a chance to assist a famous saltwater angler in a demonstration of fish-fighting skills. I played the fish's part. Instead of running and jumping, I stood about 40 feet away from the angler and held an expensive scale to which the fly line was attached. The rod that the luminary used for his demonstration was an old J. Kennedy Fisher 12-weight fiberglass stick. In his younger days, the instructor had used that rod to best many 100-pound-plus tarpon. Each student took a turn pulling on the rod to see how much force he could produce. The results surprised and humbled everyone but our teacher.

On his first attempt, each angler held the rod upright in the classic trout-playing position and reared back, imitating the silhouetted angler in the old Orvis logo. Our teacher encouraged him to pull harder and not worry about breaking the rod. So the student pulled harder, until the handle of the big rod was angled rearward and the blank was nearly bent into a semicircle. The old fiberglass stick wiggled and jiggled, reflecting the trembling of the angler's arm muscles as he strained against the scale.

With one exception, a bloke who weighed on the heavy side of 300 pounds, none of the students pulled the scale to the 7-pound mark. None of us could maintain 6 pounds. Remember that we were pulling with a super-heavy-duty big-game rod that the instructor had given us permission to break. But except for the big guy, none of us could exceed the breaking point of good 3X tippet material.

Then our teacher showed us how to pull on a big fish, using the butt of the rod and sideways pressure, and we did better. Even so, only the big man, whose arms seemed as thick as my thighs, could maintain 10 pounds of tension. The rest of us had to bust a gut to keep the scale close to 9 pounds—with a tarpon rod, correct form, and a great coach advising us.

Because of its length and the position of the grip, a fly rod is a poor tool for pulling. In expert hands, a fly rod can apply enough force to a 200-pound fish to eventually defeat it—but most anglers are not experts. When he needs to persuade a strong, determined fish to change direction, the average freshwater fly fisher can't do it.

Do fish-fighting skills matter in fresh water? Most of the time, no. We play with trout and bass rather than fight them. Sooner or later, though, everyone needs to muscle a fish—an unexpected

3-pound brown in a weedy stream, a 5-pound largemouth hooked near a deadfall, or even an exceptionally rambunctious 16-inch rainbow determined to reach a tangle of submerged brush. And when the once-a-year whopper takes your fly and heads for trouble, your usual technique will not work.

ANGLE OF ATTACK
When an unexpectedly strong fish charges toward a blowdown or weed bed, your natural reaction is to raise the rod and pull straight back. That reflex puts tremendous strain on the tip section of the rod, but it doesn't put much pressure on the fish. With the butt of the rod pointing skyward, you give the fish the longest possible lever to use against your wrist, and you let the fish pull against the most flexible part of the stick. It *feels* as if you're really leaning on the fish, and the deep bend in the rod wows the crowd, but you're not having much effect.

You'll make a stronger impression if you bring the rod down parallel with the water and angled to the side, using the butt to pull on the fish. When a skillful big-game angler fights a tarpon, the tip of his fly rod isn't bent at all. At least the top third of the rod is straight, pointing down the fly line and directly at the fish, held in that position by the tension of the line. The bend begins in the rod's midsection, which means that the tarpon has a shorter lever to use against the angler, and the fisherman has a stiffer weapon with which to beat on the fish.

Trout aren't tarpon, of course, and a trout-fishing leader doesn't have a 16- or 20-pound-test class tippet. But the low-rod, fight-with-the-butt technique still has many uses in freshwater angling. Sometimes you need to steer a trout or bass away from a hazard; occasionally you have little choice but to horse a fish and hope that the tippet holds.

And chances are that it will hold, at least if you tie good knots. These days, even 6X tippet material has a breaking strength of 3 pounds or more, and we're talking about pulling with a relatively limber rod, not with a tarpon stick.

To test my instincts, I took a 9-foot, 5-weight graphite fly rod, a digital scale, and my younger daughter out in the yard. After I

The panic position, with the rod straight up or angled to the rear, applies very little force to the fish. Here, I'm exerting only a few ounces of pull with a fairly stiff 6-weight rod. A high rod helps protect a fine tippet, but it will not wear down a fish or make it change direction.

attached the line to the scale, Amy backed up 35 feet, sat down, and held on while I pulled. For the first test, I reeled until the rod was pointing straight down the taut line, and then turned from the hips, doing my best impression of the down-and-dirty style of fighting a tarpon. The top half of the rod remained straight; the butt end developed a considerable bend. I cranked down a bit more, until I was straining more than I have ever strained against a trout. I asked Amy what the scale said.

"Two-seven," she replied. Two pounds, 7 ounces—and I was pulling *hard*.

"Let me know when it gets to three." I reeled down a little more and pulled harder, still with good down-and-dirty form, until I began to worry about actually breaking the butt section of the high-modulus rod.

"Two-twelve," Amy said. The rod was bent all the way down to the cork, but the tension still hadn't reached the breaking point of top-shelf 6X tippet material. I never hit the 3-pound mark. I was afraid of blowing up a perfectly good trout rod.

Just for grins, I tried pulling with the rod straight up. I backed up until the top two-thirds of the blank had a deep bend.

"Seven ounces," Amy said.

I pulled harder, angling the handle to the rear and bending the blank into a semicircle. If the rod was going to bust, this was the time; I have never hooped any fly rod so severely while fighting a fish.

The scale read 11 ounces for a second, then dropped back to 10. Out of fear for the graphite, I relaxed the pressure.

If you don't believe me, you can duplicate the experiment. But don't try to hit the 3-pound mark with a trout rod that you want to keep.

Later, I performed the same tests with a 9-foot graphite rod billed as an 8/9 weight. It seems happier casting the lighter line, so let's call it an 8-weight rod. That's a popular rig for saltwater, steelhead, salmon, bass, and pike fishing. My wife held the scale while I pulled with the rod. With the rod upright, I was able to momentarily get the scale to 1 pound, 3 ounces, but only by using both hands and bending the blank into slightly more than a semicircle. Why it didn't blow up is beyond me; it was a textbook example of abuse. With only one hand on the rod, I couldn't produce more than 13 ounces of tension.

Remember that we're talking about an 8-weight fly rod. We've all seen photos of a steelhead or salmon angler steering a big fish toward the net or tail gaff, one hand on the rod grip and the other up near the stripping guide, the blank hooped into about two-thirds of a complete circle. When he does that, even with a very stiff, powerful rod, an angler generates *maybe* a pound and a half of lift on the fish. That's right: the end game with a 12-pound salmon probably involves 24 ounces of pressure, or less.

In the down-and-dirty position, my 8-weight stick exerted more force on the scale—but not as much as you might expect. In fact, I couldn't beat the numbers I'd produced with the 5-weight rod. Straining hard, I could keep the scale at 2 pounds, 10 ounces. If I'd thrown caution to the winds and used both hands on the rod, I suppose I could have pulled the scale to the 3-pound mark. Maybe.

Again, don't take my word for it. Try to dead-lift a 20-ounce bottle of Coke with a fly rod. You can't. Or have a little girl standing 30 feet away hold the end of the fly line between her thumb and forefinger while you point the rod skyward and try to pull the line out of her grip. The little girl will win.

The low-rod, down-and-dirty style of fighting produces a lot more force than an upright rod does. By taking the tip out of the fight—or "shortening the lever," as saltwater anglers describe it—I can comfortably maintain twice as much tension as I can with the rod vertical. But even with my best form (and I've had lessons from great saltwater fly fishermen), I did not create 3 pounds of tension with a fairly stiff 5-weight rod or even with an 8-weight. In fact, the saltwater rod's stiffer midsection probably makes it a less effective pulling tool than the more limber trout rod. That seems counterintuitive, but think about the physics. A softer rod that bends almost all the way down to the grip gives a fish a shorter lever to use against your strength, whereas a fast-action rod with a stiff middle and butt gives the fish more leverage against your hand and wrist. The stiff rods that we use to cast heavy lines actually magnify the strength of saltwater fish that we hook. Indeed, sportsmen who use light-line rods for tough fish—a 6-weight for redfish, say—might accidentally have chosen superior fish-fighting tools.

All of this pulling and leverage stuff doesn't matter when you hook an 11-inch trout, but it has a number of applications with bigger game. When you need to *move* a fish, drop the rod, angle it to the side, and use the bottom end. The butt of the rod should be at no more than a 45-degree angle to an imaginary line running from you to the fish. Do not, however, point the rod straight down the line; if you do, you'll have no cushion and can exert too much force, perhaps enough to break the tippet. If the rod is perpendicular to the fly line, you won't put much pressure on the fish.

The second implication of all this should inspire humility. Except for a handful of big-game experts, fly fishers simply don't put much pressure on fish. We defeat a bragging-size brown trout

This is how to apply muscle. With the rod low and at a shallow angle to the line, you can exert at least twice as much force as you can with a vertical rod. When you fight a strong fish this way, change the angle of pull often, disorienting the fish and forcing it to switch directions.

with *ounces* of resistance; your doubled-over 5-weight rod can't produce more than that. We overpower trophy bass with maybe 2 pounds of force. It seems incredible. But the saltwater expert whom I assisted with his lesson assured me that 10 pounds of pressure applied relentlessly and at the right moments will have a 160-pound tarpon whimpering at the gunwale in half an hour, tops. He's proved it scores of times.

So train yourself to drop the rod and fight with the butt when you need to show a fish who the boss is. Get rid of the panic reflex of rearing straight back with a vertical rod. Practice the low-rod, down-and-dirty method on fish that don't really need it, and learn how easily you can make a trout or bass change course. Spend some time pulling against a scale to learn how much (and how little) force you can exert with your favorite rods.

Fighting with a low rod not only lets you put more pressure on a fish, but also lets you apply muscle in the right direction—from the side. A determined fish can make good headway against straight-behind resistance. A little pressure from the side, however, will quickly turn a fish's head. Once you've turned a fish and moved it a little, swing your rod to the other side so that you're pulling from a different direction. If you had the rod on your left side, move it to your right to turn the fish's head again. As the fish recovers from that maneuver, swing the rod back over to the left. Pump and reel, using short, smooth strokes to keep the fish coming your way. Then change the angle of pull again. Yep, it's dirty pool. But this kind of alley fighting quickly wears down a big fish, disorients it, and brings it to the net before it's gasping for breath and overly stressed.

Some years ago, a colleague and I spent a day fishing a private stretch of a big river out west. After we'd been fishing awhile, our host and guide urged me to try his outfit, which was rigged with the magic fly, a Western Coachman. A big, fat trout rose to my fifth or sixth cast, ate the fly, flashed past us, and bored downriver into rough, fast water. The reel sounded like one in a magazine article, howling in protest as the fish peeled off line.

"Let's go," my friend said. "We're gonna have to chase him."

I let my friend know that I do not run on slimy rocks covered by rushing water. Laziness has nothing to do with it. By my mid-thirties, I'd decided never to risk broken bones (or worse) for the sake of a fish. It's a rule I don't violate more than a few times a year.

"But we *have* to chase him," my friend said. The trout was now into the backing and still going.

"Nope. Let's see what we can do from here." I palmed the reel hard, angled the rod to my left, and began horsing the trout. I'm sure it wasn't pretty to watch. But the butt of the rod quickly muscled the fish into the relatively calm water near shore, where I was able to regain line by repeatedly changing the angle of pull as I pumped and reeled, always with the rod low and slightly to one side. The fight had all the class and style of a barroom brawl. In a couple of minutes, though, my friend slipped his net under a fat, 19-inch cuttbow.

After turning the fish loose, we decided to replace the soggy, slimy Western Coachman with a fresh one. That's when I discovered the wind knot in the 6X tippet. Conventional wisdom says that a wind knot can reduce monofilament's strength by half.

Sure, I got lucky that time. Had it not been stuck in a hard part of the trout's mouth, the size 14 hook might have torn free. And tearing out the hook (or in the case of a tiny one, bending it) is probably your biggest worry when you lean hard on a fish. Unless you lock up the reel and point the rod directly at a fish, exceeding the tippet's breaking strength just isn't all that likely with a tippet heavier than 7X.

THE OBVIOUS QUESTION

If a fly rod is such a crummy implement for pulling, then why do anglers still break off fish, including some that aren't particularly big?

No one likes to admit that he ties lousy knots, but many fly fishers do. Most of the guides with whom I've discussed the subject agree that after feeble casting, poor rigging skills are the most common failing among fly fishermen.

Practice your knots until tying them becomes not second nature, but first, and *never* tie a knot in a hurry. If you can't cast well and tie excellent knots, everything else you do and know as an angler is pointless.

Check your leader often. Nicks, abrasions, and the euphemistically named wind knots greatly reduce a tippet's strength. Streams and lakes are full of hazards, and monofilament that's only 5 or 6 thousandths of an inch in diameter can't take much of a beating.

When you lean on a fish, do it smoothly rather than with a sudden jerk. It's difficult, indeed almost impossible, to break good tippet material by applying steady pressure with a light fly rod. But a violent yank can part a tippet, particularly if the jerk coincides with a lunge by the fish. Just as a tarpon angler bows to the beast when it jumps, a trout fisherman has to know when to back off for a second. But then, like the saltwater angler, you have to come back with merciless pressure.

And remember that luck plays a role. Trout don't have big teeth, but they have lots of them. When a small fly ends up completely inside a trout's mouth, the end of the tippet rubs against the fish's rough jaw. Sometimes you can do everything right and still break off a fish. Cry or curse, according to your disposition, and move on to the next pool. I once had a small brown trout, a fish that couldn't have weighed half a pound, snatch a foam ant from the surface of a mountain brook and instantly take to the air in a horizontal jump. The little fish shot across the pool only a few inches above the water. His leap used up all the slack in my leader before I could react, the 6X tippet broke with a loud *pop,* and the trout reentered the brook with my ant in his jaw and no doubt a crick in his neck. My fishing buddy laughed so hard at the expression on my face that he had to sit down on a rock.

Some things are just beyond your control. But when the next good fish eats your fly and heads for a trouble spot, be ready to play dirty. You and your tackle are simultaneously weaker and stronger than you think.

15

Painless Extractions

In the late 1980s, one of the fly-fishing magazines—I think it was *Rod & Reel*—had an issue with a cover line that said something like "Catch and Release: The Salvation of Our Sport." While I'd hazard a guess that environmental laws might also have helped preserve such sport as we still enjoy, that cover line makes a good point. If we didn't exercise restraint, we anglers could kill fish, or at least some kinds, faster than they can breed. Fly fishers embrace catch-and-release regulations, preferring a satisfying experience and the chance to hook a few wild fish to a creel full of hatchery-raised flesh. The ethic is spreading among other anglers, though some folks will never get the message. In some places, more regulations and more stringent enforcement offer the only (though politically unlikely) chance of progress.

Of course, catch-and-release angling makes no sense if the fish dies. The ethic alone is not enough; skill matters as much as intent. And here some of us fall short. It's one thing to keep a few fish; I don't do it often, but I'll kill and eat a trout or a mess of crappies without a qualm. They're tasty, and I need the atavistic (albeit delusional) satisfaction of catching my own food once or twice a year. But it pains me to see fish die because of my or anyone else's ineptitude in handling them. They're simply too precious to waste. Besides, they've done us no harm. When we release fish, the least we can do is send them on their way with as little trauma as possible.

Barbless hooks are the obvious first step, and we all should use them exclusively. Some anglers worry about "losing" fish if they switch to barbless hooks—a strange idea, considering the context. How is a fish lost if one never intended to keep it? And are we children who need to touch and handle a thing to enjoy it? Sure, it's nice to get a good look at a fish, and I wouldn't like for every one to slip the hook while it's still 15 feet away. But a few long-distance releases don't bother me. Besides, relatively few fish slip or throw barbless flies, and I'm convinced that barbless flies produce more hookups because they penetrate more easily than barbed hooks. We have nothing to lose by going barbless, and the fish have much to gain.

A hooked fish gets a strenuous workout. The faster you bring it to hand and release it, the more likely a fish is to survive. Big, strong fish are precisely the individuals whose genes we want to keep in a river, but they're also the most difficult fish to play quickly. This is another reason for tying strong knots. Good rigging and fish-fighting skills don't merely provide material for fish stories; they are in fact conservation skills. If you know how to apply pressure and tie knots that can bear the load, you can release a good fish before it's utterly exhausted. There's little sportsmanship in tugging on a trout until it goes belly up in the current.

Whether to net a fish is a question without a definite answer. A landing net can scrape off some of a fish's protective slime and injure its fins, gill covers, skin, or eyes. I've read about a couple of studies in which researchers found that netting increased the mortality rate of released fish. On the other hand, a net does contain and subdue a strong trout so that you can remove the hook without having to grab the fish's body.

With many fish, the netting question is moot. You can hold a black bass by its built-in handle (but don't hoist a big bass completely out of the water by its bottom jaw; the fish's mouth wasn't made for that kind of strain), and you can safely grab a panfish by sliding your hand over its body from the front. Trout and pickerel require you to make a decision. Their bodies are very slippery and relatively soft, and you can't lip-land either fish. But netting a trout or pickerel can injure it, particularly if the fish thrashes around in the net.

Some anglers always net trout; others never do. A case-by-case approach makes more sense. If you can see the fly on the edge of the fish's jaw, leave the trout in the water, reach down, and push or pluck the fly out with your fingers. It's easy with a barbless hook. The fish rights itself and swims away, untouched by human hands. If the fly is inside the trout's mouth, then you have to handle the fish, though whether to use your net depends on the trout's behavior. Some are more docile than others. If it's a small to medium-size fish that's behaving itself, try to roll it over in the water so that you can lift it upside down—belly up, that is. Trout seem to thrash less in this position, which lessens the likelihood that you'll squeeze the fish too hard or drop it. A fish that's not behaving itself will sometimes calm down if it's allowed to rest on a slack line for a few seconds; the pause also gives you time to grab your hook extractor. If a trout persists in thrashing wildly or if it's too big to lift and balance easily in one hand, use the landing net.

Generally, though, the net is my last resort with a trout. I'd rather keep the fish in the water and avoid handling it at all, though I will support a tired fish in the current until it revives enough to leave under its own steam.

Pickerel are loads of fun to catch, but not so much fun to deal with at the end of the fight. They usually go berserk when netted or hoisted from the water by the line, and a pickerel caught on a crankbait with two or three treble hooks is a nightmare to handle. But a fly has only one hook, and you know where it is—in the fish's mouth. If you can see the fly as you bring the fish close, try to use forceps to pop the hook out while the pickerel remains in the water. Try to avoid handling a pickerel unless it has taken the fly completely inside its yap. In that case, try the roll-it-upside-down trick with a small fish, turning the pickerel over and grabbing it firmly at the back of the gill covers. When a big pickerel inhales a fly, a landing net or a Boga Grip is the only option. Do *not* pick up a pickerel or pike by its eye sockets. Sure, the fish will calm right down—because you've blinded it.

Forceps are the most popular hook-extracting tools among fly fishers, and they usually work very well. Sometimes, though, a disgorger that pushes on the inside of the hook bend works better. Bluegills have small mouths, but they also have a knack for completely inhaling poppers. A narrow hook disgorger fits more easily than forceps in a bream's small mouth, and since it doesn't grab the fly, a disgorger can't damage the head of a popping bug. Disgorgers don't crush small trout flies the way that forceps can, and they often push hooks out more easily and with less damage to the fish. I carry both tools in my vest. With panfish, the disgorger gets

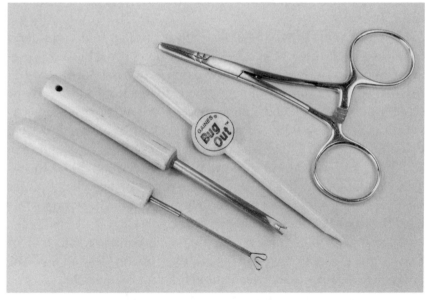

Forceps are the most popular hook extractors, but a disgorger sometimes works better, particularly with panfish that have small mouths or with a trout that has been hooked deep inside its mouth. Unlike forceps, a disgorger won't crush a fly. I carry both. The Gaines Bug Out is a good, lightweight plastic disgorger. Two of my homemade tools, one made of brass rod and the other of stainless-steel wire, are below the Bug Out.

more use; with trout and bass, it's about fifty-fifty. The Gaines Bug Out is an excellent, lightweight disgorger with a shirt-pocket clip. You can also make small disgorgers out of steel wire or brass rod, with pieces of ⅜-inch dowel for handles; the photo shows a couple of mine.

If you fight fish aggressively, you'll rarely tire one until it goes belly up. Trout seem more likely than other freshwater fish to exhaust themselves and to suffer the effects of lactic-acid buildup in their muscles. A trout's gills are less efficient than those of a bass or sunfish, and a trout in relatively warm water tires quickly and has trouble recovering. Be particularly careful with trout in marginal streams and in the hottest part of the summer. If a trout seems exhausted as you bring it to hand, try to keep the fish in the water as you remove the hook. Then cradle the fish with its nose pointing into the current. Don't swish the trout back and forth; just hold it and let it breathe. It will let you know when it wants to swim away.

Use your best lifesaving skills with every fish that you intend to release, regardless of species. For reasons beyond my comprehension, some anglers take infinite pains with trout but treat other fish like trash. Some trout fishermen deliberately kill chubs or whitefish. I once watched a particularly vocal member of a conservation club, a guy who regarded eating a trout as a sin at least equal to cannibalism, yank a hook out of a small bluegill and then heave the fish 30 feet out into the pond with an overhand throw. Trout anglers aren't the only offenders. I've also seen bass guides beat the brains out of every pickerel brought to the boat, and a few bass anglers still kill every bowfin they catch.

Nothing justifies or even excuses such behavior. Most of us enjoy some fish more than others, but there are no "lesser" fish. The antiquated distinction between game fish and coarse fish makes no sense; it's one of the mutant offspring of a rigid, Old World class system in which everything occupied a fixed spot in a hierarchy.

Some years ago, my dad accompanied a couple of biologists on an electrofishing survey of a small lake in Florida. Among other fish, the shocking brought up several bowfins, armor-plated, toothy members of an ancient and extraordinarily aggressive species. In Florida, many folks call them mudfish. Dad asked one of the biologists what he thought of anglers who kill bowfins on the grounds that they compete with the more desirable largemouth bass.

"I don't get it," the biologist said. "Mudfish fish are older than old. I think that we just have to respect something that's been around since before the dinosaurs."

A fine sentiment, and one that we should apply to fallfish as well as to brook trout. The better our catch-and-release skills, the better we can conserve all fish.

Index